Reviews and endorsements for
WHO'S THAT SITTING AT MY DESK?
by Jan Yager

"Solid advice about how to get along and make friends at work, as well as many relevant quotes and stories from people describing their own experiences with their co-workers, make *Who's That Sitting at My Desk?* a useful guidebook to creating more productive work relationships."
—*Soundview Executive Book Summaries* (www.summary.com)

"Carefully noting that workships often protect one's career and even help it survive, Yager describes their benefits (e.g. increased morale, teambuilding, and worker comfort), advises readers on which relationships to cultivate and which to abandon (with an eye toward identifying helpful alliances) and shares structured lists (e.g. ten principles for beginning a model workshop) that help frame the discussion."
—*Library Journal*

"Anyone seeking to improve workplace relationships will benefit from reading this book."
—*ForeWord Reviews* magazine (Leonard F. Charla)

"*Who's That Sitting at My Desk?* is the best researched and most useful book on getting along with friends and foes at work I've ever read. Don't go to work without it!"
—Don Gabor, author, *How to Start a Conversation and Make Friends*

"A terrific and enlightening guide to understanding the various types of relationships that exist in the workplace and the ways your career can benefit from them."
—Josh Piven, author, *The Worst-Case Scenario Survival Handbook: Work*

"Jan Yager offers an invaluable guide for maintaining your workplace relationships in a genuinely rewarding and balanced manner. Bravo!"
—Nella Barkley, President, Crystal-Barkley Corporation

"A much-needed book about an important subject that is often discussed but rarely understood. *Who's That Sitting at My Desk?* will provide readers with new insights and skills to improve their workplace relationships and their careers."
—Mark Sanborn, President, Sanborn & Associates, Inc.

"A must-read for anyone who needs to manage workplace relationships."
—Whitney Fleming, Managing Vice President, Environics Communications

"Dr. Jan Yager seamlessly integrates scholarly research results with clear examples and practical advice. The result is brilliant: an accessible book that will empower its readers to improve their relationships with co-workers and hence to further their careers."
—Rebecca G. Adams, Ph.D., sociology professor, University of North Carolina

"Jan Yager shows us how to create and cultivate the unique relationships we build with our colleagues, clients, and virtual teammates. Soloists at all levels of experience can gain valuable insights from this book, and use it to expand the impact of their business—both in economic terms as well as personal satisfaction."
—Terri Lonier, founder, WorkingSolo.com

"A good read, full of great examples. Use this book as a reference for managing your critical relationships through the journey of life called your career. Keep it permanently in your business library."
—Laurence J. Stybel, Ed.D., Stybel Peabody Lincolnshire

"Jan Yager has explored an arena, workplace relationships, and redefined it by clarifying it in a refreshing and eye-opening way. While reading *Who's That Sitting at My Desk?* I kept thinking, 'Aha, *now* I see.'"
—Jane Pollak, author, *Soul Proprietor*

"This book is destined to become a classic. If you are involved with any form of business, small or large, if you own your own business or are an employee, you will find gold in these pages."
—Carl Sanger, principal, Serenity Wealth Management, LLC

WHO'S THAT SITTING AT MY DESK?

Selected Other Books by Jan Yager [a.k.a J. L. (Janet) Barkas]

<u>Nonfiction</u>
Grow Global
Productive Relationships
The Fast Track Guide to Speaking in Public
Work Less, Do More (2nd edition)
When Friendship Hurts: How to Deal With Friends Who Betray, Abandon, or Wound You
Friendshifts:® The Power of Friendship and How It Shapes Our Lives
Friendship: A Selected, Annotated Bibliography
Road Signs on Life's Journey
Business Protocol: How to Survive & Succeed in Business
Creative Time Management for the New Millennium
Creative Time Management
Effective Business & Nonfiction Writing
Making Your Office Work for You
The Help Book
125 Ways to Meet the Love of Your Life
Single in America
Victims
The Vegetable Passion: A History of the Vegetarian State of Mind
365 Daily Affirmations for Creative Weight Management
365 Daily Affirmations for Happiness
365 Daily Affirmations for Friendship
365 Daily Affirmations for Time Management
Sleeping Well (co-authored with Michael J. Thorpy, M.D.)
The Encyclopedia of Sleep and Sleep Disorders (co-authored with Michael J. Thorpy, M.D.)
Career Opportunities in the Film Industry (co-authored with Fred Yager)

<u>Fiction</u>
The Pretty One
Untimely Death (co-authored with Fred Yager)
Just Your Everyday People (co-authored with Fred Yager)
The Cantaloupe Cat (illustrated by Mitzi Lyman)

WHO'S THAT SITTING AT MY DESK?

WORKSHIP, FRIENDSHIP, OR FOE?

Jan Yager

Hannacroix Creek Books, Inc.
Stamford, Connecticut

Published by:

HANNACROIX CREEK BOOKS, INC.
1127 High Ridge Road, #110, Stamford, CT 06905-1203 USA
www.hannacroixcreekbooks.com   e-mail: hannacroix@aol.com

ISBN: 978-1-938998-08-9 (trade paperback)
ISBN: 978-1-889262-96-3 (e-book)

Author's note and disclaimer:

Quotes in this book not attributed to a secondary source are from the original research conducted by the author, in the form of interviews, written communications, or completed questionnaires, and are reprinted verbatim. However, if editing of a quote was required for sense, clarification, or length, care was taken to preserve the meaning and integrity of the quoted material; if appropriate, additions or changes are indicated with brackets. If anonymity was requested, a fictitious first name has been provided; identifying details have also been changed to maintain that anonymity.

Secondary sources cited within the text have complete bibliographic entries in the Bibliography.

This publication contains the opinions and ideas of its author and is designed to provide information in regard to the subject matter covered. It is sold with the understanding that the author and publisher are not engaged in rendering professional career, legal, psychological, or other services. If expert assistance is required, the service of the appropriate professional should be sought.

Publisher's Cataloging-in-Publication Data
(Provided by Quality Books Inc.)

Yager, Jan, 1948-
     "Who's that sitting at my desk?" : workship,
 friendship, or foe? / Jan Yager. -- 1st ed.
     p. cm.
     Includes bibliographical references and index.
     LCCN 2003114699
        ISBN 18892622943

     1.   Psychology, Industrial. 2. Interpersonal
         Relations. 3. Industrial sociology. 4. Success in
         Business. I. Title.

     HF5548.8.Y333 2004   650.1'3
                                           QBI03-200872

This book is dedicated to my loving family –
my husband Fred, our sons Scott and Jeffrey, grandson Bradley –
and to my caring extended family, workships,
and devoted friends

Contents

1

Who's That Sitting At My Desk?
An Introduction

> "The real question about the workplace is: Who are your friends, who are your enemies, and how do you tell the difference?"
> —Patricia Schroeder, former congresswoman,
> Former president and CEO, Association of American Publishers

Foes or enemies may be a lot harder to spot than friends in the workplace, and at times it may be difficult to understand why they even became that way. I am reminded of an anecdote shared by a business executive who wasn't getting the help and support he needed to do his job:

I had just started at the company and was making the rounds, meeting with other managers with whom I would be working, when I did something that would impact my entire career at that firm. The person I was scheduled to meet was in a meeting when I arrived, so her secretary invited me to wait in her office.

A few minutes went by. I read all of the plaques on the wall and then, figuring I had a little more time, I sat down behind the empty desk to admire the spectacular view of New York Harbor. That's when I heard a female voice ask in a harsh tone, "Who's that sitting at my desk?"

As she entered, I quickly got up and moved to another chair. Unfortunately, the damage had already been done. I didn't know it then, but over the next few years, it became apparent that I had created an adversary who would attempt to undermine my every move.

At one point it got so bad that someone in another department said to me, "We don't know what you did, but for some reason she's told us not to assist you in any way."

Scenarios like that happen every day in the workplace; even small seemingly insignificant slights can have immediate and long-term repercussions.

What could that business executive have done differently once he became aware that he had somehow crossed the line? He had an opportunity that he unfortunately overlooked to try to rectify the situation since he knew from the tone of the woman's voice when she addressed her secretary that she was upset.

However, it is also possible that even if he tried to undue the damage he had done, that executive, on an unconscious or conscious level, was going to have it in for him. Just being cognizant of that would have at least given him more of the competitive edge that he lost by initially ignoring the animosity he had unleashed.

As an expert on business protocol and relationships, I became aware through my research that there is a need to understand the emotional impact of what we say and do to those around us at work. There are consequences to ignoring the clues that you have crossed a line, or pressed someone's hot buttons in the workplace. These seemingly innocuous slights can fester over time and grow like an untreated cancer, turning what could have been a strong ally into a foe who threatens to get the promotion you deserve, or to harm rather than aid your job or career.

Has something like what happened to that business executive ever happened to you? How about any of the following situations?

- Do you wonder why others seem to advance more easily or faster than you given your similar capabilities?
- Have you ever thought someone you worked with was a friend only to discover that you were being pumped for information so that the other employee could use what you shared to catapult his or her rise to the top?
- Do you wish you had at least one Mentor or an Advocate to help your career?
- Have you ever been fired or held back from promotion due to a jealous employer or co-worker?

- Has a co-worker tried to sabotage you because he or she felt slighted or ignored by you?
- Have you often wished that you could just "do the work" and not have to bother with the relationships at work that you need to deal with, yet knowing that improving your "people skills" would take you much further?

Who's That Sitting at My Desk? Workship, Friendship, or Foe? explores an important but often misunderstood issue—the impact that positive or negative actions and relationships have on your career or even your survival in the workplace. It is the culmination of two decades of friendship and workplace research. Over the last three years, I conducted additional research on work and friendship including over 100 interviews, in person or by phone, and 400 extensive friendship surveys completed by 325 women and 75 men. The majority of respondents filled out the survey posted at my website, http://www.janyager.com/friendship/survey.asp.

To better explain these relationships, I am using a new word, *workship. Workship* refers to those workplace relationships that haven't yet developed into full-blown friendships but are closer than mere acquaintances. These colleagues share the important and unique bond of work; you also feel a connection to each other that mere acquaintanceships lack.

Some people use the term "office friend" or even just "friend," but I consider *workship* a more precise term since the relationship may not extend beyond work or business. That does not mean that for those who are mutually agreeable to it, a workship may not, over time, develop into a friendship.

But workships serve a purpose even if the relationship remains at that level. For instance, workships help you, your career, and even your company to prosper. As Cindi Bigelow, Executive Vice President at the family-owned company, Bigelow Tea, puts it:

> To me, the relationships you create in your business are critical to the growth of the organization. I think it is important to share a piece of yourself with the people that you work with, share stories of family, hobbies, whatever. I believe that I have extremely close relationships inside our company, but these are still "business" relationships. I try to keep the socializing to a minimum to keep healthy boundaries. That does not mean we

3

do not do things together. We do. We go to an occasional ball game, or for a dinner, or even a round of golf. But it is still kept more on a business level. For me, I like to keep the worlds separate. I think it is healthier.

Today, more than ever before, people want to do business with, or work with, those they feel they know and trust. In general, a workship is an ideal workplace relationship because it is not too intimate but not too distant, either. A workship gives you a distinct Point of Reference—POR—that all-important knowledge about someone and his or her abilities so you are not a total stranger.

In times of economic downturns and massive layoffs, one of the most important reasons you need strong workships, as well as friendships, is survival. As the 52-year-old former Vice President of Communications at a major corporation says:

> If I had better relationships with the right people at work, I might still have a job. Because I didn't, I was laid off while those who made the right relationships are still there. It has nothing to do with competency. They're no more competent than I was. But they had stronger workplace relationships and they protected each other.
>
> I had a strong relationship with one senior executive but he got fired, so my protector was no longer there. After he left, I didn't realign myself with anyone else at that level so when the restructuring came along, I had no one upstairs to protect me.

This book also deals with what types of relationship boundaries are appropriate and beneficial in workplace and business settings. A 48-year-old married male executive confided:

> I've been married for seventeen years and my wife has never told me that she loves me out of the clear blue sky. Then this woman, my assistant, comes along, we become close and share intimate things about each other and she says she loves me as a friend. [Now] I think I'm in love with my assistant and if I don't get this under control, it could destroy my marriage.

What this executive also needs to realize, before it's too late, is that this workplace "friendship" might cause him to lose his job. It might also lead to an accusation of sexual harassment by the object of his affection, particularly if she feels he is misusing his work authority to pressure her into a romantic liaison.

In this book, you will learn which workships to nurture, how close to get to them, and how to avoid certain types of potentially harmful workships. We'll discuss how to handle those workships that become friendships, whether you continue to work together or one of you leaves the company or even goes on to a different career, and how to identify and cope with the occasional foe you encounter along the way.

Some workships can last for several months, a year or two, or even for decades. Some of these bosses and employees, or co-workers, have rarely if ever gone to a movie together; some have never socialized outside of work. Still, the importance of these workships may only become evident when they are no longer there, as one 35-year-old happily married woman with two school-age children reports:

> This week has thrown some curves my way. My distracted/insecure feelings stem from a relationship that I've had for over two years. He is retiring and I won't be able to bounce ideas off of him any more as the relationship never extended beyond the workday world. I completely understand the situation, and accept it, and wouldn't really want to change it. And yet, at the same time, a feeling of loss and grief keeps sneaking up on me.

The distress that woman expressed over the impending departure of her familiar workplace associate is typical. Whether someone is the departing worker or the one left behind, saying goodbye takes its toll.

In *Who's That Sitting at My Desk?* you will find help with understanding and dealing with those shifts. (See especially Chapter 9, "Coping with Endings.")

Workships, Friendships and Foes

Workships are pivotal in every work situation, not just the traditional nine-to-five "outside" office. For instance, for entrepreneurs or the self-employed, whether they work from home or in an outside office with just a few employees, these workships may mean the difference between having someone to toast their latest career success with, or to recommend them for a new project, and truly going it alone.

But for others, some of these workships do develop into friendships, albeit a casual, close, or best friend, and there are no problems at work or outside of work because of that friendship. Even after one or both leave the job, their friendship persists; the fact that they once worked together becomes just the initial point of reference for their enduring friendship.

By contrast, for others those workplace friends turn out to be foes who use their friendship just to get ahead. Here's one woman's story:

> I have been burned so many times by people I have worked with who I thought were close personal friends. One was a colleague who was also my boss who I considered my best friend and soulmate at one time. [But] when push came to shove, he and all the rest walked all over me to get their own way. We never see each other anymore outside of [work]. I've known him for twenty years.

In sharp contrast to that woman's negative experience is this account of a friendship that started at work but transcended it and endures two decades later:

> We met twenty years ago when we both worked for a department store. Despite a rough beginning (she thought I was bossy!), we became good friends, then best friends. Our friendship saw us through many life changes, including failed relationships, job changes, and family crises. We were like sisters.

It's not enough any more to do a good job or great work, or have innovative ideas to get ahead in today's workplace. Now you need strong workships that will protect you when others try to bring you down out of jealousy or fear, or simply maliciousness. If possible, you also need carefully managed friendships at work or from work that persist—even if you no longer work together—to provide the connections in the adult years that friendships at school offered during the formative ones.

A despondent California woman reminded me of how crucial work relationships are for career success when she wrote to me: "Which seminar or book is useful for a person who is continuously being fired or held back from promotion due to jealous female employers?" I wondered if her experience is typical. Was it more common for women to sabotage each other at work, or did male co-workers undermine each other as well? What about examples of wonderful work relationships including close or best friendships? I had been blessed with numerous positive work relationships including friendships. Others had them, too. What are some of the conditions that increase the likelihood that positive workplace relationships will ensue, including friendships, rather than jealousy, betrayal, sabotage, or rejection?

I encountered the importance of both friendships and workships when I was a fulltime assistant professor at a Long Island college. When I became pregnant with our first son, my husband left the decision up to me about whether or not I would return to work after a maternity leave or take a few years off to raise our son.

Although the main reason I chose to take time off was based on a parenting style preference, another factor was the lack of concern by my co-workers or the department when I gave birth. Flowers or visitors did not arrive at the hospital or at my home—let alone gifts or phone calls. Even cards from well-wishers with whom I worked were absent. I had thought during the two years I taught there that I had formed many positive workships, perhaps even a friendship or two, with faculty and staff, but I realized I had misjudged the situation. Although it was difficult to walk away from the status and income associated with my assistant professorship, as well as the intellectual and educational benefits of teaching, it was quite easy to walk away from a job where I had failed to form any meaningful connections with my peers.

Fortunately, over the years, that experience was more the exception than the rule. I recall how I met Gail, who is still my friend, when we both worked at Macmillan Publishing Company three decades ago. I also met my friends Mary, Marcia, and Sharon through work-related experiences. What were the conditions that made it possible for those friendships to start and flourish in contrast to the rejection I'd experienced working at that particular college?

Although I have researched and written about work and friendship before—my first book on friendship, *Friendshifts*®, has two chapters on work and friendship, my second book, *When Friendship Hurts*, has a chapter on betrayal at work, and another book, *Business Protocol,* has two chapters on workplace relationships—it is so pivotal to our self-esteem as well as our productivity and satisfaction at work that I decided to conduct additional research and devote an entire book to the subject.

It's no secret that a major key to success in any career involves the relationships you form with people you meet along the way. Even in this technology and information age, it's as much about who you know as what you know. And although the "good old boy" network has undergone a metamorphosis with more women breaking through the glass ceiling, getting your foot in the door, and whether you climb up the ladder, or find that you need to work your way through a "new girl" or "old boy" network," is still greatly impacted by the connections you develop at work and in business.

Who's That Sitting at My Desk? is a prescription for survival and success in that jungle known as the workplace where a different kind of predator may be lurking. This predator will use and abuse a relationship with you to get ahead in his or her career at your expense. Basically it comes down to: Who can you trust? Is that person sitting in front of your desk a friend or an enemy? Is he or she going to support you in your career or sabotage you?

This book will help you to form the right alliances. It's not just what you know or whom you know, but whether or not those who you know are really on your side.

The goal of *Who's That Sitting at My Desk?* is to empower you by examining the different types of work relationships: what each one is, what the benefits and risks are to that relationship, as well as what relationship challenges you may face and how to better deal with each one. It also explores how friends outside of your job can impact on your career and life, even in whether or not you get the job or assignment in the first place.

2

Types of
Workplace Relationships

> "There's a big difference between being an office friend and a real friend. Even if the whole group goes out for a drink, that's all work-related. It may be friendly but I don't call it friendship."
> —52-year-old Bonnie, single East Coast office worker

Picking the right workplace relationship may be just as decisive in determining your career success as your achievements. So whom should you have a workplace relationship with? Let's take a look at the various categories of potential workplace relationships:

- Those you work with.
- Those you work for.
- Those who work for you.
- Association members of groups you belong to.
- Vendors you do business with.
- Clients.
- Customers.
- Whoever it is that you need to interact with to be successful in what you do; this will differ for each occupation and job but you probably know who those people are at your job or in your line of work.

I've narrowed down to five the general categories of potential workships (or friendships) that you are likely to form at work:

1. Co-Worker

Co-workers can be either positive workships or competitors who constantly try to make you look bad, or even sabotage you, who act more like an adversary than a co-worker, so they look better.

Usually this negative Machiavellian behavior has more to do with the co-worker than it does with you, but sometimes you are able to set the tone and the atmosphere with a co-worker that can be mutually beneficial and upbeat. For example, be careful not to intentionally or unwittingly upstage your new co-workers. Whether it is out of insecurity or bravado, bragging about your accomplishments or outshining the most recent hire will not contribute to the "we're in this together" mentality that encourages a positive workplace relationship to develop.

With a new co-worker, be friendly, competent and humble, but keep your eyes open. Share information about the job at hand and about yourself, as needed, but make sure someone's friendliness is not setting you up for his or her professional gain and your loss.

That's what Deborah wished she had done when a new woman was sent to her department to be trained so she could assist in Deborah's department. Deborah, a 44-year-old consultant, had been seriously hurt on that job, but she came back to work anyway. She explains what she learned was really behind the new employee's eagerness to befriend Deborah, a relationship that definitely hurt Deborah's job:

> I thought we got along just great. We even had lunch together often. I showed her all my files, one by one, and explained how, why, and when to do things. When she felt confident that she had a strong handle on my job, she suddenly became a supervisor and fabricated a string of reasons why I should be fired.
>
> I realize now that the company did not want to be responsible for chronic back problems that happened on site, but they also know I was defenseless. They were behind her actions for liability reasons.

She had been planted. That was an emotionally painful realization.

Holding back information or personal details as you assess who your co-workers are and what their motives might be could be a positive step toward preserving your job while facilitating a favorable workplace relationship.

2. Boss

Being liked by the boss is often an excellent predictor for career advancement. As workplace expert Andrew Sherwood, Chairman of Goodrich & Sherwood Company, a human resources management firm, says:

> It's most important to work for someone who really likes you. If your boss doesn't like you, you don't get mentoring, you don't get training, you don't get promoted, you don't get raises, and if you leave the job, you don't get a reference. So, if you're working for somebody who doesn't like you, get that changed, either get them to like you, get transferred to somebody in the company who does like you, or change your job.

But while it is important to be liked by your boss, that does not mean you have to become friends. In fact, a friendship with the boss may backfire. (However, carefully managed boss-employee friendships are definitely possible. Friendship with a boss is dealt with in Chapter 5, "From Workship to Friendship.")

In general, a workship, not a friendship, with your boss is the less complicated strategy for career advancement. Trying to force a friendship may be viewed with even more disparagement than trying to force a friendship with a peer since you may be accused of opportunism, however unfounded. Friendship with a boss could make it harder for your boss to be objective and for you to know when it's time to leave the job and move on or up.

If a friendship naturally grows out of your association, you and your boss will find a way to deal with the status or management issues that might surface. [For a discussion of friendship with a boss, including some helpful guidelines, see "Pros and Cons of Befriending a Boss" and "If You Become Your Co-Worker (and Friend's) Boss" in Chapter 5, "From Workship to Friendship."]

But you and your boss may not make a positive connection. If that happens, here are some possible reasons and what you can do about them:

- The boss has an *Authoritarian Personality*. He or she delights in telling employees what to do.

    Solution: If you still want to have a workship, let your boss make the overture that indicates moving to a closer connection is okay.

- *The Jealousy Factor*. Insecure bosses may be threatened by employees they fear are more competent than they are. They may be inclined to keep you at a distance because they are intimidated by your abilities and do not want to do anything to help you get ahead since they fear that might make it more likely that you could steal their job out from under them.

    Solution: Play down your abilities including any credentials that might make your boss feels threatened. Show respect and admiration for your boss' knowledge and skills and make it clear that you are the employee and he or she is the boss.

- *The Fear of Change Factor.* This boss liked another employee, who you are replacing and even if the boss did not like that employee, he or she was used to him or her and you are the new kid on the block.

    Solution. Give it time. Have some patience. Give your boss a chance to get to know you and get to like you at a pace that works for him or her. Change is hard for many including change in staff. If your boss had an extremely positive or, the reverse, a very negative relationship with employees who have left, it may take that much longer to earn his or her trust.

- *Keeping a Distance is the Thing to Do.* This boss, because of previous work or personal experiences or just a personality style, believes in keeping work relationships at a distance to an extreme. The boss' remote style of interacting is so business-like that you could feel as if you are disliked or unappreciated.

    Solution: Realize this has nothing to do with you but is the way your boss is with everyone. If you do not take it personally, continue to do an excellent job, and show patience as well as an acceptance of your boss' distant personality, he or she may, in time, come round and become friendlier. Of course this assumes that your boss is acting this way with everyone. If he or she is playing favorites, try to figure out why other co-workers are having workships with the boss and you are still just an employee, and what you can do to try to change that.

- *You Remind Me of My Parent.* Because employees are changing careers or jobs so often today, and women who stayed home to raise children are reentering the work force at older ages and sometimes at lower levels, the boss may be the same age as his or her employee's children. The boss, who finds it hard to relate to the employee as a subordinate because the employee is the same age as the boss' mother or father, may go overboard keeping a distance as well as overdoing the leadership role.

  Solution: If you are careful not to undermine your boss' authority or treat him or her in any way that could be misconstrued as parental, your boss may in time become secure enough to begin a workship. Even if you are well aware that the problem is caused because of the age disparity, it probably will not help to state the obvious, "You know I'm old enough be your mother but I definitely still see you as my boss." Instead, just act like a subordinate and if you do it long enough, the artificial barriers may break down so an appropriate boss-employee workship could ensue.

3. Subordinate/Employee

What if you are the boss and you want to know how to form effective workships with your subordinates or employees? This is a challenge because you want to relate with your subordinates or employees in a way that is respectful and friendly without undermining your authority.

In order for a boss-subordinate workship to ensue you have to keep in mind that work has to come first, then the relationship. As workships develop, you will be finding out more personal details about your employees, and vice versa. The key is to avoid letting this interfere with your ability to work together and get the job done. If you find that the employee with whom you have developed a workship is taking your requests less seriously, you may have to revise the way you interact, putting a greater emphasis on the "work" in workship than the "ship" (from relationship).

In time, however, the workship may become a friendship. Jim and Dan, for example, spend at least eight hours a day together, and often call each other in the evenings and on the weekends when there are urgent work-related matters to discuss. They have worked together for seven years and Dan's wife jokingly calls Jim his "other wife," but Jim and Dan, except for an occasional out-of-town business trip, rarely get together outside of work, or to include their spouses and children in a weekend barbecue. (They always mean to but something always comes up.)

While they still work together, avoiding those family get-togethers might be wise. The workship that Jim and Dan have is optimum for their jobs. Since Dan is Jim's boss, socializing after work, especially with their families in tow, could compromise the delicate balance of power and authority in their business relationship, which, by necessity, is their primary concern. "If I ever had to fire Jim," explains Dan, "it would be harder to do if we were really close friends."

Although boss-employee friendships have disparity that might spell disaster in some situations, if carefully managed it might be a factor in tremendous career advancement. (You might also read the section in Chapter 5, "Pros and Cons of Befriending the Boss.")

4. The Client or Customer

One of the best ways to increase sales and build a business is to form workships with your clients or customers. In fact, this is a key theme to Dale Carnegie's best-seller *How to Win Friends and Influence People*.

Some people are very comfortable with this. As a 36-year-old married successful entrepreneur with two children and a mail order business notes:

> I take time with my customers to become friends with them if there's that open door. I can't take my business with me when I die, but those relationships that I build along the way will last a lifetime.

It is probable that she is using the term *friends* loosely and would have called these relationships workships if she had known of such a term.

A flourishing Atlanta salesperson also befriends her customers but she distinguishes those relationships from personal friends:

> I've built my business by building relationships with my customers. Are they "friends?" Of course not. But many are "friends-through-business" whose company I genuinely enjoy and who fulfills the social void full-time employment can create.

Lillian Vernon, founder and CEO of the retailer Lillian Vernon Corporation, is typical of successful business owners. She runs her business so those customers feel like they matter. Vernon, with 26 million customers in her database, notes:

> There are a number of techniques we use to strengthen the bond with our customers so they will remain loyal to us. I write a personal letter in each catalog and I include a picture of myself so our customers know that I am a real person and we are not a faceless, anonymous entity.
> Our website, www.lillianvernon.com, has a page called Lillian's Corner where I share my biography, tips on shopping, gift-giving and decorating, my favorite recipes and even news about my dog, Mopsey, who also appears on the covers of our catalogs.
> I encourage our customers to write or e-mail me in my letters and on our website so I can serve them better and shop for what they need and want. We respond to all these letters and e-mails in a timely fashion. We train our customer service representatives to treat each customer like a friend.

Of course for many businesses it is impractical to try to befriend every customer or client. As the salesman for an electric toothbrush said to me about his customers, the dentists who buy his product: "I have four thousand potential clients, so it's kinda hard to get personal with someone. I may see them two or three times a year." For this salesman, and for everyone who deals with dozens, hundreds, or even thousands of customers or clients as part of their job, it is key to distinguish between being friendly, which most need to be, and trying to develop a workship with every single person.

Who are the key decision-makers, the movers and shakers, who will help your business flourish? As you focus your time and energy on developing those relationships, it may be necessary to delegate to administrative assistants or others the forming of workships with the dozens, hundreds, or even thousands of clients or customers.

5. Vendors or Suppliers

Yes, you give your money to vendors or suppliers so they should provide goods or service since that is their job. Still, just as forming positive workships with co-workers, the boss, or employees impacts on your job, how productive you are and whether you get promoted, befriending vendors or suppliers may influence how quickly you get serviced, especially when you have a rush order.

Take the time to learn the names of your vendors or suppliers as well as even the smallest details about them. Connect one-on-one and it could make a difference in your career—especially if you rely on service providers to help you complete projects and "look good" to your customers or boss. Whether it is an account executive who needs a video production company to produce an excellent video news release for a billion-dollar company he services, a speaker who depends on event planners for work, or a publisher who relies on printers to create the books they sell, developing workships with vendors and suppliers is a valuable asset.

While few workers can take the time to develop a workship or friendship with every vendor or supplier, you should be able to develop a workship with as many as possible, especially those who are directly responsible for your account, for your job's success, and whose prompt and excellent attention to your needs will most likely help you to get ahead—as well as to the top of those companies. Send a card at the holidays with a brief personalization even if you just write that person's name and sign your own. Consider sending an reasonable yet tasteful gift, if that is appropriate and permissible.

You might also want to review the information shared in Chapter 15, "Personality Traits You May Find at Work," to help you assess the kind of personality you may be dealing with within the above five basic categories of workplace relationships—boss, co-worker, subordinate, customer or client, or vendor/supplier.

3

How to Start, and Maintain, a Workship

> "Every time I enter a new office, I'm amazed at how much time people spend talking to each other about their families, politics and a whole range of other subjects that have nothing to do with their jobs."
> —Minda Zetlin, "Mixed company: Balancing business and friendship," *Management Review*

How can you tell if a workplace relationship will ever become a workship? Will you be able to recognize it once it does? What's the difference between a workship and a friendship at work?

Workships are no-nonsense work-related relationships that usually exist for the purpose of aid or support at work. The only question that needs to be asked and answered in the affirmative is "Can we help each other?"

No matter how much you like someone at work, there are considerations that often make it difficult, but not impossible, to cultivate and maintain a friendship. For example, you might befriend a co-worker, only to find you are competing for the same promotion later on.

With a workship, you are able to let down your guard a tiny bit and allow someone to get to know you beyond the perfunctory niceties that we associate with dealing with acquaintances. But if you let your guard down too much, as you might with a friend, there may be severe consequences ranging from embarrassment, someone else taking credit for your ideas or projects, or hurt feelings, to getting ridiculed, or even getting fired.

By contrast, if you first form a workship and then, carefully, slowly, and naturally, that workship evolves into a casual, close, or best friendship, there is a greater likelihood that the friendship will help, not hinder or derail, your career.

Of course there are also some jobs and professions that have to be more mindful about separating friendship from work to avoid any influence peddling allegations, such as government employees, teachers, company human resource professionals, journalists, or critics. For those jobs especially, workships are the perfect alternative to either extreme of total isolation or accusations of compromise.

With high-profile catastrophic corporate collapses, allegations of insider trading, and sensitivity to even the hint of influence peddling possibly tied to friendship, it is pivotal to examine when friendship is appropriate at work, when it is to be avoided, and how to know the difference.

For example, the adage, "It never hurts to ask," has to be reconsidered in the light of work and friendship. When it comes to work and friendship, sometimes it *may* hurt to ask, especially if you are looking for a job, for yourself or for a family member, or if you are trying to acquire new customers or clients.

It helps to understand the dynamics behind those situations so you have guidelines about who to ask, and what requests you may want to honor, as well as how and when to politely decline offers for help, even if it is volunteered.

How Do You Recognize a Workship?

You can usually tell if you have a workship by the tone of someone's voice, or if you have a gut feeling that you have connected with someone. Besides the first business encounter that you are forced to have with each other, you now like each other enough to want to do business again, and perhaps even spend time together over lunch or dinner. If you exchange e-mails, you can tell that a workship is developing because the initial e-mail exchange continues at the same pace, or even a faster pace.

If the time that it takes for your e-mails to be answered dramatically slows down, or you find your e-mails are being ignored all together, unless someone is away on a business trip or there is another extenuating circumstance, a workship has probably failed to develop.

Benefits of Workships

Workships enhance teambuilding. Having a workship means you are connecting with other co-workers, superiors, or subordinates, and that you all perceive yourselves as part of a team with shared goals for advancement. Knowing that others are going through the same things you are dealing with at work, that they care, and that they are "watching your back" also helps to reduce stress.

Another benefit to workships is being able to share thoughts and feelings about work, or everyday concerns, to others that are in the same situation.

You may want to move a workship along to a casual, close, or best friendship, or you may want it to stay at the level of a friendly colleague. The choice is yours. The chapters that follow will help you make that choice. They will also help you understand some of the problems associated with being friends with employees, colleagues, or bosses.

Unlike a friendship, which requires openness and a "no holds barred" approach to information sharing, a workship permits withholding of confidences as well as any personal history irrelevant to the job at hand. Since a workship occurs at work, there is usually an instinctive evasiveness about certain facts, thoughts, feelings, and details that would probably be shared with a friend outside of work. However, the work role has to be protected at all costs; the role of workship or friend is secondary.

For example, if someone has just received a job offer, especially if he has not decided whether or not to accept it, few, if any, workships at the office may be told. Or if someone has just learned she's pregnant but needs to delay announcing that fact until it is in her best interest at work, she may temporarily withhold that information from her workplace associate with whom she has shared so many lunches and workplace gripes over the years.

Other sensitive topics might include challenges at home or medical issues to be dealt with, such as "elective surgery," which is really a major operation. Handling such personal matters with relationships at work is often distinctive from the way it is shared with a friend in one's personal life.

Initiating a Workship

There are four ingredients necessary for a relationship to grow from stranger to acquaintance to workship:

- Visibility
- Accessibility
- Having a shared work-related experience
- Having a shared wish to do so

Every workship begins with a shared situation. Before the Internet, except for the occasional long-distance pen pal, even if your first contact with someone in business was via a phone call or business letter, moving the relationship along to something more personal usually required a face-to-face meeting. But today, more than ever before, men and women are becoming acquainted online as well as in face-to-face meetings when they work together or attend a conference or a trade show.

But whether the initial contact is in cyberspace or physical space, two people have to interact out of all the myriad of choices of connections available to each of them every day. Workships, therefore, like all relationships, are really part of a process.

When you walk into a completely new situation, whether it's a new job or meeting with your latest client, you may be nervous, fearful, and anxious. You're even unaware that you're gritting your teeth, rather than smiling. You are surprised by the anger and unfriendliness you are sensing from the new people you were so looking forward to meeting and working with. You feel defeated and even upset since the situation seems so doomed from the start.

It's a maxim that you can't be guaranteed of changing anyone but yourself, so start there. Work on how friendly you are when you meet someone new. The friendliness has to be sincere; it cannot be forced nor can you be "too friendly" or it will seem like desperation, and backfire.

How do you show appropriate friendliness when you meet someone in-person, over the phone, or through written communications? I am amazed at how many people may be pleasant and upbeat when they meet someone at a conference but they answer their phone with hostility and unfriendliness, and then wonder why their relationships and business are not growing.

One of the best reasons to get out of your office and into "the field" so you can meet and greet in person is that communication experts have learned that the verbal part of communication may be as small as 7% of the message that is conveyed. The rest is non-verbal cues, such as posture, body language, and tone of voice. So it's what you say as well as how you say it, and it's how you present yourself and the impression that you make in those first few seconds, that may be everlasting.

The fourth condition noted above that is necessary to start a workship is the shared wish to do so. Unless that shared wish to do so is present, you will have to put up with just being work acquaintances. If there is a shared wish to become a workship, you may find yourself developing positive workships with co-workers, the boss, subordinates or employees, clients or customers, vendors or suppliers.

Ten Principles for Beginning a Model Workship

1. Start the new relationship by being friendly, having an open mind and an agreeable attitude.
2. First impressions do count so make a positive one in terms of how you look, talk, being on time, and responding to the cues and comments that this person makes to you.
3. Avoid "coming on too strong" whether it is out of insecurity, bravado, or a need to impress others with your credentials or knowledge. It will usually backfire.
4. Proceed with a "wait and see" attitude, taking in information and observing your new potential workship whether co-worker, boss, subordinate, client, or customer.
5. It may be helpful to assess this new person and figure out what personality trait you may be dealing with. That may help you to figure out what aspect of your personality and workstyle to highlight and emphasize. (For further discussion, see Chapter 15, "Personality Traits You May Find at Work.")

6. Listen. What are the work values this person is sharing with you? What is his or her background that will help you determine if this person will be an ally or a competitor?
7. Avoid getting into a me-versus-you approach fraught with potential jealousy and competition. Instead, try a "We're in this together, how can we help each other?" strategy.
8. Take the long view. Unless you're a temporary worker literally going from job to job, you will hopefully be working with this person for weeks, months, or even years. You don't have to go from stranger to acquaintance to workship in minutes or even days. Positive bonding takes time.
9. If you take an instant or visceral dislike to someone, try to figure out if it is based on the other person or coming from a distant, possibly unconscious place. (See the discussion below for help with how to deal with someone taking an instant dislike to you. For a discussion of how previous experiences could be called into play when you meet someone at work, see Chapter 8, "Dealing With Conflicts.")
10. Be open to valid feedback. Discuss it without overreacting.

Overreacting to comments or criticism, or even rejection, is something you may have to deal with soon after meeting someone for the first time to ensure that it doesn't sabotage your new relationship. This new work relationship, even if he or she brings up old feelings, is not a replica of your critical parent or a scary teacher. This is a work relationship that needs to be dealt with in the present tense. (See Chapter 13 for a more extensive discussion of the possible root causes of these current reactions.)

Sometimes the ability to take criticism without hostility or resentment may mean the difference between those who get promoted and those who are held back because of resentment and anger. Be careful that the feedback is heading you in the right direction. You need to be secure enough in your judgment that you know what criticism to accept and when you need to take a stand.

How to Deal with Unfriendly People at Work

But what can you do if someone you just met with whom you have to work (or work for) takes an instant dislike to you? Dealing with new relationships in the present is especially important to giving each new person you meet at work a chance to develop into a positive workship with you. For example, this person talks like someone from your formative years who made fun of you. If your negative feelings toward this new person are based on feelings and experiences unrelated to the present, deal with those feelings so you do not unwittingly sabotage this new relationship and possibly your career.

Chapter 13, "Workplace Relationships Begin at Home" and Chapter 14, "School as a Training Ground for Work Relationships," explore these issues in greater detail. At this point, it is worthwhile to examine this issue since it is not that big a leap from the unfriendly person at work to the foe, a leap you want to avoid having to take, if you can.

Here are some suggestions to try to deal with the situation and even turn it around:

1. Accept that the unfriendliness probably has nothing to do with you personally but with the person who is acting that way toward you. Unfriendly people tend to be angry and it's probably not because of you but you get their displaced anger.
2. If the unfriendliness does have to do with you, try to figure out what you did (in words or in actions including even facial expressions) to set this person off so you can either undo it or at least learn from the experience.
3. Realize that if you ignore the unfriendliness it will neither go away nor get better. However, you can decide to try to deal with the unfriendliness now. Or you may want to wait a while to handle it at another time and in the way that you think would be most effective whether in-person, over the phone, or through a written communication, such as a memo, note, card, e-mail, or even through sending a token good faith gift that is appropriate and not compromising to you or to the recipient.
4. If you decide to do something about the unfriendliness, try to diffuse it by going back to the person who is unfriendly with a friendly comment. For example, someone meets you and two other people. She says to the two others, not you, "It was nice to meet you. I hope you come back soon," leaving you out of the conversation. Instead of walking away and ignoring a comment

that has obviously hurt your feelings, or being defensive or aggressive, turn to the person who said that and say, in as nice a tone as you can muster, "It was nice to meet you, too, and I look forward to coming back again as well."

5. Once you are back on a friendlier basis, quickly follow-up and reaffirm that friendly tone and connection.

6. If you decide to delay confronting the unfriendliness, devise a plan that you will implement for dealing with it.

7. If the person does not seem receptive to your new overtures, or you decide you cannot or will not spend the time and effort it might take to win him or her over, just let it go. Try to resist the impulse and instinct to "bad mouth" the unfriendly person. Remember that the person you found unfriendly could be nice to everyone else so you will be seen as the bad-mouthing rejected party rather than a team player. Try to learn from what happened and do better with this person and others in the future so unfriendliness happens less frequently or has less of a devastating impact on you.

Examining Possible Causes of the Unfriendliness

Sometimes it helps to look at a behavior and understand that what might be causing it has nothing to do with you. Here are some possible reasons for unfriendliness:

1. Temporary unfriendliness related to a trauma or recent event— Someone may just have learned that her job is on the line, or that a family member has an incurable disease. The unfriendliness may be temporary and have nothing to do with you but to some catastrophic event that this new person is coping with.

2. Shyness—Being unfriendly may be this person's defense mechanism, a way of coping with shyness. By being unfriendly, no one will approach this person so he or she does not have to deal with his or her shyness.

3. Fear of rejection—Afraid a new person will reject him, he becomes the rejecter, protecting himself through his unfriendly behavior.

4. Excessive competitiveness or jealousy—You have something that she wants and the jealousy is so overwhelming that she is unable to be pleasant and friendly.
5. Unresolved relationship issues—Problematical relationships in his personal or business life make him fearful of beginning any new relationships. The unfriendliness acts like a sign that says, "Keep out."

Seven Ways to Turn the Negativity Around

If you really feel there is hope and you sincerely want to actively try to mend the situation, here is a list of ways to try to turn around unfriendliness:

1. Send a card.
2. Write a note.
3. Invite him or her to lunch.
4. Invite him or her to dinner.
5. Get an extra set of tickets to the theatre, opera, or a concert and ask him/her along with a spouse or date, as appropriate.
6. Rather than confront this person about the unfriendliness, let the situation ride. See if, with time, the unfriendliness turns around as you realize this person was really just having a "bad day" that had nothing to do with you.
7. Get past the unfriendliness and act friendly anyway. He or she just might copy your friendly behavior rather than escalating the unfriendliness to the level of being a foe or enemy.

Networking to Start Workships Outside of the Workplace

When you work with someone, day after day, you at least have the opportunity to observe someone as you decide whether or not you want to move your work relationship along to a workship or perhaps even to a friendship. Whether you are co-workers, boss/employee, or vendor/customer, you usually have a multiplicity of opportunities to listen, observe, and reflect on the person you are getting to know because of your workplace association.

However, whether you have a traditional job in an office or are a self-employed consultant working from home, you will also have an opportunity to grow your business and advance your career by work relationships you make through networking when attending trade shows, conferences, meetings, or parties.

This chapter offers guidelines for making the most of those networking opportunities for developing new workships out of those shared work-related experiences.

Making the Most of Out-of-Town Meetings or Trade Shows

Meeting after meeting, trade show after trade show, there are those who are able to make the time and effort they put into attending those events worth it to their careers, their businesses, their work relationships—and there are others who find it a waste of time, energy, and money. For some, the experience is even worse, especially if it negatively impacts feelings of self-worth and self-esteem. This may happen to those who show up thinking that they will meet, and befriend people, but instead are treated as outsiders. They are often ignored, dismissed, or left out of the private conversations, dinners, or even the seating arrangements that distinguish those who are "in" from those who are "out."

The way to turn this around is to face the unspoken truth about large meetings of hundreds or thousands, whether it's a conference of shared interest such as the annual meeting of an association, or a trade show of industry exhibitors. That unspoken truth is this: *you have to do the relationship building in advance so by the time you arrive, there are people who know and care about you.* As long as you have a group of workships and even friends at each trade show or conference who will include you in their private get-togethers, and introduce you as their colleague to those they know, you can work from that base of strength, and expand.

So your first step in making the most of large meetings or trade shows, whether in your town or city or out-of-town, is to give up the myth that you can show up, network, and make the experience work for you without any pre-workshop or trade show relationship building.

Of course there are exceptions to these "rules." You may be someone who can literally show up a total stranger to an event and at the end of a day or week have made enough contacts or relationships to make you feel your time and effort was worthwhile. But for many, pre-conference or pre-trade show relationship building will make the difference between time and money that is well spent and the feeling of rejection and even self-doubting that accompanies being ignored by peers.

When you attend a trade show meeting, or conference, since there are usually hundreds or thousands of attendees, it is necessary to break that mass of people up into units of one. That way you eventually connect to numerous peers or leaders, who are looking forward to reconnecting with you, because you have already established a connection to each one individually.

This takes time in advance. But, in the long run, your life will be so much richer because you are building relationships with the awareness that you will be meeting each other at the trade show, meeting, or conference, adding to those efforts the knowledge that you will also be meeting face-to-face.

This strategy of pre-relationship building before large meetings includes befriending total strangers in advance, through e-mail, phone calls, letters, or even get-togethers in advance of the meeting, as well as reconnecting with those you already know who will also be at that event.

Everyone today is pressured for time, more than ever before, but, if you put the time and energy into forming, or re-cementing, these work relationships before a meeting, the time and money you spend at the meeting will make up for these efforts. Furthermore, you have a greater likelihood of having more fun at the meeting, staying for the entire conference, rather than leaving early, as well as finding the experience extremely positive and beneficial.

Trade shows, meetings, and conferences are, of course, excellent opportunities for making new business connections that may, in time, lead to a casual, close, or even best friendship, but anyone you meet at such a meeting will start off as a stranger, unless you have done pre-meeting relationship building. Of course it's absolutely fine to meet new people at these trade shows or annual meetings; new friendships may evolve from those new relationships.

But, as you now know, new friendships take time to develop, time and trust that builds slowly through shared information, feedback, and communication. Trying to rush it along usually backfires so it's better to come to such a meeting with some friendships already in place and to add to those pre-existing relationships new connections that may or may not become something more.

Before the Conference or Meeting

Let's say you are planning to go to the annual meeting of an association that you just joined. You can go to the website of the association, or check its literature, or even call its headquarters, and find out when the next annual meeting is going to be (and perhaps even one to five years down the road). Write down in your planning calendar or in your hand-held PDA (personal digital assistant) the days you will be at the trade show including the travel time to and from the meeting.

At least three months in advance of the trade show, make a list of anyone you already know in the association that may be attending the meeting. Is there someone who already considers you a friend? It's possible, since people often join associations because a friend suggests that they join. (Some organizations or associations even require that a new member has at least one or two other members recommend them for membership.)

Ask if those you already know in the association are attending the annual meeting. If they aren't, find out about other members who *are* attending and to start an e-mail, letter, phone call exchange or, if they live in the same community, even get together and have a cup of coffee, lunch, or dinner in advance of the meeting.

You may be tempted to ask for a roommate for the meeting thinking that this could be a way of having an ally at the meeting. For some, this is a splendid idea and it will definitely increase the likelihood that you'll have someone to go to breakfast with, as well as spend some or all of your time at the meeting. Since you will be rooming together for a day, weekend, or as long as a week, you will definitely have more time to explore each other's personalities and to see if a friendship might ensue, or even give a new friendship a running start.

For others, however, having a roommate at one of these conferences can turn out to be a negative experience. If you do not get along, and the hotel is sold out, you are forced to live with someone you cannot stand or go home early. If you choose to remain roommates even though you are like oil and water, it can taint the entire conference experience for you.

If you still want to have a roommate as a cost-saving measure since hotels may offer a discount to those sharing a room, you could pre-screen whatever roommate has been selected for you. You could also try to find a roommate on your own, so you only agree to be roommates if you think you could get along for that period of time.

Asking someone who is already your friend to be a roommate has certain benefits: you know you like each other. Living with someone for a weekend or week, however, may not match how you get along when you go to the occasional movie or dinner out. So be prepared that your roommate experience may help cement your pre-existing friendship or add strains and pressures to it that you did not foresee occurring.

Making the Most of Your Networking Time

Once you have determined how long you will be at this meeting, get a schedule of what each day will hold. If you are attending an association's annual meeting, the program is sometimes set up one, two, and even three to five years in advance. The day is probably divided up as follows: breakfast, after-breakfast speaker, lunch, and luncheon speaker followed by breakout afternoon workshops, dinner (on your own or as a group), with an evening activity or free time. Are meals as a group with assigned seating or do you just sit anywhere? The seating arrangement may impact on how easily you are likely to develop new relationships that could become friendships as well as whether or not the time is pre-planned or "on your own."

If there are a lot of "on your own" time slots to the meeting's program, it is especially well-advised to have some plans in place before you even arrive. Once you arrive, you may be unpleasantly surprised to learn that most attendees have dinner plans already in place; they do not ask you along because you are an "outsider."

The best way to make the most of the time, energy, and money you spend to attend a meeting, conference, or trade show is to create your own "insider" scenarios in advance of your arrival. Yes, it takes time and planning but the increased relationship benefits to these meetings will more than repay you.

Of course there is plenty of good information shared at these meetings. Some annual conferences of scholars have literally hundreds of papers presented that enable attendees to be on the cutting edge of their profession. But with the ability to read these papers before or after the meeting, the intellectual value of these meetings is definitely enhanced only by the interaction with peers and leaders including the discussions that occur in the hallways, at meals, or during the free time periods.

The information that speakers share at the panel discussions is only part of the reason someone takes the time and spends the money to attend these programs. It is also the relationship building that occurs that distinguishes which trade shows or meetings are worth the time and effort from those that are not.

Find Out In Advance Who's Going to the Meeting

The National Speakers Association, one of the associations that I belong to, has an annual meeting attended by thousands from throughout the United States and from around the world. If you pre-register by a certain date, you will be included in the list of registrants.

One of the benefits of registering early and being on this list, as well as requesting this list, is that you can look over the names of those who are registered and see if there is anyone listed whom you already know or would like to meet. You can communicate with them in advance and start the process early of trying to start a new relationship so by the time you both attend the conference, you are one step beyond stranger or even acquaintance.

The Bouchercon, an annual conference of thousands of mystery writers and fans, also publishes a list of pre-paid attendees right on the website for each conference. Once again, it is possible to see who is attending as well as speakers who are on panels.

Get There Early or On Time, Never Late

The key networking times will be before registration, when the meeting or conference is set to begin, as well as during the breaks. If lunch is together, that will be a prime time for connecting as well. If a seminar has an 8:30-9 a.m. timeslot for registration and networking, get there no later than 8:30 so you can schmooze. Avoid showing up at the last minute, or late, eliminating most opportunities for interacting with either the attendees or the seminar leader, who just might be one of the movers and shakers at your company or in your industry.

During the breaks or at lunchtime, avoid spending all the time on your cell or mobile phone, trying to retrieve messages from your assistant or voice mail. Use that time to interact with other attendees, the staff, or the presenter.

If lunch is part of the seminar time, try to get to know those to the left and right of where you are seated. Suggest going around the table and having everyone introduce himself or herself along with a 10-second description of what they do. If appropriate, consider walking around to other tables and interacting with those attendees or speakers. There is no law that says you have to stay in your seat for the entire lunch, unless of course there is a rule about that because of the possibility of colliding with waiters or waitresses if there is not enough space between tables.

During the Conference or Meeting

- Put a smile on your face.
- Stay after the meeting is over to network and socialize.
- Keep your name badge on so others can more easily begin a conversation with you.
- Ask questions of those you meet showing a genuine interest in who they are.
- It's fine to give out your business card and of course ask others to give cards to you, but it's more about making connections that are meaningful rather than how many cards are exchanged.
- When you do get business cards, put a note to yourself on the back of each card, highlighting something that was said or anything memorable about this new person so you could refer to those comments or bits of information when you do your follow-up after the meeting. For example, did someone mention he attended the same college, or grew up in a nearby town?

Follow-Up: After the Conference or Meeting

You met dozens of people. You have 50 to 100 business cards in your suitcase or tote. Now what do you do to build on those relationships?

Sort the cards according to:

- Hot leads
- People I really liked and want to get to know better
- Nothing urgent or that memorable but still hold on to the card

After you sort the cards, decide how you will follow up on each person you wish to cultivate for business, for friendship, for both. If possible, follow-up immediately; certainly within the first few days. Send an e-mail, a note, a letter, or a sample product or brochure with a hand-written or typed note or letter, as appropriate.

Make a phone call, if that is more comfortable, although be prepared to get voice mail and, if you do, to either hang up and try again later or leave a short, succinct, and informative message. If you do want a call back, state your phone number clearly and slowly, as well as the optimum time you might be reached (to help avoid that time-consuming and annoying situation known as "telephone tag"). If you only wish to talk to the person you met, and so to reconnect by phone, it is certainly acceptable to hang up on voice mail or a phone machine. It is not the same thing as hanging up on a person. But if you are nervous about hanging up without a message, you might want to block your phone number from being displayed on the other person's phone if they have caller ID. (This helps to avoid the somewhat embarrassing situation of an over-eager recipient of your call returning your call—even though you did not leave a message—because your name and/or number was displayed.)

By controlling what information you give out, as well as how the next communication occurs with the leads you are following up, you have a better chance of moving your relationship forward.

If you hear from someone that you did not put into your "desirable" stack, certainly be pleasant, receptive, and, if it feels comfortable, open to giving this person reaching out to you another chance. Since business relationships as well as friendships and workships need to be reciprocal, the fact that this person has reached out to you is definitely a situation worth considering.

But of course, you do not want to let down your guard or throw yourself into a business relationship, friendship, or workship with someone that you just met simply because he or she is calling you. It could be the start of a wonderful business relationship, friendship, or workship, or it could be an overture that eventually spells disaster. Since your initial instinct was to put this surprise caller in the "Don't follow up" pile, be extra cautious about what conversation and possible interactions ensue from this overture.

Reaching Out at Local or National Associations

Trying to form workships outside of the company in which you work refers to meeting people in business situations or at the business functions as well as local or national association conferences that you attend. It used to be necessary to camouflage the wish to "network," or meet new people, or reconnect with business acquaintances, as a secondary motive to the educational seminars. Today it is more acceptable just to declare that you are attending a function to meet new people.

One key to forming workships outside of your company is to volunteer to become part of a committee so you meet people as part of your job function. You may also want to expand your horizons by joining associations that will put you into contact with those who are where you want to be, in terms of status or type of job, and not just where you are. Senior executive career consultant Laurence J. Stybel, President of Boston-based Stybel, Peabody, and Lincolnshire explains how participating in the suitable associations may be crucial for success today for several reasons:

> We are seeing the rise of two trends in our clients' careers: job tenure is getting shorter, a reflection of even shorter exit strategies demanded by investors, and non-compete contract enforcement is getting more stringent.
> The combination of the two means that in a world where good jobs are highly perishable, reputation is everything. The platform for establishing your reputation is the work you do in trade/professional associations.

Your work relationships are there with you for the duration of the assignment/job. Your association colleagues are there for you for the duration of your professional/career lives.

But our clients are also time starved, just in coping with the challenges of their demanding job and a family. So you need to be highly strategic and selective in developing an association management strategy. Failing to develop a strategy, your career is going to be stuck. Spending too much fruitless time with association matters and you will not have time to pursue excellence in your job.

Stybel asks, and answers, a crucial question: how do you achieve the right balance?

Join an association that is beyond the industry [that you're in]. Maybe it's a function, like sales and marketing or purchasing, and get involved with a committee assignment, which would position you with external relationships.

For example, get involved on the membership committee where your job is to meet people. You will obviously help the association as you're expanding your network.

Another client of mine was in sales in chemicals. He got involved in an industry association with the pollution committee, repositioning him in the environmental area.

In some highly competitive fields where most workers are self-employed and there are more talented individuals vying for very few jobs, networking, through association activities as well as other events, such as meetings, holiday or non-seasonable parties, conferences, and private functions, is crucial to letting others know you exist. These networking opportunities also open up the possibility that those connections may, in at least some cases, lead to workships or friendships.

Freelance writer Alix Strauss, in her article, "Schmoozing Without Losing: The Art of Networking," published in the *Dramatists Guild Quarterly*, makes a strong case for networking to advance a career. Strauss, who writes, "I'm a confirmed believer in networking, schmoozing, and making contacts. It's hard, it's scary, and it's time-consuming, but it's the single most important thing you can do for your career," also notes:

I have spent a lifetime learning the art of
networking, and I've amassed an impressive
portfolio of people who have the power to
further advance my writing career. My Christmas
card list is longer than Santa's, and the money
I spend on postage could feed a large starving
country. But in the end, it's all worthwhile.

Over the years I've observed this about networking: that if your
current network is not helping you get the visibility or information,
or even the relationships that you need at your job or in your
business, it is time to throw your net wider. In that way you will start
to meet and get to know more men and women who might be able to
help you to advance as you offer them assistance and camaraderie as
well.

Do You Want to Keep the Workship Going Even If There are Work Shifts?

What happens to a workship when roles change for you or your
colleague, or if one of you becomes the other's boss? Will you
continue the relationship if the person with whom you have a
workship leaves the company, or if you take a different job
somewhere else? Will a workship survive a shift in the work place
relationship?

Let's assume you and your colleague started as co-workers at
the same level but now you are the boss and he or she is your
subordinate, reporting to you. Will your workship continue the same
way or will it change and become a more formal and perhaps even
less friendly relationship?

Here are some tips for surviving status shifts so your workship
is not jeopardized:

- There are requirements associated with being the boss that have
  to be met and addressed so don't take those changes in your
  relationship personally. Whoever is now the boss may even find
  it necessary to be referred to by a different surname, at least in
  front of others, from being greeted on a first name basis to a
  more formal, "Mister" or "Ms," or even leaving the nicknames
  behind.

- Supervising someone may take its toll on your workship, temporarily or permanently. Take some time to see how your relationship adjusts to the changes before assuming it cannot survive.
- Consider going out to lunch, outside of work, in a neutral situation and discussing the change in your workship and how you both plan to adapt so your jobs and relationship are in tact.
- If there were behaviors you engaged in as co-workers, such as gossiping about others at work, you cannot be part of that now. If necessary, set those ground rules. Your workship, however, could still survive just as coupled men and women, who might have gossiped with each other about dates when they were single and unattached, usually learn that certain information is now "off limits" after they become a romantic couple.

Some workships, however, will not easily make that shift when status changes occur; the workplace relationship will be forever changed. That is what happened to 51-year-old Margaret, who had a hard time once her co-worker/workship became her boss. "I never could really look at her as my boss, as being superior to me in any way, as my having to report to her in any way," Margaret explains.

Did it impact on her job? Margaret felt the prior friendly relationship she had with her boss when they were co-workers actually got in the way of Margaret's advancement.

After a few years, although she had been with the company for sixteen years, realizing her advancement was blocked, Margaret left and started her own business; her boss remained and is now the company's president. Says Margaret: "I felt maybe [her] jealousy wouldn't allow me the opportunity to advance. I think some of the things that I wanted to change and improve upon within the company were blocked because of [our prior relationship] and [also] because of the personalities involved."

You could work at a job or have clients or customers with whom you have a rewarding and mutually beneficial workship for years, or even decades, and that will definitely serve your career well. (For a discussion of workships that become friendships at work, see Chapter 5, "From Workship to Friendship.") For guidelines on how to keep your workship going even after one or both of you leaves the job, or goes into a different line of work or career, see Chapter 9, "Coping With Endings."

In summary, workships will help you feel connected at work and, through your association memberships, in your profession. It's a relationship that is a big step above acquaintanceship but potentially less complicated than a friendship at work. To increase the likelihood that your workships will be win-win relationships at work, it's reasonable to expect that those involved in a workship will:

- Respect each other.
- Believe you can learn from each other.
- Believe it is good business to connect.
- Believe you can help each other's career.
- Accept that some jealousy and envy is present in every relationship including workships and see it as information and motivation (for wanting to get for yourself what someone else has, or vice versa) rather than a reason to avoid the relationship.
- Organize your workspace and workday so it is conducive to interacting such as encouraging breakfast, lunch, or after work get-togethers for food and socializing.
- Celebrate work-related achievements within each department or for individuals as a group or with workships.
- If appropriate, do good deeds together during the holidays and all year round.
- Do not tell associates or friends information shared with you by a workship that could compromise you or your business, or your friends, or even put them in legal jeopardy.
- Keep business secrets to yourself. (A "whistle blowing" situation is a whole different story and should be handled in the appropriate manner.)
- Make sure you're clear about just who your workships are. Don't be too quick to trust or too fearful to connect when it's prudent.
- Reexamine the workplace with socializing considerations. If cubicles keep everyone isolated, consider common rooms for opportunities to connect or converse, such as a corporate library, or a snack area if an on-site cafeteria is impractical.
- Share the belief that workships and the interacting associated with these workplace relationships usually foster creativity as

well as productivity; co-workers may provide information and insights for each other.

But what if you're not a "people person" and you just want to "do the work" and to avoid developing workships? What if you are friendly but the sentiment is not returned? In general, your career could suffer because most people want to work with people they like and who likes them. You may have to find a way to turn the situation around or in some cases consider finding a new job.

In certain creative careers, such as an artist, photographer, writer, actor, singer, or sculptor, among others, there is another alternative: it is possible to delegate workships to an agent or manager. You of course need to have that one workship with your agent or manager, but he or she is the one spending day and night making and maintaining at least some of the key workships that are necessary for your career.

4

Four Key Positive Workships

> "Mentors are so convinced that you have greatness in you—their vision of what is possible for you is so clear and powerful—that they convince you, too."
> —Business executive Lou Tice, "Learn to Win and Mentor Others," *Personal Excellence*

Within the five general categories of workplace relationships, there are four potential but pivotal workships that will help advance your career: Mentor, Advocate, Researcher, and Trailblazer.

1. The Mentor

He or she takes an active interest in your career and your advancement. This is someone who takes a liking to you and wants you to succeed. He or she is usually more experienced and typically, but not always, older.

The Mentor may be assigned to you, or you may ask someone you consider a role model to mentor you. The Mentor is a selfless colleague or boss who takes pride in inspiring his or her co-worker or employee to learn and excel. When The Mentor and you have a workship, it is more than the "role" of teacher-student. It is a powerful and positive relationship that can help the mentored advance farther and faster.

An interview by Gregory Bossler with playwright Eve Ensler, who won the Obie for her play, *The Vagina Monologues*, addresses the role actress Joanne Woodward played in her life. The two met when Woodward was teaching at the Neighborhood Playhouse and Ensler asked if she could write something for her. Ensler praises her Mentor and the career-changing experience that occurred:

> Joanne Woodward changed my life. I could almost cry talking about her. She was one of the first people to say, "I believe in you." She was my mentor. I wouldn't be here without Joanne.

In a survey I conducted of 257 human resource professionals and their companies, I found that only 13% had a formal mentoring program. So chances are, you're going to have to seek out your own mentor.

Sociologist and mentor expert Michael G. Zey, author of *The Mentor Connection*, noted that mentoring may actually rule out friendship: "Because the protégé is never the mentor's equal, the mentor relationship is always one step removed from friendship."

Yet the Mentor is a very distinct type of relationship that every worker needs. As I reflect on the jobs I have had over the years, I am reminded of one of my first mentors during my early twenties when I got my first job in publishing as an editorial assistant at Macmillan Publishing Company in the School Division. My boss, Nancy Creshkoff, was more than a boss; she was a Mentor, because she took an active interest in the development of my skills for the job and in helping my career in publishing as I moved up from editorial assistant to assistant editor in six months.

Nancy held weekly editing workshops for me and the rest of her staff of editors, around half a dozen of us, as well as assigning us books to read that would help us to improve our editing skills. She had lunches for her staff and took the time to sit down with me if I had concerns I needed to share even though in those days she was still living in New Jersey so she had a long commute back home from the company's office in mid-town Manhattan.

Do you have a Mentor? If you don't, whatever stage you are in your career, it's not too late to find one. You can also be a mentor to someone else, as he or she works his or her way up the ladder. It's a cliché that you get by giving but it is definitely true when it comes to mentoring.

At your job, look around and see who you admire who might want to mentor you. Ask human resources if there is a formal mentoring program that you could participate in. If you belong to a professional association let them know that you would like to be mentored. Be specific about what skills you would like to work on so you can be matched with a mentor who is the best fit.

Contact your graduate school, college, or high school guidance or career offices and let them know you're looking for a mentor from a previous graduating class who has expressed interest in helping alumni. You can also let them know if you have skills that you would like to share with current students or graduates as you offer to be a Mentor.

2. The Advocate

The Advocate spurs you on. Unlike The Mentor, who is a coach and a teacher, The Advocate inspires you to be the best that you are capable of becoming. The Advocate's role is not skills-related; nor is it involved in teaching you the ropes. Rather, The Advocate is more of a cheerleader than a career adviser.

This positive workship offers words of encouragement through an e-mail exchange, one line on a post card, a short message on your voice mail, or over breakfast, lunch, or dinner. Whatever the medium, The Advocate makes it clear that he or she is cheering you on as you rise to the top. The Advocate keeps propelling you forward whether that means sending along clippings of articles that you might find of interest or sharing your name and credentials with potential customers or clients. The Advocate just does this because he or she cares about you; you do not have to ask why. And if you did ask why, it might backfire because The Advocate is not acting out of any ulterior motive.

Over the years, I have been fortunate to have many workships who have been Advocates. In my twenties, when I was first developing my freelance writing career, Cele Lalli, who was then managing editor at *Modern Bride* magazine, was an Advocate. I still have the wonderful encouraging letters she would write to me, related to my assignments or my research, including her prophetic note that I was doing so much original research on couples who work together that I had the basis for a book. It meant so much to me that she took me to lunch at an expensive Japanese restaurant in a hotel on the East Side of Manhattan on Park Avenue. It made me feel so valued in the highly competitive world of freelancing that Cele wanted to get to know me and to honor me through that lunch.

We kept in communication over the years as Cele always cheered me on when I returned to graduate school to get my doctor and, four years later, when I got my degree, or when I published a book, as well as when I married and started a family. She even suggested that my husband and I consider buying her house in Connecticut when we were house-hunting; she and her husband were moving further north so they could have more land. I lost contact with Cele for quite a few years but always meant to reconnect.

Then, a few years ago, I was reading the local newspaper and much to my shock and sadness, I learned that at the relatively young age of 69, Cele had died in a car accident. I cried for my late Advocate with whom I have an eternal bond. Her nurturing, her attention, and her efforts went well beyond the call of duty.

Another Advocate I was privileged to have was C.H. Rolph, a well-regarded writer in England, fifty years my senior. We corresponded for two decades when he read my book on crime victims, *Victims*. He admired my writing as well as my commitment to helping crime victims. Without being asked, he found a British publisher for my book. He was not an agent; he just did it because he was my Advocate. We almost met once when he visited New York City but he returned to London before I got the message that he was in town. Our next chance to meet was not to be either; when I wrote to tell him that I was finally to travel to England, his son replied with a fax, that his father had died the year before.

3. The Trailblazer

This workship is often a few steps ahead of you and keeps pushing you along. The Trailblazer is not overly competitive and enjoys setting an example that you are inspired by or that you follow. You may even find yourself acting the role of The Trailblazer for your colleagues and that may be rewarding.

In the course of my research, I have learned about workships who were Trailblazers for other employees, changing the course of their careers by showing them, by their example, that it was possible to do something differently, or even to change careers.

I am reminded of a job seeker who went to a former co-worker with whom he had a workship from a previous job, and who was now working at a company where this man was hoping to get hired. But his colleague was in a different division than where the job seeker hoped to be employed. The former co-worker assured him that neither of them had a chance to get work in that division.

The job seeker ignored the advice of his former co-worker and applied anyway. When he got the job, his former co-worker applied for a transfer to the other division, and his change was approved. For a year, he and his trail-blazing colleague worked together before the new hire moved on to a completely different career. The Trailblazer had inspired a very positive, "If he could do it, so can I," motivation in his workship to make changes in his own career and to and forge ahead.

4. The Researcher

The Researcher helps to keep you in the knowledge loop whether it's related to what's going on at your job or in your company or, in a broader business connotation, in your business and even in the world. The Researcher, unlike The Gossip (as described in Chapter 10, "14 Types of Foes You Might Encounter") gathers and shares information in a positive way. The information-gathering helps you so you can do your best at work and in your career.

You can count on (but not become overly dependent on) The Researcher to know the paid vacation days for the next two years as well as where the annual meeting is going to be held, or what books in your field are getting the most attention. The Researcher knows who the players are at work and in your business, and he or she generously shares that information out of a genuinely favorable work connection and a sincere pride in being informed and informative.

I have several workships who are Researchers. Without being asked, they keep me informed via e-mail of news items related to my areas of interest. They provide extra eyes and ears into the world that adds so much as I feel far more connected and informed than I would in a vacuum. (I also act as a Researcher for other workships as well, clipping articles, sharing publicity leads, passing along helpful information because it is rewarding to give back to others since so many give so generously to me.)

Leslie Banks, Marketing Director at Dearborn Trade Publishing headquartered in Chicago, and Betsy Lampe, president of Florida-based Rainbow Books, Inc. are Researchers who generously share with me information that they think might be useful to my research or my career. I asked Betsy why she does it and she explained:

> This business, like many other businesses, depends so much on each of us sharing with the others that it seems only natural to share contacts. We're a community, an extended family of sorts. And I know that what goes around almost always comes around.

5

From Workship to Friendship

"Friendship is when you have the home number and you're free to use it."

—52-year-old Bonnie, single office worker

Work is an economic necessity, which is probably why instinctively so many keep their coworkers, bosses, employees, or suppliers at an emotional distance. That may help explain why whenever I asked how someone met a current closest friend, he or she often would say "at work." Then it would be noted that at work they weren't all that close until one left the job and only then a close or best friendship developed. Work had provided the opportunity to see a future intimate friend in action.

For example, 36-year-old Sally is a sales assistant whose current best friend started out as her supervisor at work. "But we didn't become friends until I was promoted and didn't work for her anymore. And then we didn't become much closer until a few years after that."

Sally's description of the path taken by the relationship with her current best friend is typical of the work-based interaction followed by a workship, once they are no longer boss-employee, followed by a casual friendship at work that eventually becomes a close or best friendship that transcends work.

Sometimes a workship does not develop further. For instance, two men who used to work together met by chance on the street. The first one was with his wife on their way to a restaurant. The second man was walking with a group of new work associates. The second man introduced his old work associate to his new colleagues by saying, "This is my former friend." It was an awkward moment and everyone either gasped or chuckled until he said, "I mean, this is my friend, and we used to work together." But what he initially said emphasized that the true relationship they actually had was probably a workship not a tried-and-true friendship since it had failed to extend into their current unrelated work experiences and personal lives.

Avoiding the forming of friendships, especially close or best, until no longer working together, may be a question of competition or survival and whether or not there will be a job and income to provide for oneself or one's family. Some, however, would like to move a workship to a friendship while still employed and they would like to know if it is possible to do so without jeopardizing their job. For some, it is easier to have clear guidelines about such situations; the military, for example, has a clear "no fraternization" policy between officers and enlisted men or women basically ruling out boss-subordinate friendships. In non-military situations, each boss or subordinate has to decide if he or she can handle a friendship without adversely impacting on the supervisory role.

This chapter explores both situations: workships that become friendships while you still work together and friendships that only evolve after the day-to-day work relationship or workship is over.

Just how common is it for a current close or best friend to have met at work? I posed that question to several e-mail discussion group lists that I am on, and thirty-three answered about how they met their closest current friend. Here are their answers, listed in order of decreasing frequency:

Work	15
School	12
*Other	6

*"Other" includes: through Neighborhood (1), another friend (2), through house of worship (1), through Mom-tot class (1), or camp (1).

Movie producer Diane Sokolow shares how it is the nature of a business like hers to come together with people and work intensely for a period of a few months, only to move away and onto the next job. Some relationships become enduring friendships, and some may not:

> The business I'm in, there's very little consistency in that you don't work in a job for twenty years. So you become very close to people over the course of a project and sometimes you're fooled into thinking it's a real friendship. Once in a while, someone pops out of that and you stay friends and that stays in your life.
>
> A real friendship is when you are comfortable and happy in the company of the friend, and they are comfortable and happy in your company. Trust. And that sometimes happens, and sometimes it's one-sided. I have a lot of friends that are true friends in my life that I have met through business and I have friends I have met not through business.

Some workships can last for a month, a year, or decades, and you never go to a movie together or socialize outside of work. Still, those workships help you advance at your job, find better jobs elsewhere, and continue to provide all the benefits of workships.

But there may come a time when you and your colleague want to move the relationship from a workship to a friendship. There are obvious benefits to moving a workship to a casual, close, or best friendship, namely the intensified connection that comes with a friendship as well as the increased loyalty to each other. Friends are expected to keep confidences and secrets. Friends working together might be a very positive development; there are some, however, who find friendship at work just complicates their job.

What Exactly is a Friend?

There are three conditions that usually accompany the transition from a workship to a more intimate friendship:

- A shared wish to move the workship to that next level of intimacy.
- Expanding the work-based workship to a non-work experience.

- Testing out the new friendship with the increased demands on it because of greater time pressures or structural changes as well as trust or discretion issues.

As noted in *Friendshifts*® and *When Friendship Hurts*, there are three distinct kinds of friends: casual, close, and best. A friend is someone you are not related to by either marriage or birth. Friendship is a noncompulsory relationship not bound by legal ties that is characterized by trust, honesty, loyalty, and a shared liking. Friendship, by definition, does not include a sexual or romantic relationship; if it does include those dynamics, it has become something other than friendship although there has been a trend, especially among younger men and women, to experiment with friendships that also include a sexual component, the so-called "friends with benefits."

Succinctly, *casual friends* are definitely friends, not acquaintances or workships, but you are not that intimate with each other. Information is shared but it is rarely privileged. *Close friends*—and some do use this term synonymously with best friends—are those who are dear and intimate in your life, but you may have several close friends. However, it's easier to have several close friends than it is to have two or more "best" friends. A *best friend* for most refers to the highest level of intimacy. A best friend knows all about your activities and relationships, your hopes, dreams, and fears. Even if is possible to have more than one best friend, especially a best friend who lives nearby and a best friend "from before" who lives far away, "the" best friend is considered the premiere chum. (Over the years, on average, as noted in *Friendshifts*® and *When Friendship Hurts*, I have found that a typical personal friendship network consists of 1-2 best friends, 4-6 close friends, and 10-20 casual friends.)

Here is how June, a publicist, summed up the categories of casual, close, or best friends, explanations that most will relate to:

> *Casual* is someone you wouldn't really confide in but whom you might get together with socially or at a party. A *close* friend is someone you would trust with events or issues in your life. A *best* friend is someone you talk to all the time and who knows the intimate details of your core.

When I was interviewed about friendship for the CBS News *Sunday Morning Show* for a series on friendship that they were producing, Russ Mitchell asked me what are reasonable expectations for a friend and friendship. I replied that it was an intriguing question since we do have very clear guidelines, even vows, that a husband and wife exchange when they marry, and there are expectations for a parent's duties. I thought about it and decided that a Friendship Oath might be useful to consider and even to share with friends. Afterwards, I composed the following:

Friendship Oath

By accepting the responsibility of being your friend, I promise to be honest and trustworthy. I will try to work out any differences or conflicts that we may have and will try to put the time and effort into our friendship that it requires. I know we both have work (or school), family, and personal obligations, and we will respect each other's other relationships and commitments, but I will also be committed to this friendship. I will try to only give advice if you ask for it, and I will also try to be your friend, unconditionally.

I will keep your confidences. However, I will also share with you if it is my policy to never keep anything from my spouse or any other primary relationship, with whom I entrust all my secrets. I will try to remember your birthday and be there for you when times are tough and when times are grand. Making time to talk, communicate by mail or e-mail, or getting together is a priority. I will celebrate your achievements even though I know a tiny bit of envy or competitiveness is normal. I will bring fun and joy to your life as much as I am able to as I cherish our past, present, and future friendship.

Another key finding to my friendship research is that it takes, on average, three years from the time when two people meet until they have gone through enough time and "tests" that they consider each other tried-and-true friends. If after a couple of years you and your workship no longer work together, that would definitely be a test: do you still keep in communication or get together even though your relationship is no longer as convenient or based on work?

How many friends should you have at work or in business? The answer to that question is similar to the answer I provide when someone asks how many projects they could accept before they are doing too much at once: as many as you can handle. Some may be able to handle one casual friend, one or two workships, and one best friend; another can handle 25 casual friends, three close friends, two best friends, and five workships.

In my most recent survey of 400 men and women, the average number of friends at work reported was 7-10. Those friends were divided into the following categories:

Best friends at work   0-1
Close friends at work   1-2
Casual friends at work 6-7

Compare these average number of friends at work to the average number of personal friends, mentioned previously, of 1-2 best, 4-6 close, and 10-20 casual and it is clear based on my research that the number of personal friendships, on average, outnumber the work-based ones.

Your definition of closeness is another factor. One's ability to be intimate with others is highly subjective. One person might label someone a "close friend" while someone else, with a different capacity for closeness, might label a similar relationship a "casual" or "best" friend.

Gender difference is also a factor. There is a great deal of social scientific and anecdotal research to support the generalities that women are more open and verbal in their friendships, providing for emotional support, whereas men tend to relate through shared activities. Those gender differences may impact on how a workship or workplace friendship is perceived.

For each relationship, questions have to be asked. Is it an acquaintanceship, a workship, or a friendship? There is, after all, a status given to the relationship we call *friendship* because it is an earned or acquired status. Whether in one's personal life or in business, friendship is viewed in a favorable light until it becomes apparent that the word is being misused to gain favor rather than to express a genuine relationship or feeling.

There are of course those who have an inflexible policy against having any friends at work, whether it is casual, close, or best. Those who feel strongly about that are entitled to that point of view and they can make it clear if someone wants to befriend them, or if a friend wants to work at the same company and they do not think it is a good idea. "Nothing personal," just a policy. That can help offset any bad feelings that you are rejecting that individual (or, if you are the one being rejected, help minimize your feelings of rejection).

For example, public relations executive David Hochberg of Lillian Vernon Corporation has such a policy. Hochberg explains: "I don't mix my personal life and my business life. I don't like to do business with friends and I certainly never hire friends."

The Process of Friendship Formation

Before discussing the pros and cons of workships that become friendships while you still work together, it is useful to review some of the fundamentals about friendship formation. When an acquaintanceship becomes a workship it is because the two individuals are no longer relating to each other through only universalistic roles, such as "co-worker" or "employee." Instead, their relationship has become particularistic and specific as they relate as individuals, with names and personalities, like Sally and Julia, or John and Marvin.

To become friends, this particularistic workship becomes even more specific as the degree of intimacy increases and the type of information exchanged includes more self-disclosures and possibly even feelings; a higher degree of trust is necessary for the friendship to flourish.

The model of a friendship that follows, from a shared situation or activity, helps to clarify the process from stranger to acquaintance to workship to friendship always remembering that both parties have to want to start and maintain the relationship, at whatever level of intimacy, or it will be changed into a workship, acquaintanceship, or even an antagonistic relationship.

Model of a Friendship From a Shared Situation

SHARED ACTIVITY OR SITUATION
(work, school, neighborhood)
↓
ACQUAINTANCESHIP
(based on formal role, such as co-worker, employer-employee, vendor, customer or client)
↓
WORKSHIP
(becoming more familiar, less universalistic and more individualistic)
↓
FRIENDSHIP
(casual, close, or best friendship with all the obligations of that role, such as honesty and trust, and deciding if job or friendship comes first)
↓
STATUS CHANGES
(such as promotions or raises or co-workers who become the boss)
↓
REEVALUATING THE FRIENDSHIP IN LIGHT OF THE CHANGES
(the friendship withstands these tests and a strong tie results, or buckles from the pressure resulting in a weak tie or no contact)
↓
RELOCATION
(to another job , company, or community)
Passive/close tie or passive/distant (once physically separated)

In theory, work is the ideal setting for a friendship to blossom since some of the key motivations in forming a friendship, including having someone to talk to, shared interests, or providing emotional support, are all present in the mutual work setting. Not since high school where everyone could share about the same routines, teachers, and classmates is there the potential for intimacy and commonality as in that home away from home called work.

However, work and business put extra demands and pressures on friendship, which, in theory, should only exist because two people like each other; there should be no other conscious or unconscious motive to the relationship. Some conditions that will make it easier for a work or business friendship to succeed without complications are the following:

- You and your friend have similar abilities or attributes. Neither is dramatically more gifted or talented than the other or, if you are, you each respect each other's strengths (and weaknesses) without being excessively competitive about it.
- You both have few unresolved issues from your formative years or, if you have issues, you are seeking help to resolve them. (See Chapter 13, "Workplace Relationships Begin at Home," for an exploration of these concerns.)
- You have shared values including work-related values such as a commitment to honesty, integrity, a similar work ethic, excellence in your work or product, and other issues.
- You have taken the time to discuss how your friendship and your work responsibilities may conflict and what you would do in those situations.
- You are competitive, which is fine and normal, but not excessively so; nor do you begrudge each other your achievements or successes.

Here are additional guidelines to remember if you want to increase the likelihood that your friendship that started at work or in a business capacity will thrive:
- Use your judgment about jumping in to discussions that trash the boss or the company. Your words could come back to haunt you if you are perceived as vindictive or negative or if you misjudged your friendship and you're really being set up to fall.
- Take that three-year average for forming a tried and true friendship seriously. That does not mean you can't feel someone at work or in business is a "fast friend," but guard yourself and your job till you find out if your initial instinct about someone is borne out by reality.
- Friendships based on doing things together or having someone to talk to may entail less angst and conflict than those based on

emotional support. Although it's fine to occasionally use your work friend as a sounding board, be careful to avoid overstepping the line into misusing your friend at work as a therapist since he or she is not trained to provide those services. If you need professional help, get it.

- Genuine friendship rarely is based on what future benefits the friends can give each other. If you get the feeling your "friend" is really looking for free investment advice, or a free coach (even though you charge for these services or have a policy of not providing professional services to friends even for a fee) you should be rethinking whether this is a friendship at all.
- Friendships between those who are equal in work status, such as between two co-workers, have a better chance of succeeding at work without complications or compromises than those with disparate status, such as between a supervisor and a subordinate.
- Since shared values are the best predictor of longevity in a friendship, take the time to find out what your work or business friend's values are to see if the two of you will be a good value fit as friends.

The Benefits of Workplace Friends

Casual Friends Improve Communication and Productivity

Casual friends are a step up from workships but not as intimate as close or best friends. Because the friendship is the least intimate, there is less likelihood that you or your friend will be influenced by emotion or affection to the point that your judgment may be impaired.

For example, your casual friend asks you to take over her projects for a week so she can go on vacation. If you are already so overburdened that saying "yes" might jeopardize your own work load, saying a polite "no" to a casual friend will result in less angst than if you have to say "no" to a close or best friend.

As 36-year-old Reginald Beckham Jr., Director of Marketing and Membership at the Washington, D.C.-based National Association of Housing Cooperatives, says about the benefits of a casual friend at work:

If you have a friend at the office or develop friends at the office, instead of talking to each other like co-workers in "work speak," you can talk to them as a friend. That's more comfortable in a work environment, and anyone who is more comfortable doing what they do is a more efficient worker.

A 63-year-old professor echoes the communication benefits of her casual friend at work: "We enjoy talking, but only at work and [at] an occasional dinner."

Why You May Want a Close or Best Friend at Work

A close or best friend should stand up for you at work and also act as your extra eyes and ears to deal with office politics. Failing to come through for you just might cause you to reevaluate whether someone is a close or best friend, just a workship, or even a foe. As a young woman who works for a store in Illinois, describing her close friendship with a co-worker in the same department, put it: "We look out for each other."

Friends at Work Offer Support Through Tough Times

Thirty-year-old Erika, a divorced Danish librarian, has a colleague who has become her best friend. Erika explains:

I've known her for three years. She is eight years older than me and has been a wonderful support for me over the past year. During my separation, she has been a good "partner" in telling me when she thought I was right or wrong. She always sees things from many different angles and she's the most honest person I know. I respect her with all my heart and I discuss everything with her.

A male trainer at a university in the Midwest, who feels strongly that best friendships at work are positive, shared this with me:

Having a best friend at work has helped he and I through some difficult times at work. We trusted each other and we supported each other. For many people, their emotional support is their friends at work.

A 27-year-old who is now married and a stay-at-home Mom to two toddlers shares how a friend at work had helped her through the emotional angst when she'd broken up with her boyfriend:

> When I broke up with my boyfriend of six-and-a-half years, my friend at work made sure I was going to make it. She took me to lunch, listened as I cried, gave me advice, bought me a plant, and helped me through the first two-and-a-half months.

Friends at Work May Aid Job Performance

Researchers Karen Jelin of the University of Pennsylvania's Wharton School and Pri Pradhan Shah at the University of Minnesota studied 53 groups of three people with a range of relationships. Their findings were that as long as the workplace friends were deeply committed to the goals of the group or the organization, friendship at work aided productivity. If that condition was not met, it was better if the friends did not work together.

Friendship at Work Might Motivate You to Stay at the Job

My survey found that *having fun at work* (according to 68 of the 102 respondents who answered that question) is the #1 benefit of workplace friendships*. Having fun at work is not as superficial as it might seem at first consideration. The fun factor, along with positive workplace relationships, are reasons for improved worker retention, increased creativity, motivation, job satisfaction, and customer satisfaction, all contributing to an exemplary corporate or company culture.

Close or Best Workplace Friends Can Aid Self-Esteem

We all want to be liked at work. As a 58-year-old editor notes: "I had a co-worker at work that I considered a close friend. We shared an office and many responsibilities and had a mutual respect

---

*The remaining answers were divided among "making the day go faster," "sounding board," "having a lunch buddy," "having someone to go out with after work" and "adds to productivity," in descending order of frequency.

for each other and our abilities. She was always thanking me and affirming me in what I did."

Getting to Know Each Other is Facilitated Because You Spend So Much Time Together at Work

One of the biggest challenges to forming new friendships after the school years is finding time to get to know someone if you lack day-to-day interaction. Work provides that opportunity, as do work-related situations, such as retreats or business trips. As a 27-year-old South African bookkeeper pointed out:

> My best friend is also a work-related friend. She went away with me for a weekend. The night before we had to come back, I couldn't sleep. It was about three in the morning. So when I asked her if she was asleep, she said, 'Sort of, but if you can't sleep, I'll stay up with you.' Then she actually put some clothes on over her pajamas and went to a store nearby to get us some coffee so that she could stay awake and talk to me.

The Friendship Gives You an Advantage

Despite accusations of favoritism, if your friendship with the boss is one of many factors in why you get promoted over your co-workers, that friendship may be a big plus for you at work.

In some industries, such as the film and television industries, there are so many qualified people that getting recommended for a job may be a question of who will personally and professionally vouch for you; friendship is often key. When I interviewed the late Carl Sautter, a screenwriter and TV writer, he emphasized how most of the jobs he got in Hollywood were from fellow writers with whom he had a writer's group. When one of his friends and fellow writers got a staff job on a TV series, if they were asked to recommend someone, it was always their friends that they suggested. Ditto if someone was asked to recommend someone to rewrite a feature film.

I have observed or been told in other professions and in other workplace settings that recommending a friend to get an assignment or an account is typical. In some businesses, you can get your foot in the door through a want ad, but getting the second assignment may depend on how well you did the first assignment *and* if a friendship ensued with the person with whom you worked or your boss.

Possible Negative Consequences of Workplace Friends

On the minus side, however, here are some reasons you have to be careful about having a friend at work.

Betrayal

According to my friendship survey of 400 men and women, a romantic betrayal was the most frequent kind of friendship betrayal, with work-related betrayals a close second. Of the 63% who reported being betrayed by a friend (250 out of 400), 43 listed that it was a romantic betrayal (someone making a pass or having an affair with a romantic partner or spouse) followed by work betrayals (37).* Here is sampling of what those work-related betrayals were as well as the type of friend who committed it:

- "Telling lies and coloring the truth to get ahead at work." (casual friend)—62-year-old married librarian
- "Plagiarized my work." (best friend)—47-year-old married scientist
- "Said negative things to the boss." (close friend)—60-year-old married male, radio talk show host
- "A best friend betrayed me to the point where I lost my business."—35-year-old married Canadian artist
- "A close friend applied for my job when I was on leave." —55-year-old single teacher

Friendship Makes Someone More Vulnerable Emotionally So That Hurt Feelings May Occur More Often

Friendship involves connecting emotionally with someone else.

---

*The third most frequent reason for the betrayal was sharing secrets or betraying trust (29), followed by lying (22), unacceptable behavior (14), and someone stopped talking and wouldn't explain why (13). (The total does not add up to 250 because there were additional reasons with just a few in those categories as well as no specific reason noted for the betrayal.)

Through friendship you open yourself up to acceptance, being liked, admired, respected, trusted, and appreciated. You also open yourself up, as do others when they befriend you, to the possibility of disappointment, betrayal, rejection, and misunderstandings.

With intimacy at work, the potential for emotional disappointment, unrelated to the work at hand, increases. Linda, a 30-year-old factory worker in West Virginia, was devastated when her close friends at work were not supportive when she had a miscarriage:

> I used to have two close friends at work until they turned their backs on me after the loss of my baby. It hurt me so much cause I was always there for their problems and the one and only time I needed something, it was like, "Get over it." So now those relationships are at best causal but could be close if I allowed it.

As a result, the friendships became less intimate. Linda felt so betrayed and hurt by what happened that this is how she answered the question, "What have you found is the #1 benefit of having a friend at work?" "I don't think there are benefits, only negative consequences."

Competition Over Salary, Promotions, and Position

Geraldine, a 52-year-old aerobics instructor, shared about her former best friend Sylvia and how Sylvia's "telling" on her—that she had private clients—led to Geraldine's firing:

> I met her when we were both in our late 30's. She was beautiful and a wonderful dancer. We became friends through our church. We both were teaching aerobics part-time at a health club and I was asked to be on staff but she was told she couldn't be a staff member unless she had a college degree. She didn't, I did. I think that was a source of irritation to her. She was jealous.
>
> I was jealous of her dancing too but in no way would I do anything but help her pursue her dream. She didn't feel the same obviously about trying to stop me from becoming a staff member. She signed up the director of the health club in her aerobics class and it was shortly after that I was called in and

told my teaching aerobics to individual clients would be a conflict of interest and I couldn't be a staff instructor.

I don't know what I did to cause Sylvia to betray me. I know that she felt threatened by my aerobics ability and teaching skills. I think that played a big part in her doing me in.

It's Harder to Keep the Work-Related Disagreements Separate from the Personal Relationship

Working with or for a friend seems to be a plus as long as there is agreement and disagreements about a specific project or client or supervisory issues do not come up. When those clashes occur, however, it takes enormous work for both friends to avoid those disagreements from wandering out of the "just work" area and into their feelings for each other as friends. (For suggestions about how to deal with these issues, see the sections of this chapter entitled "Pros and Cons of Befriending a Boss" or "When a Friend Works for a Friend" as well as Chapter 8, "Dealing With Conflicts.")

Tips When Befriending Co-Workers to Keep Work/Business and the Relationship Going Smoothly

Here are some tips for making it more likely that those friendships that start and intensify at work will aid, and not sabotage, your career.

- **Make sure your wish to relate on a level that is more than a workship or "co-worker" is shared.** Look for the verbal and non-verbal cues that your co-worker welcomes your wish to become friends. For example, if you say, "Would you like to have a cup of coffee?" or "How was your weekend?" take note of whether your questions are answered eagerly or in a dismissive way or, even more distinctively, ignored. You could try again, just to see if your co-worker was in a bad mood that one time. If it is a persistent pattern, get the hint.
- **Befriending at the same level is safer and easier.** If you are being rebuffed, it might be because your overtures are seen as inappropriate or threatening possibly because of a disparity in

status or abilities. Also be aware that even today some men and women are uncomfortable with cross-sex workplace relationships; if you pick up on that attitude, do not take it as a personal rejection. Just get the hint and seek out same-sex workplace friendships that may be more acceptable and welcome. (For more on this issue, see Chapter 7, "Opposite-Sex Considerations.")

- **Be careful who you trust at work and who you befriend**. Be especially cautious if there is a wide disparity in age, socioeconomic class, or status. Most friends tend to be similar, so wide disparities are a possible red flag that there may be blatantly opportunistic (non-friendly) reasons behind the attempts to move the relationship from a workship to a friendship.

- **Listen to your co-workers; don't just always talk and expect them to care about you.** Listen actively, responding to what your co-workers say and share, of course respecting their privacy as well as confidentiality if personal details are shared with you that are not intended for everyone or to be the source of office gossip.

- **Remember that everyone has a different capacity and need for intimacy.** Listen and observe to see if your needs match those of your co-worker. If not, decide if it is a long-term situation, based on personality clashes, or something temporary, perhaps related to excessive deadline pressures, work or family crises, or personal or emotional upheaval. If it is a temporary situation, you could revisit the relationship down the road to see if this co-worker is more amenable to getting closer.

- **Work on a project together**. Your relationship may become closer naturally as a side benefit of that shared work experience.

- **Stay informed.** Be up on current events, movies, books, articles, in general and related to your work. Workplace and business relationships are an excellent source of information as well as emotional support. If you become known for providing information, your friendship will be valued and coveted.

- **Avoid gossip.** Being friendly and open to friendship is very positive; being known as the "office gossip" is quite negative. Avoid spreading or generating gossip. Sharing information appropriately is distinct from gossip. Make sure you know the difference.

- **Help out for, as the saying goes, a friend in need is a friend indeed.** If someone needs to leave early, offer to provide coverage. If a co-worker has a personal or family crisis, offer to help. You are being a nice co-worker and employee but you are also planting the seeds of friendship if there is a shared connection with your co-worker.
- **Set limits.** You can be friends at work but you can also withhold certain information that you might tell a close or best friend in your personal life**.**
- **To facilitate a friendship at work, have some ground rules.** Discuss what you might do in certain situations where your relationship might be a factor in doing your job and have a dialogue about the appropriate way to handle those issues so neither the job nor the friendship is put in jeopardy. You might have a discussion about any exit plans you need. For example, a couple who works together has to consider when, or if, their romantic ties are getting in the way of doing the job. Close or best friends have to take that into account as well.
- **If you are both in agreement, broaden the basis of your friendship.** Take the friendship outside of the workplace not only as a way of moving it along from a purely work-related relationship to one that exists outside the workplace but because it will give you a wider range of experiences with your friend.

To minimize the potential for friendship conflicts, follow these guidelines:

- Keep your workplace friend's confidences.
  Whether the workplace or business friendship is a casual, close, or best friendship, or a workship, discretion is key. Maintaining your friend's trust is crucial.
- Avoid any situations that would put you or your friend in a position that might be construed as a conflict of interest because of your friendship.
- Dodge workplace or business gossip; avoid passing along any gossip you cannot avoid hearing.

- Never misuse a work or business friendship for opportunistic, self-serving reasons.
- Avoid name-dropping or bragging about your friendships at work or in business.
- Watch out for body language, gestures, and nonverbal cues at work and in business that are too familiar in a business setting.
- If you manage others, hold back information or comments that undermine your authority.

Here are services or possessions that it is better not to ask for but to wait until the offer or information is volunteered:

- Asking if you can stay at a second apartment, house, or vacation home you think is underused. (Let your friend make the offer.)
- Going behind someone's back to hire their secretary, executive assistant, proofreader, cleaning staff, or babysitter (or any support staff or employee pivotal to their work or personal commitments).
- Borrowing equipment that is essential to someone's job, such as a computer for a writer or business executive or a guitar for a musician.
- Borrowing and failing to return an item that has nostalgic value, such as a favorite book or a cherished pen that was a gift from a co-worker, romantic partner, or family member.
- Asking to borrow an expensive item, such as a car, boat, camera, or videocamera.

Pros and Cons of Befriending the Boss

Two key types of potential boss-friend-employee situations to consider are when a friendship develops with your boss, or when you have a pre-existing friendship that preceded the work relationship.

If you try to be friends with your boss, there are status considerations. If you share information with your boss, or your boss confides secrets in you, you may find yourself put in a situation of having to choose loyalty to your job over allegiance to each other. As the 62-year-old head of training for a government agency in Massachusetts put it:

> I don't believe that friendship has its place in business. It makes it very hard sometimes to promote from within if people are too friendly with one another. The role of supervisor becomes difficult when it involves friends. It can create a very difficult atmosphere especially if it involves discipline. Jealousy is another deterrent when someone (a friend) is passed over and the job given to someone else.

It is a different dynamic when you and a co-worker, who have become friends at work at equal status, now find yourselves in a new situation, with one reporting to the other.

Although being liked by a boss is usually key for career advancement, do not confuse being liked by your boss with friendship. For some, befriending a boss is impossible; there are just too many boss-employee conflicts brewing. As Richard Laermer, CEO of RLM Public Relations, with offices in New York, Washington, D.C., and Los Angeles, says: "You can't be a friend with somebody you resent. That's the first rule of friendship."

Trying to force a friendship with your boss will be viewed with as much disparagement as trying to force any friendship. If it naturally grows out of your association, you and your boss will work through the status or management issues that might arise. But if you try to harangue your boss into a friendship when the wish for such a relationship is not shared, you will make it uncomfortable and even unpleasant to work together.

By contrast, a 32-year-old bookkeeper, who is now married, reflects on the friendship she developed with her boss, who remained a friend even after she left the job:

> I was fortunate enough to once work for someone whom I had known for several years, someone who took me in when I needed a place to stay, kept me employed, and gave me a place to celebrate holidays. I still consider both him and his family to be the best of friends.

If You Become Your Co-Worker (and Friend's) Boss

Probably one of the more common situations that presents challenges is when you befriend a co-worker, but then you are promoted so you will now be your friend's boss. Is it possible for the friendship to survive without compromising your new role as "boss"?

Although befriending at the same level at work is easier and usually less complicated, it is possible to have friendships between boss and employee if both are sensitive to the challenges that a disparity in status will have on their relationship and their work situation.

Here are several discussion points and considerations when you and your co-worker workship/friendship become boss/employee:

- Sit down and have a heart to heart with your friend. Discuss what both of you now need to consider with the change in your status.
- Spell out ground rules that you think are necessary, such as the obvious one, that your friend cannot get preferential treatment just because you're friends since it is your mandate as manager to treat all employees equally.
- Let your friend know that if you need to criticize, or even praise, your friend at work, it will be based on her workplace performance and nothing else (e.g., your friendship).
- Agree to discuss any issues that arise rather than letting things fester or negatively impact on your new role as boss, your department's productivity, or your friendship.
- Avoid addressing each other by nicknames or mannerisms that are overly familiar that could lead other co-workers to resent your friend because of her friendship with you or that could lead to accusations of favoritism.
- Have a discussion about any exit plans that might become necessary. Just as couples who work together should consider what they will do if their romance interferes with their work, close or best friends, especially if one becomes the other's boss, also need to take that into account.

When a Friend Works for a Friend

Sometimes it starts off as a favor, or a good idea, to work for a friend. But sometimes it may become a choice: leave the job or risk the end of the friendship. That's what happened with Carol, a 46-year-old married zookeeper. Previously, a friend needed a secretary and Carol needed a job. Carol explains: "He paid me very highly for the position I was filling. But he also fired me after two years under stressful conditions." She thinks it was the preferred course of action since "if I'd stayed there, our friendship would have been ruined."

Public relations executive Richard Laermer, whose company, RLM Public Relations, now has 27 employees, echoes the difficulty when a friend goes to work for a friend so they are no longer two equal friends but boss-employee:

> When we were small, five or six people, I had some friends from my real life who came to work here. To fill in. One person came to work fulltime. That equation never quite worked because I could never quite be their boss.

As Laermer notes, sharing about the way he has become a close friend with those he met only *after* they started working at his company:

> The other side of it is, the core group that is here now, that has been here three, four, five years, most of those people have become my personal friends. For instance, our VP Mike, we are like two peas in a pod. We're very similar. We have the same sense of humor—his wife says she listens to us both and can't tell us apart. I consider him one of my closer friends—we fight like friends too! His parents raised him right and he has an amazing work ethic. He's incredibly polite not just to me but to everybody and then again he has a soul. He's pretty ironic and funny. Someone I would call a good person—he's very positive about everything.
>
> Our COO Brian and I are good friends. Scott, my assistant, who's worked here for three-and-a-half years—we're good friends.

However, public relations executive Harold Burson of Burson-Marsteller supports the theory that "it's lonely at the top." As Burson said, quoted in *Friendshifts.*® "I think it's a lot easier to be very socially active at lower levels of the company than at the upper levels. One of the prices that you pay for being a CEO in a company is that you give up a lot of the social relationships within the company. There's a line beyond which you cannot go."

In my friendship survey of 400 women and men, out of the 127 who answered the question about whether or not they had ever befriended a boss, the answer was more likely to be "no" (68) than "yes" (53). Of those who answered "yes," and shared more information about what kind of a friend the boss was, only four had a best friendship with a boss. The rest had friendships almost equally divided between a casual (22) or close (23) friendship.

One of the reasons it's lonely at the top is that, friendship, especially workplace friendship, is least compromising when the relationship is between equals. No one else is at the top level. Over the years, I have discovered that CEOs may befriend other CEOs at different companies, or even in different industries. By doing so, their work-related friendships may be with others at a comparable level, just not at their own companies.

When a peer becomes the boss, to avoid the change in status sabotaging your friendship, or your work responsibilities, be up front with each other (and with yourself) about how this change makes you feel. If you are the one who now reports to your friend, are you angry, jealous, or resentful? Or are you bursting with joy for your friend? Perhaps you are feeling all those emotions, and then some. Are you able to deal with it on your own? Or do you think it will be better for your friendship and your job if you just get it out once and for all about how you feel, that you were both equally qualified and you should have been promoted to boss instead of your friend?

There is no right or wrong answer to how to deal with this situation since you know how open to sharing of feelings your friend/boss is going to be, as well as whether or not airing your feelings will help or hinder your friendship or your job. For some, ranting and raving about the injustice of it all, but to a neutral or disinterested third party, may be the better strategy. Send a card, take your friend out to lunch, and send a basket of fruit to celebrate your friend's promotion, acknowledging his or her new status as your boss.

If you are the one who was promoted over your friend, be prepared that your advancement may cause jealousy. Mary, an 18-year-old who was promoted to manager at a fast food restaurant in Canada, notes that her best friend became jealous of her "when I got promoted to manager before she did."

The jealousy does not have to be the end of your friendship, but it could make it uncomfortable for your friend, or both of you. If you want to try to maintain the friendship and if there are hard feelings, you might consider initiating a dialogue with your friend. Talk about how the change makes your friend feel, and if there are any issues that need to be addressed that will help you and your friend/subordinate to work more effectively together. If there are any ground rules that you think will help your friendship as well as your new role of boss, let your friend know what those ground rules are.

For instance, if you have any nicknames for each other, you might make it clear to your friend that now that you are the boss, it would be uncomfortable to refer to you by that name in front of others, or at work all together.

Customers (or Clients) as Friends

Having a customer as a friend will usually be fraught with fewer complications if either of these two conditions are met:

- The business relationship develops after establishing a solid tried-and-true friendship.

- The friendship evolves slowly following the progression from customer to workship to friendship.

For example, a Midwestern sales executive for a cosmetics corporation now has numerous representatives reporting to her. But she started out by selling door-to door to her personal friends, handing out just thirty catalogues, to grow her business. She has since expanded her job beyond her personal friends, sending out 2,000 catalogues, but her core of friends had helped her to initially launch her sales career. This enabled her to have a flexible job that worked for her and her family while raising two daughters.

Others have shared with me how they started off relating only as client/advisor, editor/author, or boss/employee. But slowly, ever so slowly, over time, the work-based relationship changed to something more personal as socializing in non-work contexts becomes even more frequent than time spent in a work-related way. Often spouses, even children, and other friendships become part of the equation. If they no longer work together, the bond is so strong that the purely social connection persists even after the work or business association has faded.

When Close or Best Friends Go Into Business Together

There are certainly a lot of horror stories about friendships that dissolved because the close or best friends go into business together only to have the friendship end even as the business succeeded (or vice versa). But there are certainly also lots of positive examples of close or best friends whose friendship and businesses seem to be strong and active. For example, Karen Canavan and Kristin Cowart had been best friends for six years when two years ago they started their own Georgia public relations firm, KC Public Relations, which has ten employees. Canavan, 34, and Cowart, 29, met when they were both working at the Atlanta office of a PR firm. In Christine Van Dusen's interview with Canavan and Cowart, says Cowart, "There's a trust. Any true friendship has got to have that. But a business is built upon that."

Deborah Elliott-Upton and her best friend Kim worked together, and their friendship did better than survive: it flourished. Deborah and Kim, both freelance writers, collaborated on a nonfiction book about female friendships.

Deborah and Kim lived just a mile apart, but they still relied a lot on e-mail to communicate because of their other business responsibilities. Deborah explains why she thinks their project was successful and their friendship did not suffer from working together:

> The friendship came first and was more important than the book. We set out determined to stay friends so any writing issues were brought up immediately and settled before moving on to the next section.

> [Writing the book together] brought our friendship to a new level, one that many friendships never reach. Like sisters, we can disagree on an issue, but would never be able to sever the relationship. There are too many ties holding us together. Writing together is only one part of our friendship.

There's been a lot written on how to run a family business, but advice for close or best friends who wish to start a business, or work together, is harder to find.

Friends who become business partners have to be much more cautious than family members. You are taking a voluntary relationship without any formal legal or blood ties and adding to it legal, financial, and business responsibilities.

Here are some questions to ask before you work together, or start a business, with your close or best friend:

- Do you each have a clear plan for your business?
- Is your plan in writing?
- Have you read each other's plans to see if you share the same vision for your company?
- Is the funding for the company to be shared as well as the expenses and profits?
- Can you hire others to handle legal, financial, administrative, and other functions?
- Is it possible to give your plan a "trial run" before making a total commitment to the new company? For example, you work together on a freelance or outsourced project to see how well you handle the back-and-forth of working together, meeting deadlines, sharing decision-making, delegating, dealing with each other under pressure?
- Are your work styles similar or, if different, complementary?
- Have you considered how working together as well as being close or best friends will impact on your family members? Romantic partners? Other friendships? Extended family members?
- Do you have an exit plan in place in case working together or running a business together does not work out? Will you dissolve the company or will one buy out the other?

- Have you made a firm commitment to preserving the friendship first and foremost; if the business partnership is not working out, that you will take the hint before it is too late to salvage the friendship?
- Has everyone you told about this idea told you and your friend that you're "crazy" to go into business together, but you both still think it's a great idea and that it's going to work out?

If you answered "yes" to this last question, before you rush into your business or working-together venture, consider going back to the first question and making sure you've worked through all the other questions and answers.

You might also want to refer to the section in Chapter 8 entitled, "Money Issues," since close or best friends working together, especially going into business together, has as much to do with how you handle money as it will about how your personalities mess or clash.

In summary, here are ten principles to keep in mind for workships and friendships:

Ten Principles for Getting Along With Your Workplace Relationships (Workships or Friendships)

1. Have mutual respect.
2. Share a commitment to the relationship.
3. Understand the boundaries to the relationship.
4. Keep all confidences, work-related and personal.
5. Deal with conflicts or disagreements immediately and appropriately.
6. Avoid holding a grudge.
7. Beware of hubris. No one likes a braggart.
8. Before you get offended or angry, listen to the other person's explanation or perspective. There may be facts or extenuating circumstances you do not know about that help explain a situation that you misconstrued.

9. Emphasize your similarities and shared goals, interests, values, or beliefs rather than creating a wedge by dwelling on your differences.
10. Share credit, as appropriate, so you get labeled a "we" not just a "me" colleague.

6

Power Workships/Friendships and Cultural Concerns

> "The number one rule is to be as honest as you can about the relationship. You don't want to nurture a friendship because you are going to 'use' people. The whole thing here is not to use people. A friendship by its very implication can only be genuine."
>
> —Career consultant Nella Barkley, President,
> Crystal-Barkley Corporation

> "I think the meaning of friendship is being on your friends' side in good and bad days. This is the most important thing and the basis of friendship."
>
> —25-year-old married Turkish woman working in advertising

Beyond forming workships or friendships with colleagues, your boss, or clients, there is one category of potential workships or friendships that may be able to help your career more than all the others. This is the category of the movers and shakers, the power elite, some famous and some not, but who all have one thing in common—they get things done.

The first concept to keep in mind when considering a possible workship or friendship with this group is to realize that movers and shakers are usually very busy people. Trying to turn your connection with them into friendship may backfire since you could be perceived as a "high maintenance" business relationship. If you understand that their being busy is not a personal rejection of you, you may be that much closer to, in time, forging a valuable workship or even possibly a friendship. As Patricia Schroeder, CEO of the Association of American Publishers (AAP), a professional association of more than 300 publishers, who is married and has two grown children, points out, it is hard to find time for friends:

> One of the things I think I sacrificed being in twenty-four/seven jobs all my life is close friends. I've got family that I work very hard to stay in touch with because I think that's terribly important and I've got all the professional stuff you've got to do. Sadly enough, something gets lost. I really haven't stayed in touch with my college friends. Did you read *The Divine Secrets of the YaYa Sisterhood*? It's interesting. They were really close friends [but] all they [those women in the novel] had to do was hang out and drink and watch their kids.

Once you realize that powerful people are usually very busy, with lots of meetings and travel commitments, as well as their own family responsibilities, you need to find a way to interact with them that will work with their schedule. How do you do that? Find out what associations they belong to and join. If you do not want to join, you could also consider attending meetings or networking functions open to non-members at the non-member rate.

What benefits do they attend? What causes are they involved with? You probably have to pay for tickets to fund raisers; at least part of the cost (beyond the meal or meeting facility expenses) is donated to a worthy cause. If you are at a fundraiser, you at least have the opportunity to meet movers and shakers in your business or in other businesses and the community as well. As you start finding people who like you and want to be around you, those all-important invitations to private parties, breakfasts, or lunches will hopefully be forthcoming. (If it seems polite to bring a gift to those private functions, make your choices wisely spending just enough to be appropriate—not too much so it looks like an attempt at influence peddling or showing off and not too little so it sends off the negative message of being "cheap.")

You might also entertain and invite movers and shakers although it will be harder to get them to attend your event until they are actually workships or friendships. However, you could certainly ask your current friends to ask their friends or workships or even the friend of a friend of a friend, expanding your network accordingly.

If you have an event that is sensational or pleasant enough, you can possibly increase the likelihood that they will want to be there so you can at least meet and see if nature takes its course. Sensational events are of course an investment of time, money, and creativity, so be prepared to put forth that effort or delegate to someone who handles such matters at your company or to a professional meeting or event planner. The association, Meeting Planners International, has local chapters with meeting planners nationally and internationally who could help you with an event.

Here are other tips to increase your visibility and your access to movers and shakers in your business or field:

- Work hard to be the kind of person that others want to befriend. That means be a good listener and to be concerned with others and not just yourself.
- Be honest, hardworking, and the best that you can be at your job and in your field. Humility and modesty will also go a long way. Having self-esteem and self-confidence, distinctly different from hubris, are definitely assets.
- Build on what is unique about you. For example, if you are a woman, join associations dedicated to helping women to succeed. Or, consider becoming active in associations that are based on your interests, alma mater, or current position, such as the CEO club.
- Take trips with movers and shakers; if you are on a seven-day cruise for those in your industry or business there will be multiple opportunities for meeting and talking and, hopefully, for a workship or friendship to ensue.
- Attend meetings and trade shows.
- Join the company sports team (e.g., baseball, bowling, basketball).
- Help plan and host the company-wide summer picnic or winter celebration. Volunteer to be a meeter and greeter.

You are more likely to meet people if you take on a role at a function than if you are just another guest or attendee.

- Write and publish so you stand out in business so movers and shakers may contact you and ask to befriend you.

Race

Although friendships, in general, tend to be between those who are similar in terms of age, gender, socioeconomic status, race, or religion, that it is not a steadfast rule. Religious or racial restrictions to friendship are definitely melting away, but it is taking time for the adage "birds of a feather flock together" to evolve into meaning that those who share the same values and affection for each other will "flock together," rather than those who just share physical traits, status, or socioeconomic similarities.

It is friendship's unique ability to transcend race, religion, or cultural differences that makes it a powerful relationship in one's work and personal life. Befriending at work or in business across racial lines, especially if you did not have the chance growing up to have diversity in your friendships because your school or community was homogenous, offers an opportunity to break down stereotypes and myths. Linda, a 36-year-old married stay-at-home Mom, shares about the friend whom she met eight years ago; they became best friends a year later:

> I knew I liked her the first time I met her, which has never happened to me before or since. My best friend is black. I am white. She is a Democrat. I am a Republican. Her husband is a college professor. Mine is a counselor. Our differences make us interesting and fun. We have many similarities such as our Christian faith, marriage, and kids. We've learned much from each other because of both our differences as well as our similarities.

Annie, who is white and who grew up in the South, developed a network of black friends when she worked up North:

> I have a number of friends who are black and one of my best, closest, dearest friends is black. She prefers *black* to *African American* because she says her people came from the

Caribbean and although they might have gotten there from Africa, it was too long ago to matter. Several of my closest friends in New Hampshire were black men.

Annie shares an anecdote with a facetious twist: "In fact, when I retired, my friend organized a special private retirement party for me, about fifteen people, all black. She told me they had decided, 'No white people allowed.'"

Sharon Simpson Joseph, an African-American lawyer who grew up in Queens, New York and is now president of Spirit Soars, Inc., based in Atlanta, a publishing company, shared with me about race as a factor during her childhood and school experiences:

> I've always had friends of all races growing up. That's probably due to a few things. My parents are both open and progressive people who have always been committed to multiculturalism and equality. My Mom worked in the New York City school system. She started out as a teacher and retired as a principal. My Dad was a social worker in the South Bronx. He worked with youth groups and senior citizen groups and eventually ran one of the nonprofit centers in the South Bronx. When Prince Andrew can to visit, this was one of the centers he came to New York to visit.
>
> In the neighborhood itself, I had friends who were different races, black and white. One of the stories in my book, *And How My Spirit Soars*, is about a boy in the neighborhood. He and I were friends. He was white and Jewish. We would spend lots of time playing with each other. I was about four. One day, on this particular occasion, his grandmother picked me up from the school bus instead of his parents. And his grandmother said, "Don't play with her, that little —. She used the *n* word or something equivalent to it.
>
> At the time, I was confused. "I'm not Jewish? What?" I didn't know that I wasn't Jewish. I didn't know that he and I were different at all. My sense at the time was that we were the same. He and his family moved many years ago. We lost track of each other. But he was like a little buddy that I had growing up.
>
> I have friends who are African American as well as other races. We [my sister and I] always went to schools that were quite integrated or schools where we were one of the only black kids at times. But we also have a family that is somewhat

interracial. I've got a grandmother's who's half-Swedish, half-African American. There are a lot of interracial marital relationships in our family tree.

I asked Sharon if she and her "best sister friend," who is white, and whom she met when they were both students at Stanford Law School, ever discuss the fact that they are different races. Sharon says:

> We can go for a year without discussing anything or even being cognizant that we're different races. We just live our lives. [We'll discuss it if] it comes up, and if it's relevant [to what's going on]. Over Thanksgiving at her home in California, my friend and I were reminiscing about a celebration trip we took together after passing the Bar Exam. We took a day trip to St. Thomas and we had on similar outfits. We walked by [a fellow who called out], "Hey mon. It's the best of both worlds," and we just cracked up.
>
> I remember when we were at law school going to a party with this particular friend, maybe two-thirds of the way through the party, I said to her, "Do you realize I'm the only black person here?" I hadn't even realized it.

Thirty-nine-year-old Harriet, a black dance instructor who is separated from her husband, has more white than black friends. But she attributes this to her profession, an industry that she sees having very few African Americans in it. She explains:

> I just tend to meet more people who are white than black or Hispanic. Since I am an African American woman who works and lives in an environment that is almost entirely white, there have been times that I have felt somewhat isolated from my peers. I thought it was just me but I have found other African American women feel the same.
>
> Sometimes I feel that my white friends will talk about things that I just cannot identify with, which will cause some strife in the relationship. What is really awful is that there are a lot of black women that I do not identify with as well. We have nothing in common. Economic and educational differences can make it hard to develop friendships with other women who are black. They will simply not like being around me. I am too black to

totally blend into white culture and have too many Caucasian mannerisms to blend into black culture, yet I am a black woman.

Religion

Thirty-five-year-old Susan commented about how jokes about her religion have impacted on her and her friendships since childhood. Susan maintains a close friendship with a girlfriend who still does not understand why these jokes are offensive to Susan. As Susan explains:

> This is something that I perceived as being terrible but unfortunately [my friend] did not and still doesn't. I am Jewish and I take jokes about being Jewish very badly. My great-grandmother, whom I clearly remember, was held in concentration camps. As a child growing up, I dealt with some anti-Semitism from other kids. At the time, I am sure they didn't understand what they were saying, just learning it from their parents. Those experiences left me very touchy when it comes to being joked with about my religion. My friend was teasing me about my religion and I became very upset. She didn't and still doesn't understand and says I take things too personal.

Vikki from Berlin had a childhood friend and neighbor with whom she was close from the ages of 13 to 17 who was from Turkey and a Muslim. "Her parents did not think I as a German girl was good company for their daughter," Vikki shares. "They often would not allow her to see me and we would have to meet secretly." Their friendship faded after her friend moved to a town thirty miles away.

Even today, most of Vikki's friends are the same religion even though she is open to friends of all religions. She notes:

> I would not have a problem with being friends with somebody from a different religion, as long as they are nice and polite and not dogmatic about their belief. I would love to be friends with a person of the Jewish faith. I would find that very fascinating also in light of our painful history in the twentieth century that we share. But I never was a friend with a Jewish person in Germany so I can't say anything about this but let's see what the future has in store for me.

Carl is a 53-year-old social scientist who has two best friends, one from childhood, with whom he attended Sunday religious school (Reformed Judaism), and the second friend from work, with whom he taught at the same university when Carl moved abroad. "He is of a different ethnic and religious background from mine," Carl explains, but that has never been an issue in their friendship, which has persisted even after Carl moved back to the United States.

Alternative Lifestyle Workships and Friendships

William told his mother he was gay when he was 18 and he is very open about being gay with everyone he meets through work or in his personal life. He told me that what bothers him the most about his workplace relationships is that "People immediately assume that you are a specific sort of gay person. That's really annoying."

During our interview in the lobby of a hotel around the corner from his London office, William shared the following anecdote that typifies his frustrations:

> I remember a few weeks ago, a friend of mine, Brenda from America, that I met several years ago, she moved over here to start working. She expects me to be this screaming Queen. I overhead her saying to her friend, "This is my Will I was telling you about."
>
> I don't know if you've seen the sitcom, *Will and Grace*—now that sitcom comes on here—I saw about ten minutes of it and it didn't really appeal to me. "I'm not your bloody Will." I was really annoyed but I didn't want to make a big deal. But for my birthday, she bought me a kind of sequined turquoise hat and a book about a male movie star.
>
> I don't like any of these things! Why do people have one specific image in their head? When I meet new people, one of the ways women especially bond with me is by latching on to the sort of gay thing and using it as a sort of thinking. They'll know that's what you'll want to talk about. It's just people trying to find some common ground. But you can't hold it against people. For a certain amount of time, those things should take a back seat till you know people and what they're *actually* interested in.

Most of my friends are straight. I just go to normal pubs. I don't spend much time socializing in gay-specific places. I live on my own as well.

A woman of thirty shared about her work friendship that emphasizes universal themes in work-related friendships, whether the friend is a heterosexual or practicing an alternative lifestyle, such as: is the friendship reciprocal? Her friend Stuart is also her employee. For more than a year, she struggled with her intense friendship feelings for Stuart, which he returned intermittently:

In the beginning of this friendship, my friend and I had a very intensive relationship. Almost like teenage girls, we would be on the phone twice a day. We would share everything and we would hang out together very often. I don't have a loving and supportive family and for some reason have never had a love relationship with a man although I am in my late twenties. So that friendship with a man was something totally new to me.

I promoted him big time in the company. I gave him fashion advice. I brought him into my circle of friends. I wrote him letters of recommendation so that he could get some additional freelance jobs. I gave him so much because I wanted him to like me. And it worked...at least for a time.

When it did not work, I was of course very hurt and thought that he was totally ungrateful.

I have the hardest time to separate my feelings and myself from our work relationship.

So overwrought by this friendship at work, as well as determined to find out why she had never had a long-term romantic relationship, she entered into therapy. Through therapy she began to understand the dynamics behind the intense friendship she'd developed with her employee as she gained a perspective on why she was so obsessed with this friend. Then, after a few months of progress, she shared about a seeming setback in their friendship, which actually helped her to let go of some of her fixation on him:

We had a misunderstanding and I sent him an e-mail and he was terribly hurt by that. When we were forced to attend a meeting together, we sat next to each other for two hours without saying a word.

But fortunately, after the meeting we managed to talk. Well, for the first thirty minutes, we were bitching at each other before we were able to talk more civilized. All in all, the conversation lasted about three hours!

He basically told me that over the years, my e-mails and messages have hurt him terribly and that he would not answer them. That would be below his dignity.

Here we have the first misunderstanding: I always thought that he was not taking me seriously. I interpreted his silence that way. ...So this three-hour talk that we had was extremely difficult but also extremely important. When I said, "You know, after all I have done to you and written to you in the last two years, you really must hate me," then he said, "You are underestimating the size of my heart."

International Cultural Concerns

With so much business today transacted internationally, you may find yourself more than ever before, because of the Internet, open to potential relationships with men and women from around the world and not just within your department or company. Of course letters and phone calls have been ways to connect internationally for the longest time, but the Internet makes it faster, easier, and less expensive to develop and maintain international workships and friendships.

Keep in mind that there are cultural differences in how workplace and business relationships are viewed in different countries and take the time to get to learn about those similarities and differences.

A professor who grew up in France and moved to the United States in the 1960s, but returns to France every year for two months, reflects on the cultural differences he sees in work and friendship. To him, they are both complementary and divergent:

My experience in the United States has been that many friendships originate in the workplace. This has not been my experience in France. Friendships [in France] more generally originate in the family. There is a cultural stereotype in France that depicts Americans as making and losing friends with their jobs.

The friends I grew up with in France are still very much part of my life. I have done little traveling in the United States, but it does not strike me that I have made the kind of friendships here, with the exception of my wife, that I inherited from my youth.

Anette Moos, who lives in Berlin, where she works as a tour operator for an American company that offers trips in Germany, shares her observations about how Germans and Americans differ in terms of workplace relationships:

There is a popular saying: "Dienst ist Dienst and Schnaps is Schnaps." Translated this means: "Work is Work (duty is duty) and Booze is Booze." This shows it all: in Germany, business is business and friendship is friendship.

German people have their business acquaintances on the one hand and then they have their friends on the other hand. They rarely mix, especially on a client and provider basis. [For example], I have a friend who works at an advertising agency and she would never become a friend with her clients. It is just not appropriate.

We Germans are much more comfortable if we don't know our clients too well. We prefer to stay with the formal "Sie" instead of the informal "Du" which you would use for your friends.

In the United States, "small talk" is something that everybody masters and that does not have a bad connotation at all. Whereas in Germany, people are not as open as in the United States and many defy "small talk" because they think it is superficial.

In the United States, people will say, "Hey, let's do lunch some time!" but they don't mean it. As a German, you take this seriously. You show up at the other person's doorstep or you call them and make a lunch appointment and then the American person is a little bit taken aback because his invitation was just a nice polite piece of conversation rather than a real invitation.

Germans take everything very seriously. If you ask them, "How are you?" then they most probably will not say, "Oh, fine. How are you?" but they will tell you exactly how they are! They will say, "Oh, well, my mother is sick and my car does not work and I am feeling a bit unhappy because my boyfriend said that

I was too chubby, blah, blah, blah..." That is a difference between the two nations.

In the inner-company relations, this is something different. In Germany, a lot of people meet their [romantic] partners at their company and a lot of colleagues become a friend over time. So friendship is possible if you are working together.

In contrast, here is the description of what to typically expect in terms of work and friendship as shared with me by a director, Elia Schneider, who has lived and worked in her native South America as well as Manhattan and, more recently, in Los Angeles:

In Venezuela, you take all your work friends to lunch as the normal way to do business. Co-workers become friends very easily and they are friends with the boss and the employees. All the company is *based* on the friendship.

I love working with people like that; the friendship is more important than if we achieve the product goal. We work to be together, to have a good time, to share our problems, and to make a little money. If you reverse this, you can be out of the game. We exchange gifts every Christmas. It is very important.

When I am in Caracas, we reunite every Tuesday night for Ladies Night. The publisher of my short stories is also the executive director of the most important cultural institutions. Also present is the production editor and some other work friends. We talk about everything and we laugh a lot.

I miss this very much when I am here [in the United States]. I find that people here are much more "in control" and always watching what they say. Precaution is basic and what [work] goal have you achieved is the only thing that matters. I believe that even if people want to be different and would like to have friendship as a goal, the money machine doesn't allow it because all the values are based on how much you make.

A married advertising executive in Spain reiterates similar attitudes toward work and friendship in her country:

It is very typical to do business here in Spain with friends. Co-workers become friends but the status is shared (co-worker/co-worker, boss-boss). Business entertaining is usually conducted in the office [rather than at home or in a restaurant.]. Business is usually done at lunch. Friends do go into business together.

A 65-year-old Danish businessman, whose work puts him in contact with men and women throughout Scandinavia as well as the rest of Europe and the United States, provided these insights into work and friendship considerations:

> We can roughly divide it into two categories, friendship between employees and a very strong network, "the old men's network". We have about 200 persons in Denmark who are members of more than 25 different boards, incorporated companies handled at the stock exchange. Very often their sons or sons-in-law are introduced to the same companies by their fathers/fathers-in-law. It is a complete mix-up of a small group of people.
>
> As to the normal workers and employees, it normally goes smoothly. There are many examples of people meeting each other, getting married, after they have met at work. As a matter of fact, [the workplace] is the most common place to meet a partner.
>
> Who do we do business with? Very much like the United States: we do business with the people we play golf/tennis/badminton etcetera with, and a big percentage are people who have known each other since they went to high school or university.
>
> In all four Scandinavian countries, headhunter firms are used to find new board members, to find the general manager plus vice presidents on the lower level, and it is then decided inside the company who to employ via their personnel office. We have also had scandals here with people getting a job, which they cannot live up to, but it is more a political question. High ranked persons inside the government or the local municipalities will often push a particular person he/she knows so that this person will get a job within the organization.

In Julia Stuart's article, "So Who Needs Friends Anyway?" published in the *Independent* newspaper, about the book, published in England, entitled *Friends & Enemies*, written by Dorothy Rowe, she quotes Rowe on the differences she observed in making new friends in England (Yorkshire and Lincolnshire), Australia, and the United States:

> For most of my time in England, I've lived
> in Yorkshire and Lincolnshire…and in those
> places, if you haven't been there for 400 years
> you're a newcomer no matter how good your
> social skills are. On the other hand, if you
> live in Australia or the United States, you'll
> make lots of friends very quickly.

In Manhattan, I interviewed a 28-year-old magazine editor who had moved to the United States from England the year before. It's interesting that her complaint about Americans was that "It's hard to know when people are being genuine." She expressed a similar point of view about Americans and the "let's do lunch" type of phenomenon as Anette Moos, the German woman I interviewed: when is it real and when is it just an expression? "It took me a while to realize they didn't [always] mean it," the magazine editor from London explained.

As I listened to the reactions of Americans I interviewed about the British, I wondered if there was a similar cultural disparity at work: was "British reserve" being misinterpreted as aloofness or unfriendliness? Robert Liebman, a writer and native New Yorker who has been living in the United Kingdom since 1984, comments on the differences he has noticed in the British and Americans and in how they approach friendship:

> Americans will confide intimate matters to strangers with an ease that just eludes the British. They don't do it but a few Brits will take advantage of the most casual of acquaintanceships to discuss intimacies and they do so in a manner that suggests that they are near to bursting with the need to open up.
>
> Here there are far fewer best friends. Even very close friends don't talk as much, or as frankly, as Americans do. In both countries, male friends tend to be more superficial and other-directed (sports, work, etc.) so the differences show up more among women (from my perspective, at least).

Liebman shares his observations on how the reaction to the death of Princess Diana temporarily displayed a softer side:

The public reaction to [Princess] Diana's death perhaps showed on a larger canvas the duality that I had earlier perceived on a smaller anecdotal scale. Tens of thousands of Britons wept and grieved openly. But even while this was happening, many British commentators utterly and scornfully deplored this softening of the upper lip. Some seemed to be personally embarrassed, as if worried that outsiders might tar them with the same brush of soppy sentimentality. But the fundamental norm is still to keep emotion under control.

When I was in Tokyo, I interviewed a single working woman in her late twenties who shared with me how difficult it was for her married girlfriends who were staying at home to raise their children to get together with her. I assumed it was because they were so busy with their young children and I cited that as a possible reason to her. No, she explained, it was because they had to ask their husbands for permission to get together with a friend.

I also asked her about any changes regarding work and friendship in Japan today. She replied:

Japanese society is drastically changing due to the Internet/mobile technology and increasing unemployment. Friendships these days, especially among younger generations, are getting broad but very thin. They think they have many friends as they communicate on a daily (or hourly) basis through e-mail and mobile [phones] to so many people. But probably they may not see each other face to face as much, not even ever meet in person. They communicate for a while, then the relationship fades out very easily and they still call it "friends." Probably the meaning of "friend" is changing now.

Working for a certain company used to mean he or she works for the company almost for a life. They were rarely fired and the colleagues were like relatives or family. However, due to the high unemployment or gradual change of society, a belief of individualism, nobody believes we work for a company for a lifetime anymore. We may get fired one day and need to find another job. Or we do not hesitate to take [a] better chance, if offered. People are seeking for [a] strong bond but sadly most people are not one hundred percent sure where to turn to and [are] struggling.

Questions to Ask Regarding International and Cultural Work and Friendship Considerations

If you are interacting with men and women from around the world, you might consider asking someone the following questions (or asking a third party for some answers so you know how to interact more effectively):

- What does the word "friend" mean in your culture?
- How do you define a friend?
- Are there terms to describe different types of friends?
- Is it customary to work for, or with, friends?
- Do co-workers socialize after work?
- Does socializing take place at a restaurant or at home?
- Are there holidays or vacation periods in your country that I should know about so I can adjust my expectations for communicating, working, or visiting accordingly?
- Since there are cultural differences in names internationally, perhaps we should let each other know, if it's not obvious from our names, whether we are male or female so we do not unwittingly use "Mr." or "Ms." incorrectly.
- Is there anything about work and friendship in your culture that I should know about to help us to more effectively do business?

Most importantly, remember that there are definite cultural distinctions when it comes to work, workplace relationships, and friendship. It is up to you to find out what those differences may be in each of the cultures you are doing business with internationally. The perspective of other cultures may be eye-opening. As the writer who relocated to California from Latin America said, "Try friendship as a goal…and you will end up having friends in a natural way and not designing friendship in the fantasy of your mind, as you want it to be, like it is not, and will not be."

7

Opposite-Sex Considerations

"My best friends are guys and I have amazing, intense friendships with them."
—25-year-old single female administrator in consulting firm

"I felt betrayed because he kissed me and threw the boundaries of our friendship out the window."
—21-year-old single British university student

How can an opposite-sex workship or friendship occur so that colleagues or clients do not lodge allegations of sexual harassment (or flirting) against you? You want to make sure your male-female workship or friendship is just that, and nothing more. If you or your workship or friend want it to be something more, and it's appropriate and welcome by both of you, that's just fine. But then your workship or friendship is really moving into an office romance, so you will have different concerns, as noted below.

To maintain the workship or friendship and non-romantic aspects of your relationship, if you and your colleague are involved with others or married, make sure you let your romantic partner know about the workship. By sharing openly about your opposite-sex workship, even introducing him or her to your mate, you avoid giving the wrong idea about your relationship. If you are open and up-front about it, and comfortable about having a workship or friendship with someone of the opposite sex, it is more likely your mate will also accept it and believe you that it's "nothing more."

Keep your get-togethers in neutral, non-compromising situations preferably at work, or, if necessary, right after work, to help reduce the likelihood that tongues will wag and that it will be assumed that your workship is something more. If the romantic partner of your workship or friendship goes out of town, be careful about offering to "fill in" if she or he needs someone to accompany him or her to a business or social event.

There are some opposite-sex workships or friendships, I was told in confidence, that have a flirtatious element, but neither colleague wants it to go any further than that. Being honest with yourself about that aspect of your opposite-sex relationship, or that you feel able to share about different issues or in a different way than with your same-sex workships, does not negate or compromise any of your relationships. Each relationship is enabling you to connect in a distinctive way.

But be prepared if you and your opposite-sex workship or friendship have a change in your romantic relationships. For instance, if one of you, who is unattached, becomes engaged or married, then jealousy, whether based in reality or just a visceral feeling, may force your opposite sex colleague to choose between your workship or friendship and the new romantic partner. If your workship or friendship has to end, or be put on hold, because of that new romantic relationship, it probably says more about your co-worker's mate than it does about your workship or friendship. While you give your opposite sex colleague and her mate time to sort things out, strengthen your other workships or friendships or find new ones.

There are some, however, who successfully maintain an opposite-sex friendship that started out as a workship. For example, Joy Tipping, a 42-year-old writer who is married and who also acts in amateur theatre, explains that her longstanding friendship with Bert which started as a workship two decades before does not bother Joy's husband or her friend's wife. In the last few years, the two couples have even started getting together. As Joy explains:

> We actually met when I was twenty years old doing theatre, "Equus" in Dallas. I lived in Dallas my whole life till four years ago. He had moved to New York around fifteen years

ago. Bert met [his wife] there and they [later] moved to New Orleans. I was invited to New Orleans for his wedding.

After Bert left Dallas, for years he would return every Christmas or New Year's and they developed a tradition of having breakfast together during the holidays. It became harder to keep the tradition going since Joy was no longer living there (she relocated to New Mexico although both their families are still in Texas) but last December, both couples met in New Orleans for a week together. Joy and Bert had their breakfast friendship tradition once again, but in a different city and this time with their romantic partners becoming part of the custom.

When Workships or Friendships Turn to Romance: Do's and Don'ts

Next to college or high school, work is one of the most common places for romantic relationships to originate. Few companies have an actual workplace romance policy, so what follows here are some guidelines to help you deal with workships or friendships that turn into romance.

When the relationship is appropriate, condoned by the company, and welcomed by both parties, it can be a positive development from both a romantic and even a work perspective. On the other hand, it could also cause enormous emotional and legal problems, not to mention pain, suffering and possible termination.

What happens when the romance ends and you still have to work together? It can make the work environment extremely uncomfortable, not only for the two parties involved but also for others working nearby.

This doesn't always have to be the case. For example, Jennifer is a 24-year-old supplies manager at the London office of an international financial services corporation. She "worked side-by-side together for a year" with a man from work whom she also dated that entire year. They worked together for a few weeks and then started seeing each other. Jennifer explains: "Then we broke up and then everyone sort of figured [that we had been dating] but no one realized it while we were doing it." Her ex-boyfriend still works at her company and it hasn't been a problem. She says: "We're civil to each other now but I wouldn't go out drinking with him. We still hang around the same circle of people so we're both adults about it."

However, some may feel that Jennifer and how she handled an office romance that ended is the exception rather than the rule.

According to a 2001 poll of 558 human resource professionals taken by the Society of Human Resource Management (SHRM) and 663 corporate executives surveyed by CareerJournal.com, *The Wall Street Journal's* executive career site, 81% of the human resource professionals and 76% of the executives noted that workplace romances "were dangerous because they can lead to conflict in the organization."

Jennifer and her ex-boyfriend (discussed above) avoided post-break-up workplace conflict perhaps because she was aware of the dire consequences if any did occur and she guarded against public displays of emotion. As Jennifer says, "If people [at work] see you have a personal grudge against someone, it's the end of you."

Helen Drinan, former CEO and President of the Society of Human Resource Management (SHRM), stated, "It's natural that when people work together closely romantic feelings sometimes emerge."

Finding a romantic partner at work, after all, is a logical place for most singles to meet just as school was the primary place to meet a date during the formative years. A recent Office Romance Survey by Vault, Inc. found in its survey of more than 1,000 professionals at companies nationwide that 47% had participated in an office romance and 19% were open to it if the opportunity was presented.

Having a workplace romance policy in place, as well as defining appropriate behavior for those working together and involved in an office romance, decreases the potential for disaster when office romances do occur. For example, a 31-year-old male has been friends with his 27-year-old female co-worker for seven years; she helped him get his current job. During the first year at work, the friendship became sexual. He now has a girlfriend but his co-worker (ex-romantic "partner") refuses to be his friend as long as he still sees his girlfriend. She's even threatened him professionally saying the she would make his life "hell and 'see to it I was fired.'" He doesn't want to leave the job because he would have to give up valuable stock options and his girlfriend is upset because he won't take her to company functions.

Tips for Avoiding Career or Romantic Disaster

Here are several guidelines for when a workship (or friendship) becomes an office romance that might help to minimize the adverse consequences to your career or workplace relationships. The information here is not a substitute for legal advice in these matters.

- When in doubt, find out if there is a workplace policy about dating a co-worker, superior, or subordinate. Consult your employee manual or find out discreetly in other ways.
- If you are the boss and you are even considering asking your employee/workship or friendship out on a date, you should consider first giving up your supervisory capacity. That's what a psychologist did when he realized he wanted to go out with the social worker who was working for him. He went to his boss, shared his intentions, and his employee was assigned to another therapist. (Within a year, he married his former employee, both jobs intact.
- Be careful not to let your romance affect your productivity.
- Avoid such obvious telltale romantic gestures and signs as kissing, handholding, gazing into each other's eyes even when walking into the office building or in the elevator. Avoid sharing food in the company cafeteria.
- Avoid calling each other by your romantic nicknames such as "Dearie," "Honey," "Sweetheart," "Beloved," or personal nicknames, especially if the company adheres to more formal addresses.
- Especially if your beloved is your boss, or your employee, avoid calling attention to your relationship to minimize the feelings of favoritism that might be provoked.
- Be prepared with an exit plan if your romance cools and it's impossible for you to work near or for your beloved.
- If you are the executive or employer and you are considering a romantic relationship with an employee, you might want to explore contacting a lawyer and having what is being called a "love contract" drawn up.

Sometimes it's one or both parties who are romantically involved and working together who decide they want to change their situation even if it is perfectly fine with other co-workers, bosses, or subordinates. For instance, Mike and Brenda had an office workship that became a romance and that led to marriage.

But Mike, after five years of working with his wife, is at the point that he doesn't enjoy working at the same company anymore. "I'm a salesman," he explains. "I feel bad about giving my wife Brenda a lot of [secretarial] work to do when I go into the office. I [instead] try to do my own work. If I see someone arguing with her, I want to kill him for her. I take her side. I'm a protective person, very outgoing, aggressive. Brenda is the opposite."

As noted in Chapter 1, a married executive's assistant told him that she loves him only "as a friend." He confides: "She does not love me, but I don't know how to break my attraction to her."

He is finding it hard to control the romantic feelings that he has started to feel. This executive is well advised to find someone to help him to deal with his feelings as well as to consider reassigning his assistant to another work situation before he has to deal with a sexual harassment lawsuit as well as one or two shattered marriages.

Other possible consequences include a workplace that becomes demoralized and negative as others become aware of the situation through gossip or observation, as well as possible lawsuits from other employees who allege preferential treatment for the employee who is the recipient of the executive's amorous feelings.

8

Dealing With Conflicts

"Competition can stop you from becoming too close to others—
revealing too much—at work."
                    —Thirty-year-old New Jersey female TV reporter

L ike most relationships, there are bound to be conflicts that
    develop with any workplace connections. For example, just
    having a workship or friendship at the office, whether it is
with a peer, boss, or subordinate, may cause jealous feelings in
others. Be careful not to flaunt your closer connection before others
who may feel left out and ignored.

Over the two decades that I've been researching and writing
about friendship and business issues, one phenomenon has always
amazed me: those who would take time to work on a marital
relationship or a relationship with their parent or child, are surprised
at the notion that a workship or friendship requires work. A common
attitude toward friendship or workships is that it should either be an
easy relationship, or it's not worth bothering with it.

But workships or friendships are relationships that, like all
relationships, may be tested. With some effort, however, it might be
possible to salvage a workship or friendship that would have been
tossed aside just because it required a bit of effort to work things
through. Furthermore, if you work together, or you are in the same
business, it may be in your best interest to repair your workship or
friendship, or at least try to. That's because the consequences to your
job or career might be too great if the failed relationship leads to bad
feelings, badmouthing, or betrayal of confidences or secrets.

If You Want to Save the Workship or Friendship

In a workplace or business situation, you need to ask yourself if there are work concerns that require you to save this workship or friendship. Here are some of the conditions under which saving the workship or friendship might be recommended:

- You still have to work together.
- It's your boss.
- It's your subordinate.
- You work in the same office.
- You work in the same cubicle.
- This person's recommendation is crucial to your advancement.
- This person has friends and other workships in high places.
- Your combined efforts are more noteworthy than each one separately.
- You have a shared history that is meaningful to you personally or to your career.
- You share work or personal relationships in common; it would be awkward if you were uncomfortable spending time together.

One of the most common problems that stands in the way of saving a workship or workplace friendship is the mistaken assumption that people are mind readers. Just because you've known someone and have been in a workship or friendship for months or even years does not mean that you can read each other's minds. In most cases, you need to explain to your co-worker (boss, subordinate, client, or customer) with whom you have a workship or a friendship what you're thinking and especially what's bothering you, and why.

If you want to try to salvage a workship or friendship, you may want to try using one or all of these conflict resolution techniques:

- **Give him/her the benefit of the doubt.** It's okay to have a different standard for work-related relationships and to let things go that you might feel justified making a big deal over in your personal life.

- **Reduce the frequency of contact.** See or speak to each other less often, go from lunch daily to every other day or once a week, but don't make a big deal over the reduced contact.
- **Gradually scale back the intimacy in the relationship being careful not to hurt someone's feelings or being too obvious about it.** Pull back from friendship to workship or from workship back to acquaintance. Give out less information about yourself and be less available for regular get-togethers without breaking the relationship off completely.
- **Cooling off.** If your workship or friend did something horrendous, let it ride for a while and see where things are when you're less emotional and have some distance from the incident.
- **Try taking your colleague's point of view.** Put yourself in your workship or friend's shoes. Can you see why he or she said or did whatever had occurred that caused conflict?
- **Agree to disagree.** Make it clear that it's okay that you have divergent ideas and perspectives. There does not have to be one "right" way of behaving or thinking.
- **Ask a third party to mediate.** If you and your colleague are at a standstill, see if someone more objective could help sort things out. In work-related situations, assess whether your human resource department would be able to help out. You might even ask another trusted friend or colleague to mediate if you are confident of that person's mediation skills and objectivity.
- **Ask for a change in your work situation.** Sometimes moving your desks apart, if you work in the same small office, or even asking to be transferred to a different department might help to minimize your conflicts with your colleague by changing when and how you interact.
- **Listen carefully to each other's side of things.** Listening is a key conflict resolution skill. It shows interest in what you each have to say, and it validates each unique point of view.
- **Let your co-worker know that you care and that the relationship matters to you.** By increasing the stakes, you might also enhance your colleague's willingness to put time and effort into salvaging your workship or friendship.
- **Use "I" statements to let your colleague know how his or her actions or words impact on you.** You are not criticizing

your colleague; you are expressing how he or she makes you feel.

But sometimes, even in work-related situations, there are conditions when you should seriously consider whether or not to continue a workship or friendship, or at least wait it out while your colleague gets a grip on her/his problems:

- If your co-worker is involved in risk-tasking behavior such as drinking and driving, use of illegal drugs, or criminal behavior. (However, if your colleague has any of these risk-taking behaviors including suicidal attempts or thoughts, you may want to contact a counseling center and/or suicide hotline to find out what you could do to help your colleague get the help she/he needs.)
- If your co-worker is abusive toward you, including physical, verbal, emotional, or sexual abuse.
- If your colleague badmouths you to your other co-workers.
- If your colleague tries to "steal" your ideas or tries to get undue credit for your work or projects.
- If your co-worker steals your possessions or if you loan your colleague your laptop or something else that is valuable to you and she/he doesn't return it and makes it clear she/he has no intention of returning what was borrowed.
- If your colleague has a negative trait to such a degree that your self-esteem and the potential of a positive workship or friendship seems completely unlikely, such as being a Fault-Finder, Blood Sucker, Promise Breaker, or One-Upper. (However, if your co-worker has a negative trait but it's just now and then, or she/he is trying to change, you may want to give your colleague some more chances.)
- If your co-worker shares information or secrets that you had made clear were not to be shared with anyone else (betrays your confidence and trust), especially if this is a pattern rather than a one-time situation.
- If you find you don't like the way you behave or act in the presence of this colleague. (Positive workships or friendships tend to bring out the best in us and help us to like ourselves more, rather than less.)

- There are more reasons to walk away from the workship or friendship than there are to stay in it.
- On more than one occasion, another co-worker, employee, boss, or service provider has expressed very real concerns about this colleague and conveys valid warnings that this person and workship or friendship is not in your "best interest."
- Your co-worker workship or friendship is a pathological liar.
- If your colleague is jeopardizing your career or your relationships.

Although it can be hard at first to walk away from, or at least spend less time with, a negative colleague, breaking the habit of being with this co-worker might be a necessary step. It could free up the time and emotional readiness to find, or cultivate, positive workships and workplace friendships.

Looking at Your Own Behavior

However, it is also important to look at your own behavior with this particular colleague. Here are some questions to ask yourself:

- Are you doing anything that may be causing your co-worker to act negatively toward you?
- Did you show up half an hour late at your colleague's presentation and then take several calls on your cell phone that interfered with his or her talk?
- Did your co-worker have a career achievement and you were too busy to acknowledge it?
- Have you been physically there but not empathetically listening when your workship or friend last met you for lunch?
- Are you too quick to criticize your colleague even if she/he doesn't ask for your opinion?

Workships and workplace friendships requires that two people like each other and want to develop, and maintain, a workship or friendship, but to end a workship or friendship takes only one person. You may be able to salvage a workship or workplace friendship if you let your colleague know something about you that should not be taken personally; it's just the way you are. That is what a 36-year-old entrepreneur with two children and a mail order business does so she does not lose work-related friendships because of a personality trait:

> I will tell you a secret. When I become friends with someone and feel we are getting close, I tell them up front that I'm not good with words, but my heart is in it. I also tell them that I might offend them and if I do they need to tell me. Then I am aware if my new friends are more silent or seem upset with me, I'll call them on it and say something like, "I can tell something is bothering you, so please tell me if I've done anything to upset you."

Are You a Good Listener?

If you are tuning out when your workship or workplace friend talks to you, whether in person or over the phone, you can unwittingly be creating distance and even hostility that can sabotage your career.

To help avoid the conflicts that could occur because of poor listening habits, here are some suggestions to improve how well you listen to your workships or friends:

- Concentrate on what your workship or friend is saying when she or he talks to you. Catch yourself if your mind wanders and bring your attention back to her or him.
- It helps to restate what your workship or friend says in your own words so you show that you have really been listening. If it seems comfortable, you might reframe what you just heard. For example, your workship or friend tells you about a time management book she' s just read. You reply: "Thanks for sharing about such an useful book." Then refer to what your workship or friend said, exploring it further, rather than immediately switching to yourself, "What was the #1 suggestion that we could use to improve how we run our meeting next Tuesday?"
- Avoid thinking about what you're going to say next instead of focusing on what your workship or friend is saying.
- Listen without judgment.

- Wait to be asked for your opinion before volunteering it. (Your workship or friend may just want to vent or share without your opinion or feedback.)
- Allow enough time for your workship or friend to talk to you so you won't have to cut short your listening because you've got to go.
- Don't be critical so your workship or friend starts to withhold information out of fear you'll disapprove.
- Hear the emotion behind your workship or friend's words, not just the words. And observe the non-verbal communication that is shared, the body language, the facial gestures, not just the words.
- Maintain eye contact or nodding your head when you agree with the person who is talking to you (if you're in person) or by occasionally making "listening sounds" (such as "I see," "yes," or even just a guttural sound if on the phone) so the other person knows you are still there.
- Whether in person or over the phone, show interest by occasionally asking questions.
- Avoid interrupting. Don't cut your friend off before she finishes speaking.
- Don't switch the subject in an abrupt and artificial way. Have a natural bridge from topic to topic and make sure your friend has finished talking and is ready to go on to the next topic.

Dealing with Jealousy

Do you have a problem with jealousy at work, either dealing with your own jealous feelings about co-workers or bosses, or do you find others always jealous of you? It will definitely help to understand just what might be causing those feelings, in you or others, as you comprehend what you can change within yourself to alter the pattern of jealousy→sabotage.

For example, ask yourself these questions:
- Are you unwittingly exacerbating the situation by arriving very early at work, even before your boss or other co-workers, making everyone else look like sluggards?

- Are you showing everyone up by completing projects faster than everyone else?
- Did you badmouth someone thinking it would be kept confidential only to find your words coming back to haunt you?
- Are you so overqualified for your job that you should be the one looking for a higher-level opportunity in another department or even moving to another company where your co-workers or boss would not be jealous of you?

For an additional discussion of jealousy, see the section on jealousy and envy in Chapter 13, "Workplace Relationships Begin at Home."

Conflict Need Not Be Cataclysmic

In researching work and friendship, I have discovered that those who have less conflict in their workships or work friendships share one or more of the following traits or situations:

- There was adequate time between first meeting and the ensuing workship (and between the workship and the friendship) to ensure that the workship is based on enough shared information so that its foundation is solid.
- One or both of the colleagues have a personality that avoids, rather than fosters, conflict. For instance, one woman whose relationships tend to be conflict-free notes: "I am an easy going person who will compromise if I need to."
- One or both colleagues are skilled at handling conflict when it does arise.

In a workplace situation, be careful what words you say or actions you take that might end a workship or friendship. Winding down the workship or friendship, decreasing the amount of time you spend together, changing the type of information that is shared from personal or somewhat personal to just business and "small talk," may be a better course of action than a dramatic ending. Some actions are so dramatic, however, so that cutting off the workship or friendship is necessary.

Here are some examples:

- "Became power hungry and used me in an attempt to climb the ladder. She told untruths and she ended up being ostracized but I was devastated and went into a depression for a couple of months."—44-year-old married health care professional
- "Stole a very important job from me by making me look like I was incompetent."—23-year-old married consultant
- "Blamed something on me that I didn't do."—20-year-old student
- "They lied and said that I was suing the company for sexual discrimination to get me out of a job that they wanted."—36-year-old married entrepreneur, referring to previous work situation
- "Taking full credit for something we worked on as a team and interrupting me when I was trying to explain something for a group of people saying, 'No, that's not right,' and then telling the same thing as me."—30-year-old divorced bookkeeper

Be very clear that ending a workship or friendship is what you really want to do since you may not be able to reestablish it.

Money Issues

There's a maxim about money and friendship that holds true for workplace relationships as well. Avoid loaning money or, if you do make a loan, decide in advance if your friendship or workplace relationships could withstand the possibility that you might not get paid back right away, or at all.

In this book, however, since it explores work and business relationships, whether those workships remain solely in a business setting or extend into your personal life, money may be an issue. Here are some suggestions to minimize the potential negative consequences of loaning a colleague money, or doing business with a friend, and maximizing the benefits so that you are dealing with someone whom you (hopefully) know quite well and whom you feel is a trustworthy person:

- **Put money matters in writing.** If you enter into a business arrangement with a friend that involves money, whether it's a loan or working on a project together, put the terms of your arrangement in writing. Even if you're tempted to do business with a handshake, having the terms of your business arrangement spelled out, even if it's just a simple letter agreement, may avoid confusion or hurt feelings down the road. If money is loaned, have an understanding of when your friend will repay the loan, and at what interest, if any, or, if you are the one who is being loaned the money, suggest terms that you can meet or exceed.
- **Do you confuse money with love or friendship?** Just because a friend has money, whether through earnings or inheritance, does not mean he or she has to, or should, loan or give it to you for your business venture, for your work emergencies, or as an investment.
- **Do you confuse money with power?** Many people associate money with power, but you don't have to. Whether your friendships are based in the workplace, or are an outgrowth of a work-related association, if you equate money with power you're setting yourself up for a fall, or possibly accusations of opportunism. All friendships should be based on the core of a person and not how powerful or rich someone happens to be.
- **Share business opportunities, as appropriate, but avoid putting pressure on your friend.** If you think you have an investment opportunity that your friend might welcome knowing about as a source of revenue, let him know what you're up to, especially if you think your friend would feel offended if you excluded him from whatever proposal or project that you're pitching.
- **Consider hiring an outside consultant or firm to act as an intermediary between you and your friend on any money matters.** The benefits of having an objective third party might help take the pressure off you or your friend so you can focus on your friendship and leave the money and business aspect of your transactions to an expert.
- **Play out in your mind the worst-case scenario and see if your friendship could survive it. If it could not, reconsider if you want to involve your friend in a business venture or anything related to money.** Whether someone is a millionaire or trying to

survive on an entry-level salary, if you think he or she could not absorb the financial loss if a loan is not repaid or if a business venture goes bust, reconsider if this is the right course of action. Friendships that might have persisted for years or even decades could fall apart over seemingly inconsequential amounts of money. If you fear this might happen to you and your friend, politely explain that your friendship is more important to you than the money or the business venture, and keep the two separate.

- **Be careful to avoid emphasizing the monetary contrasts between you and your friends.** Whether you are the one who has suddenly inherited huge wealth, or gotten a big bonus from your job this year, focus on the non-materialistic ways you and your friends appreciate each other. If you are the one feeling envy or jealousy of a friend's perceived greater wealth or possessions, work on your feelings. Yes, a little jealousy and competition is natural and predictable in all friendships, but so much that it turns you green will definitely make your friend uneasy around you, so she will be forced to spend time with friends for whom the money issue is not a problem.

- **Avoid the attitude that automatically equates money problems with failure or sadness, and wealth with competence or happiness.** The most successful executive could fall on hard times, and the man or woman earning a minimum wage may feel his or her life is fulfilling and successful. Be careful about projecting on to others your own attitudes about wealth and success or it will get in the way of your friendships.

Entertaining: Should You Mix Friends, Family, and Business Associates?

Each year, as the holidays approach, whether it's Christmas, New Year's, seasonal or religious celebrations, there seem to be more social and business functions to attend than there are days in the week to schedule everything. Especially during December, it may be tempting to combine family, friends, and business associates at a dinner party, or even a gala holiday dinner dance. Or maybe there's a family wedding that you wonder about including workplace or business friends or workships? What are the pros and cons to consider if you do decide to mix business with family and friends?

One possible benefit of inviting family and personal friends to a holiday function that also includes business associates are the economic and time concerns. Is such a party a legitimate business expense and deduction? According to an accountant that I interviewed, "I would go by percentages," she said. "It makes sense that businesses would have holiday parties for their business contacts but you would want to have a much higher percentage to be business contacts in order to deduct it." She suggested 75% as a ballpark percentage. "If you invited the business contacts and said, 'You could bring a friend,' that would be part of the seventy-five percent who are business associates."

So a holiday event that combines business with family and personal friends could be a legitimate business deduction. It could also mean finding one restaurant for the event, or, if you entertain at home, dealing with just one caterer rather than having several events. That could save you time and money.

But do you want to combine family and personal friends with workplace relationships whether it's your boss, co-workers, or employees?

If you are going to combine business and family or personal friends, have some ground rules. For example, let your family and personal friends know that there are certain topics that are "off limits" to discuss at the holiday party, such as whether or not you're disgruntled and possibly even looking for a new job, or how much weight you've recently lost or gained.

You want to strive to treat all the guests equally. However, a big kiss for Uncle George may not be that comfortable at a holiday party with business and family and friends if it could be misinterpreted by co-workers who have not seen you publicly treated in such a familiar way before.

Although combining business associates with family and personal friends may seem like a timesaver and a cost-effective way of accomplishing several goals at once, you might just want to re-evaluate whether you will lose more than you'll gain. Keeping business and your personal life separate, even if it means having two different parties, just might be a more comfortable solution to what to say and what not to say for you and your loved ones. Of course if you and a co-worker are also husband and wife, or it's a family-owned business, that's a different story since some of your business associates are also your family members.

Helping the Friendless Worker

In the past, some high-level working women avoided workplace friendships because they could not substitute a less intimate approach to friendship, as working men were prone to do. Rather than risk saying or doing anything that might compromise their workplace situation, some opted for no friends at all. But now, the benefits of workships and workplace friendships have been shown to outweigh the potential negatives. An inability to form friendships, regardless of gender, has emerged as a factor that may be holding men or women back from more satisfying workplace relationships as well as hurting their career advancement.

What can be done to help those friendless workers who want to cultivate friends at work and in their business? You can offer friendship to a friendless worker, but he or she has to share your goal for a relationship. "Take it slow" is certainly good advice with someone who is fearful of work-related friendships. (There is a list of associations and agencies in the "Resources" section in the back of the book that might provide direct help or referrals to overcome social phobia or shyness if you are asked for such information.)

Understanding the Possible Roots of the Conflicts

When you meet someone at work, what that person brings to the new situation, and any relationship that ensues, may have as much to do with what transpired during his or her formative years as it does with you. Similarly, your own family relationships will impact on how you connect with those you meet at work or in business.

Refer to Chapter 13, "Workplace Relationships Begin at Home." There are suggested ways of reevaluating why someone you meet in the present at work or in business may bring up certain feelings in you, about him or her, or your relationship, that has little to do with the present reality. Yet you must deal with the consequences of that person stirring up memories of previous relationships.

As discussed in Chapter 13, there may be reasons from someone's childhood or earlier friendships that are the underlying causes to the problems you have with someone at work or in business. Sometimes a workship or friendship is moved along, or halted, because someone you meet unconsciously relates to you as if you are someone else from his or her past. Uncovering those past connections can help you understand your reactions to certain events that are disproportionate to the current situation.

For example, a 63-year-old female professor in the Midwest can't seem to allow a workplace relationship to become closer. Although they "enjoy talking" it is done "only at work and an occasional dinner." Her personality and upbringing probably has more to do with the limitations on the relationship than anything her co-worker does or says: "I am quiet and introverted," the professor explains. "I also grew up in an atmosphere where the expression of feelings was not done."

The ability to share feelings is a cornerstone of relationships with greater intimacy. Developing that ability may be a necessary step for this professor to allow her workplace relationship to become closer.

If you find a workship that could become a friendship is either moving too quickly or that the road has been blocked prematurely, try asking yourself the following questions:

- Does this person remind me of someone from my childhood?
- Who is that person?
- What was my relationship with that person?
- In what ways do they seem similar? Different?
- Why is that unconscious association or comparison motivating me to befriend this person (or, conversely, discouraging me from moving the relationship forward)?
- How can I separate this new or current person from the past associations that are clouding or distorting this fresh relationship regardless of my past?

The associations could be something as superficial as hair color: a co-worker has the same hair color of a friend from sixth grade who betrayed you. It could be race: your parents discouraged you from befriending anyone who was not the same race as you. It could be religion: friendships were drawn along religious lines during your formative years. It could be the way someone smiles: you had a friend in first grade who smiled like that and you are naturally drawn to someone with the same smile. The association could be on a deeper level as well: a customer wants to be in charge of all the details of your business dealings and that reminds you of your domineering younger sister.

For a further discussion of the possible early roots of current workplace relationship challenges, see Chapters 13 and 14.

Avoiding a Feud

A feud or vendetta is the game that occurs when someone you know—it could be someone you worked for, or a co-worker, or even someone who has heard about you through someone else—has it in for you. (Or you could be the one that has it in for someone else.) Because of a real or imagined slight against you, the person with the vendetta is out to make sure you do not succeed. It may be that you were once an underling and now you are above him or her so if he or she gets in power again, you will be made to pay for that. Someone may have given you a hard time when you were fired, or said something nasty to you and you decide to "get even" if you ever have the chance.

Example #1: a woman in her fifties is laid off after ten years with a publishing company. Her job goes to a younger co-worker who is rather cold and unsympathetic about getting the displaced woman's job. The displaced woman is bitter, but all her longtime friends and acquaintances in the business are generous about giving her leads for new possible jobs. After a few months, she lands a good job as the right-hand editor to the top of a small but prestigious firm. About two years later, the first company folds and, low and behold, the former replacement gets a job working under the very woman she had formerly replaced. The angry woman makes it clear she has a vendetta against her former superior-turned-underling. She tries to make life miserable for the younger co-worker at the new job, blocking proposals she tries to get through, and almost sneering at her whenever they pass each other in the hall.

Example #2: A young woman is sent by her company to decorate the office of a business owner. The businessman calls her company and requests a different decorator without offering an explanation. It turns out the man remembered the young woman as a former friend of his daughter who, a decade before, had hurt his daughter's feelings by ending their friendship. He chose not to do business with that young woman, without an explanation, out of his own belief that it was the only way to show his loyalty to his daughter.

The woman who shared that anecdote with me—whose father it was who had refused to do business with her former friend—did not know if there were any consequences to her former friend because of that incident. Certainly, if nothing else, her former friend had to wonder why her services were refused.

Feuds or vendettas are counterproductive. Companies function best when departments and people work with, not against, each other. The woman with the vendetta in Example #1 was also going on old information. The younger woman, who initially had been cold and unsympathetic to her, could have changed. The subsequent loss of her own job could have made her humble and more tolerant now that she had gone through the experience herself.

What makes a vendetta a game, like all business games, is that it has a predictable outcome. No matter what the person does who is the subject of the vendetta, he or she will be the object of someone else's wrath.

What should you do if someone has a vendetta against you? *Get the vendetta out in the open.* Discuss what happened that led to the vendetta. If the emotions fly too high between the two of you, consider having a mutual friend, co-worker, or even an impartial third party mediate your dispute. If you were wrong, admit it and apologize. Saying "I'm sorry" can sometimes go a long way.

If the vendetta is not resolved with one airing of the grievance, give it some time and then try to get along again for a week or two. The important thing is to keep trying to eliminate the vendetta and lessen the distance between the two of you.

Call a truce and get on with the business at hand. If you work for different companies but have to deal with each other, or see each other at conventions or trade shows, be civil and friendly. If you feel you are being badmouthed or sabotaged, once again, try to get the vendetta out in the open, find out what's behind it, and try to resolve it so you can work amicably in the future.

There are, however, people against whom you have a legitimate grudge. They have done you wrong. They are despicable people. You would prefer never to deal with them again rather than confront them and try to iron out your differences. If you are lucky, they are not co-workers or people you have to deal with on an everyday basis. If that is the case, avoid those people and stay away. Do not badmouth them. Doing so could come back to haunt you by making you look bad or, even worse, they might take legal action.

Here's a hypothetical example not too dissimilar to real-life examples shared with me in surveys or interviews. Let's say someone badmouthed you years ago, actually telling your boss not to hire you. Your boss ignores his friend's comments and you are hired, but you never forget his friend's vicious and unjust criticisms.

Years later, your boss leaves the company. His friend contacts you and asks you to help him. You decide to ignore him. Ten years later, the friend with the vicious tongue becomes a celebrity. You are tempted to contact him to say hello, renew old acquaintances, see if he could be helpful to you now. But instead you decide to stay away, and do not fan old painful flames. You continue to hold your grudge since nothing he has done has caused you to change your mind. But you also decide to avoid contact with him since that might backfire and cause you more new harm.

When It's Personal, Not Business

There are times (fortunately for most, it only happens now and again, or once in your career, if at all) when someone just has it in for you. If you detect this quickly enough, you might try to get another supervisor or boss, co-worker, client, or customer, a replacement for whoever it is that is determined to sabotage you.

Sometimes it is not possible to switch. In those cases, it is helpful to find other allies at the same level at your company or in your business, even if that person is outside of your department or immediate area, such as if you work at a public relations firm and you are an account executive and your immediate boss does not like you, you befriend another boss as well as your boss's boss so you at least have some allies at the company to offset this one negative relationship. You can, of course, try to turn it around. (You may want to refer back to the suggestions about how to try to turn around unfriendly behavior, in Chapter 3, "How to Start, and Maintain, a Workship.")

You also want to create as many positive documents or laudatory situations to offset his or her negativity about you, such as recommendation letters from others within the company or from your business to whom you might turn if this person does try to get you demoted, fired, or just keeps giving the plumb assignments to someone else.

If you choose to stay in this situation, you will need to continue to bolster your ego so his or her dislike for you (which often has nothing to do with you) does not start to do exactly what he or she unconsciously hopes his or her rejection will do, namely cause you to have insomnia or to mess up or even, in extreme cases, give up your job, your career, or even more extreme self-destructive reactions.

Sometimes, even if you try your best, not only won't you connect with someone, but he or she will misuse his or her position of power over you and your work to withhold recommendations that you have earned or choose not to verbally praise you at the appropriate time so that you may start to feel insecure about yourself and your abilities.

These affirmations may help you when this type of scenario occurs because, in most cases, as long as you truly were competent and excellent, the way you are being treated has little to do with you but everything to do with what you have stirred up in this other person—uncomfortable feelings that are causing him or her to try to make you doubt yourself and even catapult you to self-sabotage. Don't fall into that trap! Stay strong and repeat the affirmations that follow that could help you through this tough situation, especially for those who are exceptionally talented, determined to succeed, and above average:

Affirmations to Help Deal With Unjustified Mistreatment or Rejection By Those Who Can Directly Impact on Your Career

1. I tried my best and objectively I know I did an excellent job.
2. I have to avoid taking this person's rejection personally. It is more about her or him than it is about me.

3. I may never know what his or her motivation is to undermine my job, career, or self-confidence.
4. My assumptions about her or his motivation may not be the real reasons so I have to work on accepting that this has happened through no fault of my own.
5. I will try to minimize its negative impacts on my ego, my reputation, or my career by highlighting the positive feedback and relationships in my career and life.
6. I have to remind myself that I cannot make everyone like or respect me and that those who do not champion me and my career may be basing it on their own insecurities and problems rather than anything to do with me.
7. I will dwell on what was positive about the relationship or the interaction and let go of the negative that has been trying to overtake me.
8. I will move on to a new project, relationship, or situation and stop obsessing over this negative one.
9. I will stop trying to change this person who has an irrational, unjustified aversion to me and move on to others who are positive.
10. I will try harder in the future to see the warning signs more quickly that this person has problems that will come back to haunt me if I give her or him any authority over me and see if I could request someone else to deal with if that is possible.
11. If I let this negativity slow me down or undermine my self-confidence, he or she will win and I will lose. I will, instead, be a winner by refusing to succumb to those mental gymnastics and refuse to let his or her negativity sabotage me.
12. I am competent, talented, bright, hardworking, and deserving of praise and success.
13. I accept that some may find me a threat or I may bring up insecure feelings in them that unconsciously cause them to try to undermine me.
14. I will focus on doing the best job I can do and accept that others may not always give me the praise I deserve.
15. I accept that many never learned how to treat people appropriately or with kindness. I will not take on this person's vicious behaviors but reinforce the value of treating people

fairly, with respect, and in a timely manner as the cornerstone of my own behavior.

16. Without blaming myself, I will use this as a learning experience: looking back, what could I have done differently that might have helped the situation to have a different outcome? How could our communication patterns have been more effective either in the way we communicated (via e-mail, phone, fax, or in-person meetings), in frequency, or in location?

If you absolutely have to end a workship or workplace friendship, see the suggestions in the next chapter, Chapter 9, "Copings with Endings," which addresses endings because of conflict as well as because of job changes.

To help minimize conflict with workships or friends, here are some suggestions about what not to share:

Seven Things You Should Never Share With a Workplace Relationship

1. Business confidences that would be a violation of trust and ethics if revealed to anyone.
2. Family secrets that put someone else in your family in any level of jeopardy.
3. Who you are currently having an affair with or who you used to have an affair with.
4. If your spouse (or romantic partner) is good in bed.
5. Anything you would not feel comfortable having repeated on the six o'clock news or reading about in a national newspaper.
6. Any negative feelings about the boss (co-worker, company president, customer, or client).
7. Comments that are racist, sexist, anti-aging, or against any religion or culture.

9

Coping With Endings

> "My close friend and I worked together for 20 plus years but after our jobs changed, we had less contact."
> —50-year-old divorced occupational therapist

The three basic categories of workships or friendships at work endings are because of a conflict, a job change, or death.

Endings Because of Irreconcilable Differences

How you end a workship or a workplace friendship may differ from ending a friendship in your personal life if will still have to have daily contact with this person. You will definitely want to end the workship in such a way that it will not be uncomfortable to see each other and even work together or attend the same meetings.

Unless there is good reason to share your innermost thoughts and feelings with this colleague, try to minimize your conflicts and just pull away, being busy for lunch or unable to attend after-hour get-togethers. Of course if you and this colleague were close or best friends, sharing everything, and suddenly you are silent, the inevitable questions may be asked, "Are you avoiding me?" or "Are you trying to tell me that you don't want to be friends anymore?"

At that point, it may be necessary, in as calm a way as possible, to explain how you feel or what's going on. You may suggest a cooling off, rather than an end to the workship, even if you are doubtful the workship can be salvaged. That's because since you work together, by suggesting a cooling off, and reassessment period, will give your colleague a chance to get used to the idea of your workship (or friendship) changing or ending. It will also provide an opportunity for your co-worker to re-connect to others so the feelings of rejection are not as devastating. If your colleague has someone new to meet for lunch, or to go out with on a Friday night, it may be easier for both of you when you do see each other on a daily basis.

If you are the one who is being told that the workship or friendship is over, accept it graciously, if possible. Remember that there are as many factors that go into why a workship ends—at least as many as why you and your co-worker even clicked in the first place. These include everything from timing, luck, and personalities, to what else was going on in your lives at that time, plus variables that are also hard to control. These can include other pulls in your life, relationships, and the type of relationship you now have at work compared to when you first formed your workship. Perhaps your colleague is now also your boss or, conversely, you have become your friend's boss. Or perhaps you are earning three times his salary, or you seem to have more workships, or the boss showed favoritism toward you.

If you or your colleague ends a business friendship and you rarely see each other, it will obviously be a lot easier on both of you than if you work together, at least in terms of avoiding face-to-face daily encounters. Although you may see each other at business trade shows or conferences, the possibility of everyday confrontations is reduced.

But with the Internet, it is key to avoid writing anything negative about your former workship in an e-mail since your e-mail might be forwarded, with a likelihood of it getting back to your former workship. This will only fuel the situation and might cause your former workship to write a negative e-mail about you and before you know it there is a vendetta going on in cyberspace that will be counterproductive and negative for all involved.

In person or over the phone, you still want to avoid badmouthing your former friend, or sharing secrets that you used to hold dear. By setting a positive example of trust and honor, even after the bond of friendship is over, you increase the likelihood that your former friend will also honor, and not betray, you.

Susan, 34 and married, provides technical support for an American company; she relocated from Canada, where she grew up. Susan had a friendship with Helen, a co-worker. Their workplace friendship had grown so that after six to eight months, Susan considered Helen to be a friend, and the relationship extended into their personal lives. But Susan had to end their friendship, as she explains:

> We were very close friends at work and outside of work. We confided in each other, we spent lots of time [together] outside work. I considered her to be one of my best friends. [But] about three-and-a-half or four years after we became friends, she betrayed me. I was using the Internet at work for some personal reasons, and she told our boss. Apparently Helen felt I was threatening her job. I do not know why because we did not work in the same department.
>
> Carole, our mutual friend, and one other colleague told me that Helen constantly spoke about me behind my back for years in a negative way, implied I was slutty (I was dating a few men at that time), bitchy, and many more things and my two colleagues felt bad for me because I was under the impression that Helen and I were close friends.
>
> I stopped confiding in her, stopped going out after work with her [but] I still had to work there so I kept her as an acquaintance.

Since Susan felt that Helen was not someone with whom she could try to work through the conflicts and salvage their friendship, she maintained an acquaintanceship with her co-worker, instead of confronting her. Eight months after the betrayal, when Susan had left the company (and they were no longer co-workers or friends), Susan shares how Helen reacted to her attempts to figure out what happened and why:

> I confronted her...via e-mail, not the greatest way, but I had to write her about it and I did say that I enjoyed her company, and that if she would just be honest with me about what happened we could try to save the friendship. I tried to be diplomatic. I also mentioned that I had made mistakes that I

regret, to try and make it easier for her to admit [to her mistakes].

But she blamed all our other colleagues in the office and blamed everything and everyone but herself. If she truly did not do [it] I feel she would not feel the need to blame everyone and everything. She said I was wasting her time and that I was not important enough to her and our friendship meant nothing to her. She had more important things to think about. Then one of my former work colleagues contacted me and said that Helen was still saying nasty things about me and my husband.

Susan and Helen no longer talk to each other. Susan still feels bad about what happened:

I care for her still and would like to be friends if we could have cleared the air, but I cannot be friends with someone who I cannot trust. What hurt the most were the mean things that three different people told me she said about me for the years I thought we were friends.

What has Susan learned from this close friendship that started in the workplace and ended? "To pay attention to signals I get instinctively about others, even friends," she notes, reflecting back to the thought she had dismissed: that if her friend were badmouthing others, would she be badmouthed as well? Since Susan's friendship with Helen started after only working together, and knowing each other, for eight or nine months, something else she learned was to take more time trusting a new friend.

My research has found that it takes, on average, three years from meeting to becoming tried-and-true friends. During that time, the new relationship will be "tested out" in various ways, as you and your potential friend will instinctively be assessing each other.

Since Susan moved to another company, and country, her failed workplace friendship with Helen did not seem to have any long-term negative consequences. The goal, if ending a friendship, whether it's a workship, casual, close, or best friendship, is to avoid having the failed workship or friendship turn into a vendetta.

Endings Because of Job Changes

Even if you and your co-worker get along famously, and a strong positive relationship ensues, in time, one or both of you may go to another company, relocate to another state, or even switch fields entirely. The reset of this chapter will look at how to decide if you even want to keep workplace relationships going—workships or friendships—once you no longer work together, and if you do, how to accomplish that even or if you change careers, as well as coping with endings because of death.

Staying Workships After No Longer Working Together

If a genuine friendship has developed from your work or business association, even if you change jobs, even if you change careers, your relationship will probably persist because you have a strong bond. But what about a workship that is not yet a friendship?

Indeed, job changes are one of the key "tests" on a relationship, just as graduating from school is a test: will this relationship survive once it is no longer convenient? Will your former co-worker travel across town to have lunch with you, or pick up the phone to call when you can no longer chat by just popping into each other's offices right down the corridor?

Workships may fade away or end once you no longer work together because changing the context of the workplace relationship may have a dramatic impact. Be careful not to force the situation; moving to another work situation may help one or both of you to reassess your workship, which may have been perpetuated as much out of convenience or habit as it was out of genuine feelings. It could have been easier to keep the workship going while you still worked together than risk the potential fallout if one or both of you decided to minimize it or even end it.

Here are questions to ask yourself to know if you should pursue a workship once you no longer work together:

- Was the main reason you kept this workship going because you were afraid to end it while you still worked together?
- Did you and your former workship have anything in common besides the job? If yes, what did you talk about besides work?
- Since you stopped working together, do you find yourself thinking about and missing your former workship?
- Do you have clear indications that your former workship shares your wish to continue the relationship?

- Do you think this workship might eventually evolve into a friendship? Do you want it to?
- Can this workship help your career even though you no longer work together?
- Do you genuinely like this person?

Look over your answers. The main considerations about whether or not to sustain a workship is that it should be a relationship you hope to turn into a personal relationship (or it already has become one) and that there is mutual respect and admiration for each other.

If it was just a work-related relationship that helped you at a specific job, don't feel guilty if you let the relationship fall by the wayside. That does not mean you have to make a big deal out of its ending; work at no longer fretting about this former workship or trying to find the time and energy to keep the relationship going.

You can also consider this former workship as a business contact. This person is someone you do not actively call upon or spend time communicating with, but you know of him or her, and vice versa, in case a job opportunity comes along. You may need to find out something that this person might know because it's his or her area of expertise, or there's another reason to reconnect.

Making the Time to Keep Workships Going

But if you do want to keep your workship going, and your former co-worker feels the same way, then put the time and effort into making that happen. Fortunately, because of e-mail (of course written with discretion since you should not put anything in an e-mail that you would not feel comfortable having published on the front page of a major newspaper), it is a lot easier, and less expensive, to keep up with old workships. Long distance phone calls are also less expensive than ever before due to free evening and weekend minutes, as well as pre-paid calling cards.

Reaching Out if the Job Change was Mandatory

Of course it may be more challenging to get together once you are no longer working at the same company, but there are countless examples of former co-workers who remain or even become close or best friends after a job change or even a career shift or retirement. (See the tips for keeping up your relationship once you no longer work together that are shared later on in this chapter.)

Distance as a Deterrent to Maintaining Previous Workships

If distance stops you or your co-worker from maintaining your workship once you no longer work together, that is one of the key tests to the longevity of this relationship. Rather than force it, take this as useful information that either you or your former colleague do not want to put the time and effort into your non-work relationship.

What if All You Had in Common was Work?

William explains why he thinks that eventually he and Brenda, who began as co-workers in London, may eventually lose contact with each other, now that they no longer work together:

> I think the relationship will probably peter out eventually. At the moment, Brenda has been gone [to New York] about eight months. We still e-mail each other relatively frequently, about every week or two weeks. But we are totally different people. A lot of what we had in common was our work, gossiping about people, the stuff we talked about. But once you're separated, you move on to different things. You don't share those same interests anymore, so there isn't that common ground.

Misreading Workships as Friendships

When work changes, the workplace relationships may not survive because of those changes. What worked in the previous situation no longer works, as Don Gabor, author of *How to Start a Conversation and Make Friends,* told me:

> What's important to remember is that certain commercial relationships require people to be friendly with one another and that's what maintains the business. Some people don't understand that if the commercial relationship changes, sometimes that 'friendship' will change too.

That's why people who have lost a position in a company all of a sudden find that their so-called friends aren't calling them anymore, or they're not in the position of influence to help them [so] they're not in the top ten list of who to invite over.

Learning to recognize, and correctly label, a relationship as a workship, and also recognizing when it ends because the work-related association changes or terminates, may help avoid undue disappointment or even embarrassment.

Tips for Keeping the Workship Going Even After You No Longer Work Together

If you and your workships decide you do want to keep your relationship going even after you no longer work together, here are additional tips to help:

- Build and forge new memories instead of just rehashing work.
- Some companies now have alumni programs for former employees. Find out if the company where you worked has such an alumni program for former employees; if not, try to start one.
- There are sites on the Internet that help those who worked together to find each other, such as Alumni.net, Reunion.com, Coolbuddy.com, and Classmates.com.
- Start e-mail lists of workships with whom you want to stay connected. For example, some of the current and previous employees at a wire service have an e-mail list to keep each other informed about job changes as well as accomplishments, and up-to-date information about co-workers, retirees, and former employees or bosses by sharing information via e-mail. The e-mail list is also a way of quickly notifying members of upcoming get-togethers, which tend to happen once every year or so.
- Put *making time for workships* a concern so you will find the time for these relationships.
- Avail yourself of all the technological advances that make staying connected easier including e-mail, cell phones, sending a fax, as well as the more traditional methods of telephone calls, letter writing, and in-person get-togethers or rendezvous.

- As much as possible, include your workships in your current life with updates about what's going on with you and your career, as well as asking them what's new in their lives.
- Remember each other at the holidays.
- Celebrate with a card, a phone call, or a reunion those birthdays or shared anniversaries, such as the day you started working together or the day one or both of you left the job.

The "We Used to Work Together" Syndrome as the Precursor to a Friendship

For some, it may be necessary to no longer have the work connection for the workship to become a friendship. At work, the friends are like foxhole buddies, joined in a workship that helps them to survive corporate combat but unable to let down their guard so they could be intimate until one is no longer in the foxhole.

At that point, however, you are, for all intents and purposes, personal friends; working together is just the shared situation that was the catalyst to your friendship. It could have been school, camp, or living nearby. You are now personal friends who once worked together. As 32-year-old Jim notes:

> With these two close friends, we were not friends while we worked together. I considered the relationships very casual. Work sort of forced us into an environment together. After I left, or the other person left the company, I felt comfortable enough to work toward establishing and developing the friendships. Since we didn't work together [any longer], the only way to maintain any relationship was to be friends.

This is a typical pattern; don't miss out on some of the most rewarding friendships you could have in your personal life, when you and a former co-worker or boss pursue a friendship once you no longer work together, fearing that it should have happened while you were working if it was "meant to be." Not necessarily so. For example, two women met when they both were teachers for the learning disabled. Even though they had a workship when they worked together, going out to dinner, shopping, or to ballgames, their friendship blossomed once Vera left to become a stockbroker.

How to Stay Friends After the Job Ends

A work-based friendship, if it is indeed a true friendship, should transcend a particular time and place. In fact, that is often the way to test if a work-based relationship really is a friendship: does it persist when you no longer work together?

The British career consulting company, Sanders and Sidney, as reported in the *Birmingham Post*, found that more than 70 percent of surveyed departing employees had "a sense of loss" because of workplace relationships that they had to leave behind. The study also found that seven out of ten men and close to nine of the ten women reported having made "lasting friendships" at their workplace.

Since you may have spent weeks, months, or even years getting along with certain colleagues, how do you keep those workships or friendships from falling by the wayside if you no longer work together, or should you bother?

For genuine friendships, job changes, or even retirement, do not have to mean the end of a work-related friendship. Especially if the job change was by default, rather than choice, such as when someone is downsized or fired, reaching out to previous friends at work can help offset the loss of the job. Although the job might have ended, knowing that the relationships that were formed at work have not ended as well can reduce the potential devastation of job loss.

When my mother, Glady Barkas, who is now 81, retired more than a decade ago after 27 years as a kindergarten teacher, she and her former colleagues, who over the years had also become close friends, made a commitment to keep their relationships going through a lunch of retirees every month. In addition, they talk regularly by phone, as my mother explains:

> We have so much in common because we taught in the same school and many of us have become widows in the meantime. We don't need any bereavement groups because we have our retirement group which acts like a bereavement group for anyone who has had a sorrow. It was originally ten retirees and now it's seven. One died. Two moved. Most of us retired after 1990 and that was when these girls all formed this. We go out to lunch and usually somebody has a big dinner in their home and invites everybody.

We go to each other's big events that happen in the families. When their children get married, we go to the weddings. We talk about everything including the old times at school, the different shows we put on in school, things like that. We discuss the graduations of the different children that we taught.

My husband Fred had a best friend, Milton Haynes, with whom he had worked at the Associated Press. When they first met, Fred was twenty-four and Milt was a decade older. Their workship became a best friendship as they spent time together outside of work. Several years after they met at work and became friends, Milt returned to school, got a graduate degree in social work, and left journalism to start a private practice. But their best friendship survived even after they no longer worked together or shared the same career, a best friendship that spanned more than three decades. As Fred says:

> We only worked together at the Associated Press for four or five years at the most. But our friendship was stronger than our workship. In fact often at work we clashed and Milt was angry once because when I took over his shift, he had to work nights and he hated it.
> We were friends in that we opened up to each other. We knew each other's fears and likes. We liked a lot of the same things. We shared a love of music, movies, and writing. We were *sympatico*. We thought a lot alike. We were both creative. We were part of a group that shared a beach house at Fire Island, Kismet. Our friendship was an accumulation of shared experiences, emotions, ups and downs. He was sort of like an older brother to me. A mentor.

Gloria says the network of seven close friends who met twenty years ago when they worked at the same bank in the Caribbean are still connected today. Gloria's best friend is Suzie, whom she also met in a work-related capacity. Although Suzie left the company after just two years, their friendship has endured more than two decades even though they live in different countries. Gloria explained why she thinks all these friendships, started at work, persist today:

We all worked in the bank's human resource department so we spent most of our days with each other. The mix of persons and personalities must have been just right; that is to say that while we had differences of opinions, we really got on like a family.

Birthdays were celebrated in the department. We'd buy pastries and share it around and the events that we had to plan as part of the human resource department were fun things for us—calypso-singing competitions, service excellence awards programs, Christmas parties.

Though most of us have parted ways with the bank, the friendships remained. We make it a point to get together at someone's house or an outside venue several times a year and we give updates or just have lots of fun remembering our "old" times and there were many.

Sixty-year-old Annie, an entrepreneur who is white, still maintains a best friendship with Laura, who is black, who was her secretary when they both worked at a telecommunications company. Annie says about Laura, even though they no longer work together and live one thousand miles apart now: "Laura is the best. She is one really, really special person! I am so blessed to call her *friend*. We're sisters."

Annie and Laura keep up their friendship through regular e-mails and instant messaging. A reunion is planned although Laura, who is twenty years younger than Annie and still working, has economic issues and Annie, who is semi-retired, has health concerns that make long trips challenging.

Some are better at keeping up with former work-related friendships once they part than others. Personality may be a factor as much as time constraints. For example, Bill explains how his close work-related friendships never go beyond the workplace situation, but that's okay with him:

I work in a corporate setting. I have had the occasion of making close friends at the office, but with the reality of relocation and the like, I do not have any at present. That doesn't mean these people mean any less to me, it is just a fact that they are no longer co-workers, and as such time and space causes the connections with these friends to thin. The fact that I have an outrageous commute makes socializing unworkable.

While I believe wholly that at any time they can call on me in a time of need, and I on them, the fact remains they and I will remain distant friends, connected by the occasional e-mail.

When a Workship or Friendship is Impacted by Death

Tens of thousands of co-workers, friends, and family from throughout the United States, especially on the East Coast, as well as from more than 100 countries, had to deal with loss and grief because of colleagues who died in the September 11th 2001 terrorist attacks in Washington, D.C. and Manhattan. Some also had to deal with "survivor guilt" when they survived and their co-workers or bosses did not.

Death is less of a taboo subject in the United States since those tragic terrorist attacks on September 11th forced the entire United States and countries around the world to try to cope with such horrific loss. Co-workers lost dozens, even hundreds of men and women who had become members of a corporate family. The youth of the victims, so many in their prime of life with so much to live for and look forward to, highlighted the tragedy of the loss.

Grief is, ultimately, a private emotion that is handled by each individual in his or her own way. There is no right or wrong way when it comes to grieving. To cry, to write a poem, to erect a memorial, or to set up a scholarship in the name of the deceased friend—these are all choices and options. But what unites those who lose someone they work with currently, every day, or someone they used to work with is that they may have shared hours, weeks, months, or years of their lives, and now that person and those memories are gone, but not forgotten. Certainly the grief of the immediate family members is paramount when a co-worker, boss, or business associate dies, but the sadness of those who worked with and also liked and loved the deceased should not be diminished or ignored. It is a loss for them, too, and the healing process will take time and dealing with it in a unique way.

When a workplace or business workship or friend dies, there is a loss but the depth of the loss is usually tied to how close you felt to your deceased friend beyond your roles of co-worker, boss, or business associate. It may also be tied to your previous experiences coping with the death of a peer. For example, Martin met his best friend, Jim, when they were both in sixth grade. "At the time our school district was growing so fast it had to rent churches so all of the sixth grade was put into one church," says Martin, who is now 42 and working in the West as an educator. Martin and Jim remained friends all though middle school and high school.

"After I graduated from college, I went to the same town where he was going to pre-seminary school," Martin explains. "That year the friendship was cultivated. We had always been in contact through letters and telephone calls. One time he lost his sight temporarily [Jim developed cancer behind his eye] and we were in contact by tape. They didn't have e-mail at that time."

Jim died at the age of 28 from a heart attack related to his cancer. Martin still misses his best friend but he says, without bitterness, "He lived a good life."

Martin also shared with me the following story about how two co-workers handled it when their beloved co-worker died:

> I worked in a nursing home in the kitchen. I was a food service worker and I was around twenty-one and in college at the time. They were all food service workers.
>
> Soon after I was hired, someone suddenly died. It was a woman who was going to retire....She became ill. She was in her early sixties. It was a sudden death.
>
> After she died, they discovered she had left her sweater at work. They never returned it to her husband for the longest time. They kept it for two years and every time they went into the cooler or walked into the refrigerator, they would put it on. It seemed that each time they put it on, they would remember that woman.
>
> Then, shortly before the nursing home closed, they gave [her sweater] back to her husband.

My husband Fred's best friendship with Milt Haynes, with whom he had worked thirty years before at the Associated Press, ended only by Milt's death in February 2002 from a stroke at the age of sixty-five. Says Fred: "I still think of him as my best friend even though he's dead."

When Crystal-Barkley's CEO Nella Barkley's beloved husband of 45 years, Rufus, became terminally ill with ALS three years ago, her work friendships and her personal friends and family helped her get through that tough time. Barkley's reflections on the role of her friendships during the two years of her husband's illness and in the months after his death, when Barkley was grieving and dealing with the dramatic changes in her personal life, include these reflections:

> Certainly my work friendships were an important part of that time. There were times when Rufus didn't want to see anyone but I'd say, "You have to let them come. It's as much for them as it is for you," and he always loved it.
>
> He couldn't talk at all at the end but as long as he could talk, he was always cracking a joke. It was an amazing time. Rufus and I had friends come to see us who we never thought we would ever see again. One couple came from South Africa to see us.
>
> The house was always full of people and you know it just made us stay in a positive framework as dismal as the whole situation was. Even in the midst of disaster and tragedy, there really are some wonderful things that happen if you just let them happen. I shall forever be grateful to my colleagues and to Rufus'. They really kept things going at work and for me at home.

Here are some tips for coping with the death of a workship or friend at work as well as friends you met through work, including the military, even if you no longer work together:

- There is no right or wrong way to express your grief or sadness to other co-workers or to the family and other friends of the deceased. If it is comfortable, express your feelings in whatever way suits you: in a card, by sending flowers, a donation to a favorite charity, or writing in a journal.
- Your everyday routine will be different without your workship or friend. Give yourself time to adjust to the changes. Give yourself time to mourn.
- If you need time off, or to see a counselor or therapist, do what you have to do. Don't minimize what you're going through, and what your needs are, because it was "just a friend" rather than a family member that has passed away.

- Create a memory book compiling some of the work-related remembrances about your workship or friend who died. It could just be from you or you could ask others at the office to contribute. Put it in a scrapbook, along with any work-related photographs or memorabilia, and give it to his or her family as a source of comfort.

Here are some suggestions for offering comfort to your workships or friends at work if they have lost a loved one:

- Express your sympathy to a co-worker or friend at work upon the loss of a loved one in the immediate family as well as extended family members, including parents, siblings, aunts, uncles, or first cousins, friends, workships, or pets.
- Ask if there are any tasks related to the funeral that you could help out with such as childcare responsibilities, making any phone calls on behalf of the family, ordering flowers, setting up at the house after the wake, funeral, or trip to the cemetery, and so forth.
- If your help is not required, consider sending a card expressing your condolence even though you did not know or have a relationship with the deceased. By sending a card to your workship or friend, you are showing support for what he or she is going through.
- If you say, "Is there anything I can do to help?" make sure you really mean it. If it is feasible and reasonable, be prepared to actually do whatever it is your workship or friend asks of you.
- If appropriate and allowed at your company, offer to take on some of the workload of your workship or friend until the funeral or grieving period is over for their loved one. (Jewish co-workers, bosses, or subordinates may want to be out one week if they are sitting *shiva*, the mourning period which traditionally lasts five to seven days but is sometimes shorter.)

10

14 Types of Foes You Might Encounter

"Another VP in the Communications Department, when she heard I was going to be highlighted in a feature in the company's internal publication that would probably help my career there, helped nix the article by saying, 'What if our competitors got their hands on the publication? They'd be able to see what we were doing.' Which was ridiculous because our competitors already knew what we were doing and it was no secret anyway. But voicing her unwarranted concerns was enough to keep the article from being published."
—52-year-old male communications executive

Unfortunately, some people we meet through work may not be those who have our best interests at heart. These are often workplace relationships, whether co-workers, bosses, or subordinates, who feel threatened by anyone who has the potential to outshine them on the job. Rather than form positive workships, they tend to perceive some or all workplace relationships as competitors in a variety of potential power struggles.

In Harvey Mackay's classic *Swim With the Sharks Without Being Eaten Alive*, the businessman and author admits:

    Like everyone else, I have accumulated my
    share of enemies in the course of a lifetime.
    It's nothing to be ashamed of.

Noting that for many the advice of forgiving your enemies may be hard to implement, Mackay instead offers this alternative suggestion:

> The only way you can achieve true revenge is not to let your enemies cause you to self-destruct.

General Warning Signs of the Foes You Encounter at Work

The first step is to recognize you may be dealing with a foe. Although oftentimes it is clear and obvious, sometimes it is subtler.

Let's take a look at negative behavior some workplace relationships may show that will give you a warning sign that they may be a workship to avoid. Keep them at the workplace relationships/acquaintance level. Certainly avoid increasing your vulnerability by opening up and sharing as you are tempted to escalate the relationship to a friendship. Avoid that temptation!

By keeping a safe but not too obvious distance from this fiendish individual, you will deal with him or her in a cordial way. However, you can avoid revealing any personal or work-related information that could be used against you as they try to claw their way to the top on everyone else's back.

Here are some typical traits used by those who will do whatever it takes to get ahead:

- They are friendly but only as a manipulation and act to get what's needed; when the need is over, the friendliness is dropped, replaced with rudeness and a dismissive attitude.
- Lying.
- Exaggerating so much that it constitutes a lie.
- Placing blame on everyone else even if he or she was culpable.
- Stealing ideas, materials, money, or relationships.
- Misusing confidences.
- Currying favors because of the relationship.
- Initiating a vendetta.
- Sabotaging.

14 Foes to Watch Out for at Work and How to Deal with Them

Here are fourteen types of foes you may have to deal with. Even if you avoid forming a workship with them or don't become their friend, you will still need to know how to identify their Machiavellian schemes. Keep in mind that a workship or friendship with any of these types may have dire consequences to your career and even your personal life.

1. The Information Pirate

Be especially leery of this type of person if you work in a business where creativity and original thought are highly coveted. Much to your surprise, someone might cultivate a relationship with you only to get close to your innovative ideas, which he or she could present to his or her boss (or your boss, if you report to the same person) as his or her own. Or, if you work on a project together, he or she takes all the credit when it should be shared or yours alone.

Exercise caution about relationships at work, especially when you start a new job or project. Be particularly careful around those who ask you too many questions whose answers would require you to reveal too much information. Also be very leery about someone who asks probing questions about information or ideas that would be considered proprietary. They should not ask you questions that they know you cannot answer, especially if you have already advised them that you are not at liberty to discuss certain ideas or projects.

Forty-seven-year-old Linda, an entrepreneur and cosmetic manufacturer, was used by three women—Information Pirates—who, in the guise of companionship, tried to find out proprietary business information that is not typically shared:

> Three casual friends got "next" to me in order to find out things I knew—suppliers of ingredients, which is a pretty protected thing—and once they got them, dropped me like a hot spud.

2. The Begrudger

Throughout this book I mention that some jealousy or envy is not only normal in the workplace but it can be used as a positive motivator by showing you on a gut level just what you want for yourself. By contrast, The Begrudger is not only jealous or envious of you and your success, or skill, or even your relationship with a co-worker or boss, but he or she begrudges you that benefit. The Begrudger is a "sour grapes" kind of person who thinks you did not deserve the attention you are getting or the accolades, bonus, or promotion.

There is maliciousness behind The Begrudger's behavior and attitudes that is lacking in those who simply feel a twinge of jealousy or envy. Most scary of all is that The Begrudger may try to get others to agree that you do not deserve what you have so your reputation and even your job may be in jeopardy.

Avoid enraging The Begrudger even more than he or she is already fired up. Recognize that you are dealing with someone who is like this and tone down any sharing that could be misinterpreted as bragging. If possible, avoid working together on projects where you might naturally outshine The Begrudger, only fanning the flames of resentment that could cause this potential workship to derail you if given the chance.

3. The Saboteur

The Saboteur is one of the most insidious and dangerous of all the potential workships to avoid. The Saboteur is usually unaware that he or she is undermining you, and you may not see the pattern of destructiveness in their advice or actions until it is too late.

This foe will be especially dangerous if he or she is in a position of power as well as trust; if you look up to him or her and depend on his or her guidance to do your job.

Practically everything The Saboteur tells you turns out to be wrong or misleading. It could be because The Saboteur is ignorant or incompetent, and that is one reason behind their counterproductive behavior. Or it could be because The Saboteur is threatened by you; misleading you, whether it is done consciously or unconsciously, is a way to derail the competition.

Since The Saboteur is usually unaware that his advice or actions are wrong, and since he or she is usually someone you report to, pointing out misinformation could look as if you are questioning his or her authority. Therefore, you have to find other ways to deal with The Saboteur. The first step is to see the pattern to the misinformation or misdirection so you know you are dealing with a Saboteur. The second step is to always check whatever The Saboteur tells you with two or more other sources so at least you can figure out for yourself if you are being misled.

Be very careful with any offers of help that The Saboteur may provide. It could be a way of setting you up; you may then be accused of asking for something that is then held against you.

Here's an example: a co-worker offers another co-worker an introduction to a friend of hers who has a business that the co-worker might be interested in. The co-worker takes the name and number and makes the phone call, flattered that the co-worker wanted to be of help. What the co-worker who placed the call failed to realize was that the co-worker turned around and told the boss that her colleague was actively looking for additional work so the co-worker's loyalty to the job was questioned. No matter how often the co-worker refuted the claim of disloyalty, the damage had been done. The co-worker had been set up but it was too late to reverse the ramifications.

Why does The Saboteur do such devious things to cause co-workers or employees to become the object of ridicule or even lose their jobs, a project under consideration, even their reputation? In many cases the answer is "insecurity." The type of insecurity that causes The Saboteur to act out such deception is so deep-rooted that you probably will not be able to turn this tendency around. All you can do is note it and protect yourself so you are not The Saboteur's next career victim.

4. The Clique Member

It may be tempting to approach someone at work who is in a clique but you should carefully consider the situation before you commit yourself to membership. Although being part of a clique, and linked to another clique member, may seem like the fastest way to feel connected at work, especially at a new job, cliques are not without consequences.

Even though workships, especially if the guidelines suggested throughout this book are considered, may be a positive relationship on the job, cliques may lead to morale problems. As hard as it is to be accepted by a clique member or a clique, it may be relatively easy to be ostracized from the clique. Working day-by-day, side-by-side with former clique members may be so uncomfortable that it jeopardizes your ability to perform your job well.

Befriending a clique member also means that you will become associated with what that clique stands for, so do your homework and know what you may be getting yourself involved in. Does the clique have a reputation for gossiping about other workers? Is the clique made up of one level of employee so you may feel held back if you want to talk about advancement or even be resented if you are promoted over the other clique members?

What are the values of this clique member and the other members? Are they negative or positive individuals? A network allows others to become part of the group; a clique tends to be exclusive, which can lead to feelings of favoritism.

Although cliques within a traditional nine-to-five workplace may be counter-productive, in non-traditional work situations, such as among those who are unattached and working alone, a clique may provide a community that is lacking. Since the clique members in those situations do not work together but get together because of a common work or business bond, the clique can be a positive opportunity for connecting rather than the potentially negative situation in a nine-to-five setting.

5. The Spy

The Spy is someone who pumps you for information under the guise of being interested in you but does not give any information back, or the information that is shared may be false, inconsequential, or misleading. The Spy may also be in a position to use the facts and opinions you have given to him or her against you, either within your own company or at a competing one.

This potential workship may be trying to get close to you because he or she is spying for anyone from your boss to another co-worker to a competitor to another department. Listen carefully to what The Spy says about what his or her job is at the company as well as what he or she plans to do with the information you provide if you do answer any questions of a somewhat sensitive nature.

6. The Bully

Since this potential workship feels threatened by you and everyone else, he or she bullies you. If you were brought up in a home where your parents were distant or abusive in any way, whether emotionally, physically, or sexually, or your siblings bullied you, you might consider it "normal" to be bullied by co-workers or bosses. It's not, so be careful about associating with the bully.

Without professional help, he or she may not be able to change; a relationship with a bully means you may be in for a long haul of disappointment, anger, shame, and self-abuse. Some bullies may even cross the line and threaten, or carry out, physical harm. For example, a 23-year-old female, who works in a store, finally had to end a relationship with a bully. She explains: "A co-worker would constantly try to fight with me knowing I took Martial Arts and then try to hurt me."

7. The Gossip

This potential workship is dangerous because you never know when his or her gossip is going to be about you rather than everyone else that you may have found yourself being told about, even if reluctantly. If you annoy The Gossip in any way, he or she can turn on you and then you will be the current topic of discussion—usually in a negative way.

Be careful of high tech gossip, as well—the kind of chit-chat that might have been shared around the water cooler in bygone days that is, in some instances, being posted in Internet chat rooms or online sites. According to Tracey Drury's article in *Buffalo Business First*, "Gossip Goes High-Tech in Offices," employees who are being "dissed" in this way are suing their employers if offensive comments are not removed from these online forums; employees are being dismissed for posting offensive e-mailed jokes.

An advertising executive shared with me an intriguing way that she figured out for dealing with the traditional office Gossip. She puts the Gossip to work on her behalf, sharing with him or her a piece of information that she would actually like to have disseminated in the office but it might look too boastful if she were to do it herself.

8. The Sexual Harasser

You would think this kind of behavior did not exist anymore because of all the consciousness-raising about it, as well as the legal remedies that can be pursued if sexual harassment is suspected. The potential workship who engages in words and deeds that are definitely examples of sexual harassment could be misusing a possible relationship as a way of getting close to you. "In the name of friendship" he or she could be telling offensive jokes, making inappropriate sexual comments or overtures, or even put-downs, that are gender-related.

9. The Overly-Friendly

Of course you are eager to have relationships at work, especially if you are new at a job or in a novel work situation, such as attending a trade show or workshop. Being overly friendly, however, is a trait that could spell trouble. This potential workship may be overly-friendly out of eagerness, loneliness, a wish to "butter you up" with the promise of acceptance in the hope of finding out information about you or what you do, or there may be ulterior motives. A female carpenter shared the following anecdote with me: "I was working under a carpenter and he seemed really encouraging of my being a women in a male-dominated field. Well he used any tidbit of information I shared over the course of our two-month tenure together to try to do me in at work….I felt really betrayed."

10. The Pseudo-Confidante

Similar to the Overly-Friendly, the Pseudo-Confidante tries to pry information out of you by appealing to your emotional side and a need for intimacy that some have and that they bring to work. "Come on, you can tell me," The Pseudo-Confidante may say to you as he or she tries to connect with you (and learn your vulnerabilities and your secrets). This type is called a Pseudo-Confidante because he or she is insincere in his or her offer to hear your problems or fears out of a genuine concern for you.

With the Pseudo-Confidante, unlike a genuine Confidante, a trusted friend you can confide in with confidence that your self-disclosure and deepest secrets will be cherished and kept, it is an act, pretending concern and compassion, only to find out things that could be used against you or, if not against you, definitely for his or her advancement.

138

11. The Compulsive Talker

This potential workship displays a neediness through his or her compulsive talking. At work, this can slow you down, lower your productivity, and even get you into trouble with your co-workers, boss, or subordinates. The Compulsive Talker, however, is not a malicious type of potentially negative workship. This is just an obnoxious trait that, through self-awareness or therapy, could be minimized or overcome.

If you do choose to maintain or pursue a workship with a compulsive talker, be careful about when and where you begin conversations so you do not hurt your own productivity or image. Move out of the hallway where the conversations are stopping traffic or preventing you from getting to a meeting on time by asking the Compulsive Talker to lunch. If the Compulsive Talker calls you, be more mindful of the time than usual, preparing to politely wind down the conversation if it goes on far longer than necessary.

12. The Liar

How can you trust The Liar? You can't. There are those who try to convince themselves and others that they can lie in business but still be truthful in their personal lives, but lying is a red flag.

Sometimes it is tempting to overlook someone's tendency to lie because the lies are either in a work setting or do not seem to concern you directly. But, in time, the willingness to lie to get out of a difficult situation may be directed toward you. For example, an educator was betrayed by a casual friend at work who was "telling lies and coloring the truth to get ahead at work."

Is a "white" lie the same thing as a lie? Is exaggerating the truth the same thing as a lie? Is withholding information comparable to lying? How about tact? Now we're into a gray area. Being tactful and deciding to say something in a way to avoid offending someone is an exercise in diplomacy and judgment, something quite different than an outright lie.

13. The Taker

The Taker is selfish and self-absorbed. He or she tends to focus entirely on himself or herself. There is little or no reciprocity, or give and take, in a relationship with The Taker. It's a one-way street with them always taking and you always giving. Beware of those who are takers (and also of being one yourself).

14. The Downer

The Downer is someone who has an unconscious desire to make you feel as bad as he or she does. Another term for The Downer would be the doomsayer. With The Downer, things are always bleak, and negativity seems to be the order of the day. They use words like "can't," "never happen," "we're dead," "what a terrible idea," and "we're never going to be able to do this."

Do yourself a favor and surround yourself with positive people, because negativity is contagious and The Downer is spreading it around. So if you want to be positive, minimize contact with or avoid negative co-workers. One of the greatest orators of the twentieth century, Norman Vincent Peale, preached the strength of positive thinking in his bestseller, *The Power of Positive Thinking*.

As career consultant Nella Barkley emphasizes: "I would put at the top of my list, avoid the negative people, the naysayers. If we want to have good, successful happy lives, we need to surround ourselves with positive people, and do it consciously. Circumvent the negative people to every extent possible."

Speaker Karyn Buxman says about avoiding The Downer:

There are some people who can walk into a room and make you feel really good. There are others whose goal in life is to see how miserable they can be and their mission is to see how many they can bring down with them. You can't really change a negative person's attitude or goal so my goal in life is to recognize the people that I really enjoy being around. If I can come up with creative ways to be with those people, I won't even have time for the negative people.

Quiz: Is She (or He) a Toxic Person?

Recognizing and then avoiding harmful relationships is always crucial, but at work the ramifications can be dramatic. Being able to pick out a toxic person at work will be to your advantage so you can avoid that person or, if you are forced to deal with him or her, you at least know the type you are dealing with.

The quiz that follows may help you make that determination. Consider a specific person when you answer the questions that follow. (Since you probably have more than one workplace relationship that you want to assess, take the quiz more than once.)

Answer "A," "B," or "C" for each question below.

1. If you had a problem at work, you would:
A. Readily share it with this person.
B. Tell this person you had a problem but that you didn't want to share it.
C. Want to share it but would remember that last time you shared she let it slip to others and it came back to haunt you.

2. If you told this person a secret she would:
A. Keep your confidence forever.
B. Try to keep it a secret but it might slip out by accident.
C. Share it immediately.

3. If you wanted to go to lunch with this person but she had a prior commitment she would:
A. If appropriate, ask you if you'd like to come along.
B. Apologize for being unavailable and set a specific time to get together.
C. Say she was busy and didn't know when she'll be free. Go into detail about her heavy work schedule.

4. Your workplace relationship tells you that another co-worker wants to start going for a weekly business dinner on the night you usually go out for a drink after work but she is going to:
A. Suggest you join them.
B. Schedule another time to get together with you.
C. Let you know that she is choosing between the two of you.

5. When you call this person she:
A. Takes your call as long as it's feasible to put aside what she was doing.
B. Tells you she's really busy but she'll try to call you back.

C. Tells you she's busy and that you should call her back another time and hopefully she'll be around.

6. When you get an award for your work, your workplace associate:
A. Stops by your office or calls to congratulate you or sends you flowers, a present, or a card.
B. Mentions a week later that she's happy for you and she's sorry she didn't mention it sooner.
C. Completely ignores your achievement and even ignores the invitation to the luncheon in your honor.

7. If you and your workplace associate want to go out to lunch:
A. You discuss what restaurant you'd both like to go to.
B. Your associate will often pick the restaurant but she asks if you agree.
C. Your associate always has to pick the restaurant and it's always more convenient for her.

8. What your workplace associate told you she likes the most about you is that you:
A. Have an excellent work ethic and you're very accomplished.
B. Excel at the same things.
C. Can introduce her to your influential friends.

9. If your workplace associate made a mistake that impacted on you she would:
A. Apologize, explain why it happened, and ask you to accept her regrets.
B. Ignore the situation.
C. Blame it on you even if it was her fault.

10. If two weeks went by and your workplace associate hadn't seen you at work or heard from you she would probably:
A. Send you an e-mail or call you to find out how you're doing.
B. Call or stop by your office and interrogate you about why you hadn't contacted her sooner.
C. Wait as long as it took for you to call or contact her since you're always the one that initiates communication and she's afraid her

concern might be your way of setting her up for being accused of favoritism.

Look over your answers. How many A's, B's, or C's did you select?

If you chose mainly "A's" for your answers, the person you are considering is a positive individual who treats you with respect, affection, and courtesy. This person seems to base your positive association on shared values and beliefs as well as a mutual respect and concern for each other. You and this workplace associate seem to have a healthy give and take to your relationship, not taking it for granted but also realizing that there are other work relationships and demands that have to be considered as well.

If you chose mainly "B's" for your answers, your workplace associate may be ambivalent about just how important you are to her. This person does value your relationship but she also seems to lean toward doing what's easier rather than what might be in the best interest of your association. There is enough concern and thoughtfulness, however, that with some joint efforts this relationship could develop into a more positive and reciprocal workship.

If you answered a combination of A's, B's, and C's, look at the B's and C's that you might want to be working on with your workplace relationship, but also remind yourself that there's still a lot of positive traits (especially A's and some B's) to this person.

If you answered mostly "C's," be very cautious about your relationship with this workplace associate because she is probably a toxic and negative person. This person tends to be opportunistic as well as to manipulate you and situations to her advantage. She will reveal your confidences and put everything and everyone before you and your relationship, so if you were to allow this association to develop into a workship or even a friendship you may be setting yourself up for a big fall.

If this person is going through a rough time, such as having work challenges, health or family concerns, or romantic relationship ups and downs, you may want to cut her some slack. In that case, you might want to adopt a wait-and-see attitude about this workplace relationship before deciding that it has to be wound down or ended.

If you hold out little hope that your associate can improve, consider minimizing the importance of this person at your job as well as winding down or ending it without unwittingly causing a vendetta.

How Do You Deal With Toxic People That You Don't Want to Encourage?

The first step is recognizing that you do not wish to pursue a workship with the fourteen types discussed in this chapter as well as any toxic people. But suppose you *still* have to work together. What do you do? Try these techniques:

- Be polite and gracious. You do not have to like everyone that you work with but you do need a cordial working relationship.
- Keep your decision not to pursue a workship to yourself. There is no reason to hurt this person by announcing that you prefer to avoid getting closer.
- If you have made overtures to extend the relationship beyond the workplace, if possible get out of it. If you have to fulfill your obligation, be careful about what information you share.
- Be very careful about confiding in others at work about your reluctance to befriend someone. Badmouthing is never polite and since the reason two people do not mesh may be subjective rather than objective, you may be the one to look bad rather than the one you are putting down.
- Take a raincheck in making a final judgment call. First impressions are not always correct, good or bad. Keep an open mind and revisit your opinion at a later date when you have more information or shared experiences to reflect on.
- You can't win every relationship every time. You may want to start a workship with someone and he or she may see you as fitting into one of the "to be avoided" categories. It may have as much to do with the other person as it does with your actual behavior, but if you think there is any validity to their negative perceptions, see if you can find out what they are, and decide if you can, or want to, change. If the judgments about you are completely wrong, decide if you are going to try to reverse them or just let it ride.

11

How Workships and Friendships Help or Hinder Getting a Job or Growing a Business

> "It's easier when friends and co-workers recommend you for jobs than if you apply on your own."
> ——30-year-old New Jersey female TV reporter

Whether you are searching for your first job, have been downsized and need to find a new position, or you are a freelancer or entrepreneur constantly searching for the next assignment, client or customer, workships and friends are a great source of referrals, direct help, information, and emotional support. If you are already out of work, or a new graduate looking for a job, let everyone know that you are searching.

But if you are still employed, be careful about what workships you confide in about your job search goals; you do not want to risk others at work, including bosses, knowing about your wish to move on before you have either had a job offer or secured your future. Furthermore, your career goals, if you do share it with superiors at work, should be shared by you rather than passed along as office gossip.

There are many ways to search for a job, from cold calling to relying on employment agencies or executive recruiters. But one of the best ways is through networking with people with whom you have formed workships.

It is well-known than some of the best jobs do not even get listed with employment agencies or executive search firms. Either the job is filled from within, through an internal search, or friends tell friends or those they have formed workships with about the opening and they get "first dibs" on the job opportunity before the general public hears about it.

In the perennial bestseller, *What Color Is Your Parachute?,* Richard Nelson Bolles lists "The Five Best Ways to Try to Find a Job." The very first way is: "Asking for job-leads from: family members, friends, people in the community, staff at career centers— especially at your local community college or the high-school or college where you graduated." Bolles suggests asking them this one simple question: "Do you know of any jobs at the place where you work—or elsewhere?" The success rate of this method? According to Bolles, a "33% success rate."

Interestingly, those results are quite comparable to the ones I obtained based on a survey I conducted of 126 randomly-selected human resource managers who were all members of the same international professional association (SHRM, the Society of Human Resource Professionals). I discovered that 37% who completed that survey got their current job through someone they knew, with the largest category being through their friends or a friend of the family (25%). The second most frequent way was through a newspaper advertisement (24%), followed closely by through an employment agency or headhunter (23%). Just three persons out of those 126 got their current job by directly contacting the company.

Hank Schmidt, vice president for eleven years at Lee Hecht Harrison, an international outplacement firm, concurs that in conducting a job search, friends or people with whom you have workships are one of the many relationships that you, or any job seeker that you know, want to contact for help. Notes Schmidt, who previously worked for 19 years at the General Foods Corporation where, for four years, he supervised their staffing and career management system:

> Friends are just one of many categories of contacts. As you network, obviously one category would be friends, relatives, and neighbors. Another category would be relationships around

common interests that might be religion or schools. Another category is community and political groups including community relationships.

Still, there are distinct benefits to the workship or friendship factor in the job search as you ask friends, and the friends of friends, for referrals. As Schmidt says:

> Friends want to make referrals. They also want to talk to you if you were referred to them because that's a confirmation of quality and of somebody [who] can be of help. Friends want to talk with you because they just want to help—if one human being can help another human being, they want to do that, as long as it's productive.

But there are considerations and differences in terms of the job search related to whether the help is offered by a casual, close, or best friend. As Schmidt notes:

> Best friends are there for you regardless. They are in your support system. They can be very, very helpful in terms of psychological support and emotional support. They can offer advice.
> Casual friends as well as close or best friends can help react to your marketing plan—which is a self-assessment of your competencies and skills—with target companies.
> Ultimately, when I make a referral, I'm putting my own reputation on the line that you won't embarrass me in any way when you contact a target company that I gave you. If someone is a close or best friend, they are very comfortable referring you on. Close or best friends would accelerate the kind of trust and knowledge of the individual looking for a job.
> [But] people are sometimes reluctant to contact close friends because they're embarrassed of their situation, they haven't thought through their positioning, they haven't thought through what target companies [they want to contact], or they haven't thought through what they can give as much as get from the call. They're afraid of rejection. [But] a close or best friend is somebody who is there for you regardless, and will return your call.

Schmidt points out that even though it may hurt if an associate (what I call a workship) or a casual friend does not call back, it does not jeopardize the relationship as much as if a call from a close or best friend is ignored. Career consultant Nella Barkley, CEO of The Crystal-Barkley Corporation, concurs that friends may help in the job search, but be cautious about unrealistic expectations about just how much they can do, or should do. Barkley says:

> Friends can be somewhat helpful, but the inclination on the part of the job seeker is almost to expect the friend to do something, and it doesn't work very well that way. Other people can't get you jobs. Other people may help you with introductions and contacts, but only you can get your own job. A third party never should take the responsibility for getting someone a job. This is a personal task.
>
> But it's very appropriate to ask, "I think I recall you have a friend who works at such-and-such a place and would it be possible to share some ideas with that person on the basis of the shared interest"? But you would never go in and ask for a job.

You may want to avoid making a "cold call" since the rejection rate is so high if you lack a previous relationship with the person you are calling. Workships or friends will help you here because it will provide the POR—Point of Reference—that you need to get your call taken or your resume moved to the top of the pile. At least have the name of someone you both know to share that could give the person that you are calling a higher level of trust about you. If you prefer to cold call, there will be less rejection if you at least have the name of a workship or a friend, or someone known to the person you're calling, who allows you to use that name and relationship as a point of reference for your cold call.

Another way around the cold calling situation is to send a resume, cover letter, and any supporting materials in advance of the call. Then you can refer to those materials, which the person you are calling may even have looked over before your call, or at least it sounds like you put some effort into making the contact.

You could also ask a mutual workship or friend to call someone, in advance, on your behalf so when you later call, it is no longer a completely "cold call."

Help from the Friends of the Job Seeker

Besides direct help in getting a job, workships or friends offer emotional support during the job search, which, in today's tough job market, may be a much more extended and difficult search than before. Now the Director of Marketing and Membership at the Washington, D.C.-based National Association of Housing Cooperatives, Reginald Beckham, Jr. is grateful for how his friends came through for him during his extended job search. Beckham, who is single and who was unemployed for eight months, relied on his friends to help him through those months between jobs. Beckham explains:

> Moral support, calling everyday, sending leads, "Just wanted to call and check on you, my treat, I'll take you to the movie." That type of rallying type-cry. I had enough in my reserve so it wasn't like a cash thing. It was more like, "Hey, Reg. How you doing today? Anything I can do?"

Beckham relied on all his friends especially his best friend Darren, who provided emotional support during his search. They've been best friends since they were twelve years old and Beckham moved into the new neighborhood "and he was the first person I ever met."

He was also offered a very helpful piece of job search advice from Stacey Riska, who was his boss ten years before and they remained friends after they no longer worked together. Beckham considers Riska, who founded her own company, DataMax Solutions, a business based in Maryland with 22 employees in two locations, his mentor as well as his friend. Beckham explains:

> The best tip I got from Stacey was that when you go to do your job search, make it a job. Keep into that groove that you're actually [still] at an office.

Riska, who is married with two children, shared with me about Beckham and his job search, offering insights into how friends can help friends to get jobs but also how key it is to keep your friends up-to-date about your career accomplishments over the years. In that way, if they do recommend you, it will be based on current information as well as a confidence about that particular friend:

> Reggie worked for me at my old association. I was always impressed with him because of his initiative and eagerness to improve himself professionally. We bumped into each other through the years and he communicated through e-mail and on the phone. We always stayed in touch. He used me as a reference and I was really so glad to see him grow.
>
> Maybe because of the type of person I am, I want to help people. Whenever I found out about leads I thought would be valuable to him, I touched based with him. Not every day but at least once a month.

As it turned out, when Beckham interviewed for the job that he eventually landed, his old friend and former boss Riska got a call for a recommendation, not from Beckham, but directly from the new employer. Riska explains:

> They're a client of ours [so] I got a call from the executive director. "An old friend of yours just interviewed here." I got the call before Reggie had a chance to let me know. But based on what I knew about that organization, since they were a client, I knew Reggie would be a good fit and I told the executive director why.

For most careers, having a well-maintained network of all three types of friends—casual, close, and best—plus workships will provide the numbers and wider net for career success that most jobs require. It is less compromising to ask a casual friend for a favor, or a job referral, than it is to ask a close or best friend. If a casual friend turns you down, there are, ostensibly, "no hard feelings." True, if a close or best friend turns you down, it may do irreversible damage to your friendship, but a close or best friend may be more likely to help you out, to take your call, in the first place. You have to weigh the career and personal risks.

Sometimes it is also *what* you ask an old friend to help you with rather than the familiarity of the friendship that might be a concern over whether or not it was the right request to place. For example, David Hochberg, public affairs vice president for Lillian Vernon Corporation has, over the years, helped old friends from college with work-related concerns. But there are certain requests he is open to and others that he eschews:

> I don't appreciate it when old college friends call and want to sell me something, but I will help them get a job. I've helped good friends with critiquing and updating resumes or helping them in a job search, not at Lillian Vernon, but elsewhere. I'll [also] help spread the word among my circle. That is something I would do and have done."

But what if a friend who is out of work directly confronts you and asks, "Could you get me a job?" Career consultant Nella Barkley suggests that a good response is, "Tell me what interests you."

But what if the response to that question is something like, "I don't know. I've been working as a sales person and I just need another job."

Barkley suggests handling it this way:

> Then I would say, very kindly, "I can't get you a job, but what I can do is help you explore your interests so you could meet the people who share them so that might lead you to a job."

Offering Help with Finding a Job, Just Not At Your Company, Please

Although you may want to open your Rolodex or electronic organizer's address book to your friends to aid them in their job search through referrals, you might not want them to work at your company or for you. One woman shared with me how she intentionally lied about job openings at her company because she doubted the competency of the woman asking her for some leads. The woman sharing the anecdote quickly distanced herself from the woman she described as incompetent by calling her an "acquaintance" rather than a friend, although she admitted to liking her.

The anecdote is a reminder of the high stakes in the whole issue of friends helping friends get work: protect your own job at all costs. What if that means keeping job openings at your company that might be right for your friend to yourself? Of course that is easier to do without having to lie (never a good idea) if you are not directly asked about possible job openings. Of course ideally you are able to protect your job *and* preserve your friendships; since you and your family depend on your income, the role of job needs to be considered before the role of friend.

Twenty-two-year-old Don experienced first-hand the dangers to his own job by getting his friend a job at the restaurant where he worked. When Don recommended his friend Paul for the job, and Paul landed it, Don warned him, "When you come to work, don't fool around."

"He comes in here and already he starts flirting with all the girls," Don says, exasperated. "Some of the girls are really upset about it. The night manager at the restaurant says to me, 'You have to talk to Paul.'" Don had not talked to Paul yet. "Today Paul was supposed to work," but he didn't show up.

Don admitted regretting the day he recommended his friend Paul for the job and the day that Paul began working there.

Don's example highlights one of the pitfalls of recommending a friend for a job: once your friend accepts that job, not only your friend's reputation, but your reputation, is on the line. If your friend does well, you will be thanked and revered. If your friend performs badly, or has to be fired, your company will be annoyed that they have to start the job search process all over again and your judgment will be called into question.

Since consciously or unconsciously we are all judged by the company we keep, a disappointed employer may wonder about you because it was your friend who messed up. Even if no one even wondered about you before, guilt by association could come into play.

"The way he's carrying on," Don said about Paul's poor job performance, "I could have just left him on the street instead of finding him a job."

Don also shared that his boss, rather than talking directly to Paul about his disappointing job performance, instructed Don, because he was the friend who brought him in, to pass along the negative comments to Paul. Not only did this put Don in the unpleasant and undesirable position of being the bearer of bad tidings, but it also asked him to perform supervisory functions that should have been directly handled by his boss.

The opposite scenario is also possible, although a lot harder for someone to own up to. That is when a friend is instrumental in helping another friend to get a job at his company, and the friend excels at the new job, "showing up" his friend. Having the friend you suggested outshine you can be as threatening to your career as the recommended friend who turns out to be a dismal failure.

Of course both these situations are extremes and, most of the time, recommending a friend for a job will prove to be a positive experience for both of you, as well as the new employer. But seriously consider whether you want that referral to be with the company you currently work for or for another company, especially if you are in a similar line of business or profession.

How you handle a friend's request for a referral could be a "crossing the line" type of situation: saying "no" or hesitating could be seen as kicking a friend when he is down and out.

Whether you are doing the asking, or the referring, here are some things to consider that might help you deal with this request:

Guidelines for Workships, Friends, and Job Referrals

- Gather as much information as possible beforehand about your friend's previous job situation and performance so you have facts, not just second-hand or even outdated data upon which to base your referral or recommendation letter.
- The truth of the matter is that you can have a personal friendship with someone for years and rarely talk about what work you do. So if you honestly need information to help you determine if you can or should make a job referral or write a recommendation, be blunt and ask for details. Explain that your referral or recommendation will be that much more effective if you have specifics that you can consider, e.g., awards or commendations during previous jobs, accomplishments that could be highlighted, and even anecdotes or examples showing your friend in a favorable light.
- If you do not feel qualified or comfortable making a direct job referral, or writing a recommendation letter to a new potential employer, tell your friend that your knowledge of her career is too spotty. Instead, offer to comment on her character, or write a recommendation letter based on your status as a personal friend.

- If you do not feel comfortable enough about your friend to make a personal, not a professional, referral you should reevaluate whether it is in either of your optimum interests to have each other in your life as friends. Your reluctance to help this friend with a referral or recommendation letter may be an indication that you have wanted to wind down or end this friendship but put off doing it. Be prepared that turning down your friend's request for a referral or a recommendation may precipitate a dramatic reaction in your friend, catapulting the end of your friendship. Be prepared to deal with that consequence if it does happen.
- If possible, if you think you have to turn down a friend's request, try to make it clear that you have a policy of denying such requests. That might help your friend not to take it too personally.
- You could also stall your friend. "I'm busy right now but get back to me in a couple of weeks," may be easier to take than "No." The benefits of stalling is that your friend will probably find lots of others who can help him right now, and he may not get back to you a few weeks later. But if he does, you may have amassed enough background information to base your decision about whether or not to make the referral or recommendation on data that gives you more of a comfort zone about your ultimate decision. If your friend does get back to you in a few weeks with a renewed request, at least your decision will be based on objective facts and not just subjective impressions and memories.
- You might offer to provide your workship or friend with a general job recommendation that you could put in your file that reads "To Whom It May Concern." Tell your workship or friend that you know that you still will be hearing from potential employers by phone or mail for a specific recommendation, but this letter is something he could at least have on file if he needed it. (You can also ask your friend or workship to write such a letter for you to keep if you ever have to search for a job.)

Building Your Business

Gerald R. Baron, a Washington-based consultant who is the author of *Friendship Marketing* and who conducts seminars on that topic, shared a story about how friendship grows a business. His wife started going to a coffee shop regularly and before long she became a friend to Carol, the owner. It turned out that the owner had three children and Baron and his wife also have three children, and the two families all became friends. Within a year, Carol's oldest daughter, who was married and had a young child, was helping her husband clear some brush from the yard when she fell into a chainsaw, and was killed.

"My wife and I went to the funeral and there were several hundred people there with about a hundred more who couldn't even get into the church."

Baron realized that many people at that funeral were like he and his wife; they had become friends with Carol by first meeting her at her coffee shop:

> The coffee shop gave us the opportunity to know Carol, the owner. The value of the coffee shop ultimately won't be measured in the money it produces. How can you measure the value of those friendships? That's where I say the relationships were the end and the profitability of the coffee shop is the means to the end. The relationships are what you're working for but you have to have the venture, and the venture must be successful, because if she failed in that coffee shop, we wouldn't have had the opportunity to build those relationships, at least not in that setting.

A 50-year-old divorced single mother shares how a friendship helped her to build her business:

> I am an entrepreneur who has succeeded thanks to a special friendship. I am a single mother who had not a dime to my name fifteen years ago. Now I am the owner of a public relations firm that is doing very well. I have to say I owe much of this to my best friend. My best friend of twenty-five years helped me obtain the career I now have by introducing me to the man who gave me my first PR job. She was always my best PR agent!

Having a strong network of workships and friendships, especially in the beginning stages of a business, may make the difference as to whether a new business or an entrepeneur swims or sinks, or any business that relies on numbers. I am reminded of a story that is told about businessman Harvey MacKay and his first book and bestseller, *Swim With the Sharks Without Being Eaten Alive*. When his publisher was deciding on the number of books they would print for the first printing, Mackay reassured them that he had thousands of customers in his Roladex with whom he had maintained a relationship. He assured them that a majority of those customers would probably buy his book because they felt a personal connection to him.

The publisher increased the first printing as well as its expectations for the book that it could be a big seller, which it did become.

Jack Mitchell, part of the Mitchell family of Connecticut who run the very successful clothing stores, Mitchells of Westport and Richards of Greenwich, has formalized a similar concept in his bestseller, *Hug a Customer*. Here is the slogan for Mitchells, reflected in the title of his book, epitomizing the customer service that is one of the mainstays of the enormous success of their retail stores: "Once a customer, always a friend."

12

Working from Home or Alone

> "I don't feel that isolated. I go to Starbucks® almost every morning. I say hello to people who are there and then I come home [to work]."
> —Paula, 48-year-old single mother working from home

The trend toward working from home and telecommuting as an alternative to traditional office settings is beginning to have an impact on workplace relationships, especially workships and friendships at work. Many people are trading the demands of commuting for the seeming joys of conveniently working from home, unaware that those discussions at the water cooler, and those "drop-in visitors" who might have seemed annoying at the time, may actually have been adding to their productivity. The connections at work may also bring out creativity and innovation; if working alone or from home is a choice or an enforced situation, it is useful to find ways to keep or develop workships or friendships even though you are no longer in a workplace setting.

About a decade ago, I was on a train from New York City to Connecticut. I struck up a conversation with a woman on the train. It turned out her name was Janice Papolos and she was also a writer and, by coincidence, also a member of a writers' association I had belonged to since my early twenties: the American Society of Journalists and Authors (ASJA). Janice had also relocated from

Manhattan to Connecticut with her husband and two sons, and, like me, she also missed the city. We agreed to start a writers' group.

The group quickly grew to half-a-dozen women, all published authors. Initially we met every month but it became difficult to keep up that pace with everyone's schedules and family commitments. Recently, after almost a year of e-mails back and forth, we finally got together, and then decided to meet again in two months. We alternate our meetings at different members' homes; for the last several years, in December, we try to have a holiday lunch. We call our group the Writers Bloc. Until my husband worked from home for two years of fifteen years of corporate jobs, including a decade of long commutes, except for teaching, consulting, or interviewing, the Writers Bloc became a key connection with work-related friends, as intermittent as it might have been.

I asked Janice Papolos to share what our writer's group has meant to her:

> Our Writers' Bloc surprised me because I found out that four prominent authors lived within the neighborhood or a town or two away. I no longer felt isolated, and the support and advice we have given each other has been incalculable.
>
> These women just happened to be there when I found out my book had been set in what looked to be 8-point type, and supported me while I sobbed to my brilliant and sympathetic editor (the point size was changed).
>
> They urged me to contact my publisher when the jacket of another book was about to go to press with a color choice unchanged and—in the nick of time—I was able to get a better, more vibrant cover.
>
> One of our group acted as reader and editor of two of my books. She straightened out my rather mangled grammar and urged me to be bold about the material. Also, she had been on a number of network television talk shows, and she kept calling me with wise advice about how to handle another network show that was fast-moving (and nerve-wracking). Her words and strategies helped me make the points and help families.
>
> When I look back, I realize that this group has been responsible for so many of the cliff-hanging decisions that set me right. What if I had taken a different train?

For most self-employed home-based workers, staying connected and not isolated is a challenge. But, making the effort to forge business-related workships and friendships will prove beneficial to the work and to you, personally and professionally.

Joanne Kabak, a freelance article and book author who is in my writer's group, shared with me her thoughts on working alone:

> I find it extremely isolating. I do not have the natural camaraderie that comes with being in an office —an experience I often enjoyed when I worked in organizations. No matter what environment I was in, I developed good friendships as well as warm casual relationships. Now, since so much of my work is done by phone, I do not feel like calling people for a friendly talk either in the middle of the workday, or when my day is done. Enough phone talk! The result is that I neither see people during my workday, nor call them.

Realizing that working alone, although it has the advantage of allowing Joanne to set her own hours to fit her children's schedules, also has disadvantages, Joanne has found ways to try to offset the negatives of working alone:

> I keep up relationships by e-mail, especially long-distance ones that I otherwise wouldn't have. I have a particularly strong e-mail relationship with a college classmate and colleague in the writing business who lives in LA.
>
> I also have joined groups of women entrepreneurs in my area and have formed very nice relationships with several of the women. However, it is much [more] based on common business issues than personal ones. On top of working solo, I have many responsibilities with my immediate family, community work, exercise routines, and ongoing education. So I find myself in a situation where there isn't room and opportunity for the kind of friendships I've had in the past. And I do miss them!

Paula is a 48-year-old single mother living in California who has been working from home for a company based in Alaska for the last seven months. Offering customer support by telephone is a job she could do from anywhere, including her home. So far Paula does not feel isolated. Her eight-year-old daughter keeps her busy; she also has a neighbor in her condominium development who lets Paula come over every day at lunchtime to use her workout equipment. Paula shares about her working from home lifestyle:

> I'm on the phone a lot [since] my job consists of being on the phone. I have other co-workers and they work at home and we call each other during the day. One of my co-workers is also a good friend. She's become a close friend. We met through work. We used to work together in the same office. She left the office four or five years ago. I just started with this new company seven months ago. But the two companies work together.

Whether someone works in a traditional 9-to-5 corporate setting, or alone in a home office, everyone needs the bonding and camaraderie that feeling connected at work and in business provides. As noted throughout this book, those positive feelings have been proven to increase productivity and workplace and work satisfaction.

As the number of workers who work from home, part of the time or all the time, increases, the necessity of somehow creating those workplace or business workships or friendships that will keep you up on what's going on in your field becomes more crucial.

Massachusetts-based consultant Barbara Callan-Bogia, like most of those I have interviewed over the years who work alone in non-traditional office settings, has found a way that works for her to get the workplace relationships that she needs for herself and for her business.

Becoming active in regional and national associations related to her career as a speaker and trainer as well as being a small business owner helps Barbara to feel connected. As Barbara explains:

> Being a solo practitioner has its ups and downs. I am a people person so I have missed the interruptions of the normal workday by colleagues stopping in to ask a question or to talk.
>
> [But] over the seven years I have been in business for myself, I have built up a network of colleagues who I can call or meet with to get "water cooler" time.
>
> When I first started my business, I purposefully joined the New England Business Owners Organization (NEWBO) to meet other small businesswomen to relate to. It's great to help other women in their business as we grow our own business.

As a member and now president of the National Speakers Association New England (NSA-NE) chapter, it is like going home. The friendships and caring by the members I haven't found anywhere else.

If You Work with Your Romantic Partner or Mate

Screenwriter Marilyn Horowitz works with her husband Arthur Vincie and it's just fine. "I'm very fortunate," says Horowitz. "I work with my husband but we parallel rather than collaborate directly and I think that's the secret. As a result, we also have an awful lot of the same friends."

If you and your romantic partner or mate work together at the same company, obviously you're going to act professional in front of employees, subordinates, or bosses. But if you and your romantic partner work together in a home-based setting, there are other concerns. For example, it is important not to become so isolated that during the workday and in your non-work time you become a "you and me against the world" force to reckon with. Even if you do mainly work together, try to schedule time with others during the workday, for meetings and for business breakfasts, lunches, or dinners, and even for social lunches.

Take the time to network with potential new clients or customers separately; avoid doing absolutely everything together so you begin to fuse your identities and lose your independence. A little bit of separation from each other is healthy and positive, for your romantic relationship as well as for your business and work concerns and relationships.

"Sometimes too much 'togetherness' may occur," notes a freelance writer and publisher who worked together with his wife for twenty years of their twenty-five year marriage before their relationship dissolved. There is a "difficulty sometimes in having fun with the person who is troubled about the same business worries you are," he wrote in his questionnaire about the disadvantages of working with his partner, a few years before their marriage came unglued.

A physician and his medical assistant wife, who worked together shortly after marrying, found more advantages than disadvantages in the 41+ years of their married, working together union. The only disadvantages were "Can't be fired," and "Difficulty at times in finding fault."

California-based Christine A. Hartline, Executive Director of the Eating Disorder Referral and Information Center, works at home along with her husband, a psychologist. Hartline is pleased with the working arrangement; she makes sure she stays connected to the friends she met in the mental health field with whom she still interacts:

> Currently, I work at home and so does my husband. He has an office downstairs and I have an office upstairs.
>
> At first the thought of spending all day with him seemed like a bad idea but things have worked out very well for us. We are a very supportive team. Both of us enjoy what we do and bounce ideas off one another and help each other quite a bit.
>
> I [also] have the luxury of having some wonderful friends I met years ago and with whom I still work with and interact with a great deal via phone, e-mail, and in person. I go to Los Angeles every once in awhile to visit them and consult on issues related to administration. They are all friends and colleagues in the mental health field. I have also met so many wonderful people over the Internet and have met many of them in person at conferences.
>
> I really do not miss going to the "office" everyday as I still get the one-on-one interaction with colleagues here in San Diego and L.A.

Before you decide to work alone, or even if you work alone already, reconsider the impact that this work arrangement has on you from a social and even a business perspective. I'll be blunt: I had a great time during the two years that my husband Fred was able to work from home as a freelancer. He decided to return to a fulltime corporate job recently but we definitely enjoyed those two years working together.

During those two years of working together, we both made sure we had time to network professionally independently of each other instead of spending twenty-four hours a day together. Although we were together most workdays, writing or researching in our separate offices on the lower level of our house, we still attended business breakfasts, lunches, or seminars that reflected our varied interests and career goals. We had meetings without each other and I belonged to a whole host of associations that I tried to get to at least every month or two. Fred has always been less of a joiner of formal associations but even he joined a new professional group when he realized that working from home made different networking demands than those with a more traditional office/corporate job.

But working together with a spouse, or even working alone or from home, is definitely not a lifestyle that suits everyone. I remember when we worked together the first time, right after we married. A woman who had an executive job at a leading credit card company, who was also married and had two young children at home, was absolutely stunned that I wanted to spend almost all of my work and leisure time with my spouse. She assured me that she could never do that and would not want to. She explained to me that getting out of her apartment, and away from her spouse and young children during the workday was one of the benefits of her job (along with her impressive salary and the professional challenges of her position). But that's what makes horseracing, as they say.

Here's a self-quiz to help you decide if working alone or from home is for you:

Working Alone or From Home: Is It For You?

Answer *yes* or *no* to the questions that follow:

1. I do not need to interact with others on a daily basis.
2. My work requires me to be out of the office and meeting people at least 50% of the time.
3. If I do need to connect with others during the workday, I have established ways to do that, by phone or in-person.
4. I connect with others through e-mail and online, but in other ways as well.
5. I have personal relationships outside of my work that keep me connected.
6. I belong to at least one professional association and I attend monthly networking meetings.
7. I have tried working in an office with others but I cannot get any work done in a traditional shared office environment.
8. The nature of my work demands total concentration and silence.

9. There are economic benefits to working from home that prevent me from getting an outside office at this time.
10. I have some outside work-related activities or meetings so I am not a complete shut-in.

Look over your answers. If you answered "yes" to at least five of the ten questions, working along or at home is an option that might work for you. You are taking into account your personality, which seems to like the benefits of working alone or from home, as well as finding a way to counteract the potentially negative social consequences of working in an isolated situation.

If you answered "no" to most of the questions, you should seriously re-evaluate if the social consequences of working alone or from home are outweighing the economic or work benefits.

You might also consider trying working from home to see if it is an effective office arrangement for you. For example, Grace Freedson of Long Island-based Publishing Network, LLC, an agent and book packager, only worked from home for the first year after leaving the publishing company where she had worked for sixteen years. She discovered she needed to see people during the day. For the last two years, she has been renting outside office space, and it's working out well for her.

Here are some alternative ways to "work alone" or in a non-traditional workplace setting, without being alone:

- Look into renting an office in an office suite wherein you share a secretary, photocopier, and mailroom services with other self-employed entrepreneurs. Rent an office with others who are also self-employed.
- Work with your spouse.
- If you outsource or use freelancers, consider sharing office space.
- For at least a few hours a day, work in your local or school library.
- Coffee shops, such as Starbucks®, offer a place to work with others around; there are even places to plug in your laptop computer.

- If you have clients with offices ask if there is space available to you on an occasional basis so you could work there, from time to time.
- Some professional associations, as a membership perk, will allow their members to use their offices to work, conduct interviews, or meet with clients.
- Join a local club for business people. For an annual membership fee, you can meet business associates for breakfast, lunch, dinner, or networking events as well as use their space for meetings and seminars, according to the policies of the club, such as purchasing refreshments for your events through their catering facilities.
- Join a local health club and meet business associates or friends there for meetings or to work out together.
- Instead of conducting business by e-mail, fax, or phone, make an effort to conduct as many meetings as possible in-person and face-to-face.
- Start a networking group. That's what a 40-year-old married publicist, who was feeling "lonely working from home" did. She explains: "Despite my hectic schedule, I value friendship tremendously and that is exactly why I recently founded a networking group, so I could make new friends who relate to me at this stage in my life."

As more and more workers work from home because they want to, or their companies require it to save on overhead, it is vital that the social aspects of work be considered. As career consultant Nella Barkley notes: "The increasing virtual manner of working imposes a huge and different responsibility on management, which very few senior managers have yet perceived."

You may have to take the first step about putting regular contact with workplace and business associates in place. "Don't wait for your boss or others to take the initiative," Barkley warns. "Make sure that you're in regular contact with those with whom you want to maintain relationships."

Most of all, remember that interacting only by e-mail, although a very efficient way to communicate with workships or friends, should not be your entire way of relating, even if your job is dependent on the Internet. We all need to place phone calls and hear someone's voice as well as get out and have those face-to-face meetings so we can exchange a smile, a handshake, a hug or kiss on the cheek, if appropriate, or even share a tear of sadness or joy.

13

Workplace Relationships Begin at

Home

> "A work friend transferred out of my office at a stressful time. I understood why this was necessary but it still felt like a betrayal."
> —36-year-old schoolteacher whose father had walked out on the family when she was 13

When you meet someone at work, what that person brings to the work situation, and any relationship that ensues, may have as much to do with what transpired during his or her formative years as it does with you. Similarly, your own family relationships will have an impact on how you connect with those you meet at work or in business.

Why is it useful to consider one's formative years as it relates to your current workplace relationships? Clinical psychologist Michael Thompson, Ph.D. and co-authors Catherine O'Neill Grace and Lawrence J. Cohen, Ph.D. share these powerful, wise words in *Best Friends, Worst Enemies*: "Children's original love relationships with their parents teach them vital lessons about how to be friends."

As psychotherapist Carolynn Hillman points out in *Recovery of Your Self-Esteem*: "As you were parented, so you parent yourself." I would add: so you parent (or befriend) others. In that chapter, "Why We Are The Way We Are," Hillman points out six parenting styles. Recognizing if your parent fits into a particular style, and what the consequences of that style of parenting, especially mothering, might mean to your current approach to workplace relationships could be a productive exercise:

- The Good-Enough Mother—A concept proposed by British psychoanalyst D.W. Winnicott of the mother who manages to give her child just enough of whatever she or he needs so the child grows up well-adjusted.
- The Over-Involved Parent—The parent who is unable to let go as her child matures, making her child feel guilty for maturing instead of embracing a natural progression from dependent infant to independent adult.
- The Distant Parent—Hillman calls this the "under-involved" parent with the consequence in adulthood of "longing for closeness, while often afraid to be vulnerable."
- The Narcissistic Parent—Those raised by a narcissistic parent, according to Hillman, "often have difficulty being empathetically connected to others" because we "cannot give what we never received."
- The Insecure Parent—Those raised by an insecure parent, as Hillman notes, "long to be affirmed—to be told that they are good, worthy, competent, and lovable, but they cannot affirm themselves."
- The Highly Critical/Abusive Parent—As Hillman notes, "Children of highly critical, abusive parents cannot help but feel that their parents are right and that they, themselves, are bad."

Do you recognize your parents' nurturing style from the above list? How about the relationship you had with your sibling or siblings? How does it fit into any of the above characteristics (substituting the word "sibling" for "parent")?

Ask yourself and then answer this question: *If the way you were parented was less than ideal, or the way you got along with your siblings was far from equitable and positive, how do those early patterns impact on your friendship choices and relationships now?*

Fortunately it's never too late to revisit your early childhood roots. You can develop new scripts for how you interact with people now, based on what you now know and who you really are, not based on the messages, often inaccurate or negative, that you might have internalized during your formative years.

It is from observing your nuclear family—your parents and your siblings—as well as by experiencing the words they say and the way they treat each other that you initially internalize the concepts of love and friendship.

How did your family members handle conflict? Anger? Rage? Criticism? Were you encouraged to share your feelings? Or to bury them? Did your parents encourage you to be self-sufficient, or overly dependent so that you need others to nurture you to such an extreme that you push people away? Were you the victim of physical, sexual, or verbal abuse by a parent? Sibling? Extended family member? Authority figure?

As noted in my previous books on friendship, especially Chapter 4, "It's All in the Family" in *When Friendship Hurts*, it may be necessary to deal with how those early childhood traumas have impacted on your personal friendships as well as your workplace relationships or the ability to form workships or friendships at work.

For example, 40-year-old Linda, who is divorced with one teenage daughter, was abused numerous times by her step-father between the ages of 11 and 16. Linda describes the long-term consequences on all her relationships: "I live almost constantly in crisis in my home, in my work, and in my relationships with the opposite sex."

Self-Quiz: Consider How Your Childhood Might Be Impacting on Work-Related Relationships (Workships or Friendships)

Answer the following questions to discover some key considerations that will impact on what kind of workplace or business workships or friendships you are capable of initiating and maintaining:

- How did you get along with your father?
- How did you get along with your mother?
- How did you get along with your siblings?

- What was your first experience with friendship? Was it positive? Negative?
- How did you deal with anger during your childhood and teen years?
- How do you deal with feelings of jealousy? Envy?
- Are you competitive?
- Does competition inspire you, enrage you, or shut you down?
- Did your family members make you feel as if you counted and were important?
- Was honesty valued in your family?
- Did your parents have friends when you were growing up? What were those relationships like?

You might also want to consider rephrasing or reframing the above questions, as well as the answers you get, as related to each workship/potential workship or friend/potential friend that you know in a workplace or business context. Depending upon the relationship and situation, you may want to ask some or all of the above questions directly or just listen carefully as your friend or potential friend shares information related to their formative years.

There is not always a direct cause-and-effect between what you experienced growing up and who you become as an adult. It is a complex journey and process involving personality differences. Other key relationships, such as extended family members like a grandparent, aunt, or uncle, as well as a family friend, teacher, clergy member, or even a team mentor, could have helped minimize the long-term negative effects of a dysfunctional, critical, or abusive nuclear family.

There is also the possibility of change through self-analysis or therapy, whether it is short- or long-term care. But certainly, without outside help, emotional deprivation in childhood may make it harder to connect and have mutually satisfying workships or friendships in later years—including workplace friendships.

Meredith, who is 28, married, the mother of a six-year-old, and living in the South, shares how the sexual abuse she experienced by her sister, when she was six, and by her cousins, between the ages of 11 and 15, impacted her friendships during her childhood and adult years. She "felt isolated at times because I was not allowed friends." Her one friendship at work (in the Army) turned out to be a very unfortunate situation. She now has only two casual friends, and not one close or best friend:

> I never had friends. Just casual acquaintances. I was the unpopular kid that people picked on and made fun of. We lived out in the rural area so family was all I was around while I was a child.
>
> I had a friend in the Army and she turned someone in for something and others girls were threatening to her. I informed her of this and she accused me of siding with them. I tried to assure her that I wasn't. I had to leave the next week on an assignment. In this case she trashed my room, while I was away, poured garbage all over the place, spray-painted on the wall.
>
> She was discharged and I never heard from her again.
>
> [Being the survivor of childhood sexual abuse] makes you feel all alone. It's hard to believe anyone else could understand. It has made me feel isolated, different. I feel that if I let anyone get to know me they wouldn't want to have anything to do with me. I believe the abuse has impaired my judgment on who could be trusted. When just about everyone has hurt you, would you really want to keep on taking chances? Sometimes I think I get scared when someone starts to get close and I pull away and start a fight so they won't like me.

Meredith has two casual friends at the factory where she works as a materials handler: One is a woman who is "old enough to be my mother and she treats me like a daughter. I think we have a mutual friendship."

The other person she feels closest to is her therapist. But "saying she is a friend would be wrong. A friend is one who you call to say 'Hey let's go shopping or to a movie.'"

By contrast, Barbara is a 20-year-old single student at a college in the Midwest. She notes that she has enough close or best friends now: she lists two best friends, five close friends, and 12 casual friends. Her relationship with her two brothers when she was growing up was "positive," her relationship with her mother during her formative years was "supportive," and with her father was "loving."

Forty-four-year-old Suzie, who lives in Canada and is married and taking time off from her corporate job to raise three children, says she is "blessed with wonderful friends." She and her husband entertain often, "and we constantly meet new people and find that these new friendships live on." Suzie maintains a best friendship with Gloria, whom she met at work twenty years ago, even though they live in different countries thousands of miles apart. (In *When Friendship Hurts*, Gloria described Suzie and why she is an ideal friend.)

Suzie, who says "friendship is very important to me, I am very loyal to my friends," attributes her positive relationships, not just with girlfriends but also with her husband, siblings, children, and the spouses of her friends to her grandmother's influence during her formative years, which even helped Suzie deal with her parents' rocky marriage:

> My grandmother had a terrific influence in my life. A fabulous fabulous foundation. Love[d] just to love and care about other people. Whenever my Mom and Dad had problems and they would separate, there's where we always went. We'd always go back to our parents, and then they'd break up. But my grandparents were a wonderful foundation for us, which we passed on to our children.

Below are key issues from childhood and teen years that may impact on your workplace relationships including workships and friendships:

- Trust
- Jealousy and Envy
- Unrealistic Emotional Demands
- Relationships with Siblings and Sibling Rivalry
- Ability to Deal with Authority Figures
- Fighting Fair

Trust

Having workships or friendships at work or in business, which involves sharing of information, requires a degree of trust in another person. Since someone's job or livelihood is usually at stake, unless someone felt his parents or siblings were trustworthy, it may be difficult to risk opening up in the workplace, even to the minimal degree that a workship might require, because a high degree of basic trust is lacking.

Conversely, someone may be so used to being betrayed by parents or siblings that he or she enters into workplace relationships with the unconscious need to recreate the betrayal. When it occurs, he or she may act shocked and dismayed, but if you study the situation's dynamics it becomes clear that the betrayal was set up. (This is part of the concept of repetition compulsion in psychology, the unconscious need to repeat a childhood trauma until it is mastered and overcome.)

"I was warned not to do business with friends by my father at an early age," notes Marjorie, a 50-year-old divorced Midwestern communications consultant. "Now I know why," she continues. What happened was that rather than pay Marjorie for the discounted services that she had provided her best friend to get her new company launched, the friend used her money for other things. "She could have seen to it that we were paid....It showed me how selfish and shallow she is."

This betrayal, however, is not an isolated incident for Marjorie, who notes: "I have been betrayed by friends I made in the business world. I have been back-stabbed, of course, by people whom I thought were friends, but clearly they weren't. It was always, however, in the business arena."

If you would like to have a workplace workship or friendship but you are resisting it, ask yourself if there are any childhood trust issues that need to be addressed. There may also be other instances of friendship betrayal at work or in business that have reaffirmed your or your colleague's decision that friendship at work cannot succeed.

These examples of failed workplace or business friendships, however, are not the starting point. Those situations are probably just additional replications of what occurred during childhood or adolescence. Being able to have a successful workplace or business friendship that does not end in deception, distrust, and betrayal may actually be a turning point in your ability to trust others, especially when the stakes are high, such as at work or in romance.

However, it is important that you increase the likelihood that a workplace relationship that becomes a workship or a friendship is a positive and not a negative experience by taking the time to find out if the person trying to befriend you is trustworthy. Especially if you are new at a job, as noted before, listen, observe, watch, see how he treats others, see how others treat him, take your time starting a workship or a friendship, but also see if your gut instincts about someone turn out to be true.

Jealousy and Envy

Childhood experiences of jealousy toward the opposite sex parent, or competition for the same-sex parent's love, or for the amount of attention divided among siblings, and the levels of feelings associated with these, may factor into whether or not an individual can tolerate workplace workships or friendships.

"Helpless infants need to be jealous of anything that diverts mother's attention," notes Barbara Lang Stern in her article published in *Vogue*, "Is Jealousy Healthy?" Fast forward to the workplace: a co-worker could be seen in a more favorable light by the boss (mother figure). A co-worker could get promoted over you, or praised more than you, or you could be the one who becomes teacher's pet and gets promoted over your co-worker. How would that make you feel? If you are just co-workers and not friends, it may be easier to ignore your colleague's jealousy, or, if you are the one who feels jealous, you may feel less guilty about those feelings because it's not someone you care about. It's just a "co-worker."

Fifty-two-year-old Geraldine, the aerobic instructor mentioned in Chapter 5, was the victim of her best friend and co-worker's jealousy, and it cost Geraldine her job:

> My best girlfriend was jealous of me and my talents and therefore sabotaged me every chance she could. It was not healthy for me to continue in the relationship. Because of her jealousy, [she] convinced the company we worked for to let me go, that my [consulting] business was a conflict of interest.

Geraldine's former friend acted on her jealous feelings, derailing her friend's career, and ending their friendship. However, some degree of jealousy, as long as it does not lead to harmful actions toward another, is natural and normal in every relationship. When jealousy is extreme or excessive, however, it is time to wonder about someone (or yourself) and ask the difficult question: how do you and your friend really feel about one another?

But, allow yourself to have some jealousy of a co-worker when she is praised by your boss; or, accept as typical that a co-worker will be jealous when you get a $200 gift basket of goodies for the holidays from a major client and she is ignored. This level of jealous feelings does not mean you cannot or should not be friends. As Barbara Lang Stern notes in "Is Jealousy Healthy?" that "If jealousy is about loss, envy—its twin—is about gain: how much we want what someone else has and fear that we can't get it."

Robert C. Solomon, in "The Passions," calls envy one of the seven deadly sins (along with pride, sloth, covetousness, lust, anger, and gluttony) and says that it is an "essentially vicious emotion, bitter and vindictive." Solomon continues: "Envy is among the very strongest competitive emotions, thus virtually shutting out all possibility of intimacy (except in alliance with fellow losers)."

I am reminded of the failed friendships that ensued, as told to me by the victorious professor who lost his other friendships, when he was one of four colleagues and friends at the same college. Only one of the four could be granted tenure and when he got it and his colleagues/friends did not, unchecked envy ended the friendships.

I asked Geraldine, the aerobics instructor mentioned previously, what she knew about her former friend Sylvia's childhood that might help explain why Sylvia "told on" her, leading to Geraldine's firing:

> Sylvia told me that her mother used to hear voices. She told me that her Dad called her a whore all the time. I have tidbits about her childhood but they seem to add up to an abusive, dysfunctional, family environment.
>
> As far as my background, I was raised the youngest of three children. A brother six years older and a sister 14 years older. I grew up in the shadow of two very high achievers academically.
>
> I was also Daddy's girl. I had a loving father but my Mom was restrictive in discipline and love.
>
> I do feel that Sylvia felt threatened by my aerobics ability and my teaching skills. I think that played a big part in her doing me in.

If jealousy or envy are getting in the way of your workships or friendships at work, here are some steps to take:

- Jealousy is an emotion that is felt toward friends more commonly than you might have thought. For example, in my survey of 400 men and women, of the 346 who answered the question, "Has a casual, close, or best friend ever been jealous of you?" 48% noted that a friend had been jealous, while 38% answered that they didn't think a friend had been jealous. Of those who were asked, "Have you ever been jealous of a casual, close, or best friend? almost as many admitted to being jealous of a friend (46%) as there were who denied having jealous feelings (50%).
- Accept that jealousy and envy are normal emotions that need not rule out a workship or a friendship.
- See the jealous or envious feelings as information. It says that someone wants what someone else has got. That information could be used as motivation (and not to begrudge a friend's accomplishment or justify an attempt to sabotage someone's job).
- Reflect back to the possible childhood roots of the jealous or envious feelings, understanding that the past may be influencing someone's response to the present.
- Since jealousy and envy may be more prevalent when it is between those who are most like each other (see sibling rivalry, below), it may be necessary to befriend those who are dissimilar. For example, rather than be friendless at work or in business, befriend at another level, higher or lower, even though, in most instances, friendships between co-workers who have their jealousy and envy in check are more common and fraught with fewer potential status-related problems.
- Befriend outside your business, such as someone in the movie industry, if you're a teacher, or someone who heads a manufacturing company, if you're a book publisher.
- Acknowledge the jealous or envious feelings, and move on. "I'm jealous that you got the promotion and I didn't." "I envy how you exude confidence whenever you make a presentation at the weekly meeting and I quake in my boots." As one writer noted: she was jealous that a friend got a bigger advance than she did "but I got over it."

Unrealistic Emotional Demands

Expecting too much from a friend in adulthood because someone did not get enough from loved ones during the formative years will spell trouble. Friendship thrives when it is between two emotionally self-sufficient people who do not expect a friend to make up for what was lacking in their childhood—although positive friendships can certainly help to provide contemporary nourishment.

So the trick is to learn how to give to yourself, and not to overly rely on friends to give to you what you never received, or received in too small a dose, when it is from those very friends that you might gain additional emotional support.

The good news is that since you can have multiple friends, you can get and give a lot of feeling to friends without suffocating one of those relationships.

That might help you to avoid the sort of unrealistic emotional expectations that created conflict for 30-year-old Vikki. A single consultant, Vikki tried to turn her relationship with a man who reported to her at work into an intimate friendship that he could not handle. She had turned work into a battleground for herself and for her employee. But through therapy, she was able to understand she was hitting a brick wall with her employee as she understood that they were basically very similar in their relationship challenges:

> I found out that my work friend has very low self-esteem and that he does not think that he deserves friendship. He has a huge problem with "taking," with accepting friendship, love, and affection. I also have this problem but I am realizing that he may have it more severely than I!

Vikki no longer has to send long e-mails to her friend at work, who is also her employee, criticizing him for not giving her the friendship that she needs. They are able to work together now; Vikki is trying harder to cultivate her non-work, same sex friends as she tries, through therapy, to unlock the relationship issues that so far have prevented her from also finding a mate.

The ability to take friendship for what it is, no more, no less, especially in the workplace, may be a key factor in allowing it to blossom in the first place. Friends at work and in business make work a more connected place to be, improve teamwork, and make you feel there's a cheering squad for your efforts.

Friendship, especially at work or in business, need not be the relationship into which you dump all your anger, fears, regrets, rage, romantic relationship frustrations or triumphs, parenting challenges, or deepest childhood secrets. You have non-work-related friends, romantic partners, and family members who can provide that for you.

Relationships with Siblings and Sibling Rivalry

Early relationships with siblings will have an impact on future workplace friendships and workships although, of course, there is always the chance to change current patterns. Here are some examples from my research:

- "When I was growing up, I didn't have strong relationships with my siblings, and I don't have strong relationships with people at work either," says a senior executive.
- A 32-year-old security guard does not have any friends at work; she describes her relationship with her siblings when she was growing up as "distant."
- Forty-year-old Mary is a divorced manager with four children. She describes her relationship with her three siblings as "distant" since they were split up and raised separately when she was seven years old; her relationship with her mother when she was growing up was "abusive" and with her father as "distant."

As Adele Faber and Elaine Mazlish point out in *Siblings Without Rivalry*, the interpersonal skills that siblings learn during those formative years are crucial and last a lifetime. They write: "Even if their personalities were such that they never could be friends [with each other], at least they would have the power to make a friend and be a friend."

Similar to the previous discussion about how you dealt with jealousy, and how your family members dealt with feelings of jealousy growing up, is the issue of sibling rivalry. Did you and your siblings get along? Fight? Did you compete in a positive and healthy way, or were you always made to feel that if one person won, the other person lost?

If putting yourself first without being apologetic or devious was not a value during your childhood, friendship at work may be anathema to you. Conversely, if competition and rivalry ruled in your home, you may be duplicating these behaviors in the workplace.

If you were an only child, you may still have issues related to sibling rivalry because, ironically, without having had the chance to work through jealous feelings in childhood, it may be that you (or your co-worker who lacks siblings) are acting them out in the workplace.

Unresolved sibling rivalry may be the reason you choose one type of workplace friendship pattern over another, or why your friends are more comfortable in a friendship with just one other friend, rather than a three-way friendship.

Friendships can be two-way, three-way, a group of four or more. There is no right way for friendship groups to form but your childhood issues about your siblings may be called into play if one configuration of friendships is more comfortable and workable for you than another, especially at the office or in business. For example, if you were the youngest of four children, five years younger than your siblings, who only had one year age difference, you could have grown up feeling very left out "from the group."

Unless you resolve those feelings through self-analysis or therapy, or work through them on your own in actual similar situations, it is likely that friendships with more than one person trigger a "sibling rivalry" that is hard to get around. So at work or in your business friendships, you may find fewer conflicts if you befriend just one other person, and go out for lunch with just you two, than if you try to also add two, three, or more friends to the friendship group.

Ability to Deal with Authority Figures

You grow up with parents as authority figures and for some that never changes. For others, once they become young adults in their twenties, their relationship with their parents shifts more toward a relationship based on friendship or mentorship than on authority.

If you always feared your father or mother during the formative years when they were authority figures, especially if either one was abusive to you, it may be harder for you to see how you could befriend your boss or, if you are the boss, how you could be both an authority figure and a friend to your employees. If you felt that your parents were authority figures but you could talk with them about anything, even if you knew they would disagree with you, it may be easier for you to see how a boss could also be a friend.

In *Siblings without Rivalry*, Adele Faber and Elaine Mazlish share the following anecdote provided by an attendee at a sibling rivalry workshop, which characterizes how authority figure behavior in childhood, whether with parents or among siblings, may foretell adult business relationships and associated decisions:

> I'm a person who has to be in charge. And I'm sure it's because I was the oldest of my three brothers. I was the benevolent dictator over the younger boys. They always looked up to me and would do anything I told them. Sometimes I beat them up, but I also protected them from the bullies in the neighborhood.
>
> Even today, I have to be "on top." Recently I had an excellent offer to sell my business. The deal was for me to manage it for the new owners. But I know myself. I'll never do it. I've got to be the boss.

Fighting Fair

How do you fight fair? Here are some rules that may help you to avoid vendettas and retaliations:

1. No name-calling.

You know that old saying about "sticks and stones may break my bones but names will never harm me"? Well, it's not true because names DO harm! Being called a name is cruel and hurtful and it can stay with someone for a very long time. (While name-calling is better than doing anything physical—which is absolutely not permissible—name-calling is still not a mature or acceptable way to fight fair.)

2. Use the "I" approach—"I felt hurt by what you said because...." or "I feel as if you're...." Emphasize that this is *your* reaction, *your* feeling, not "the" only explanation.

By telling your friend or foe that what she or he did hurt your feelings, or upset you, and sharing the reasons that you feel that way, you depersonalize the anger instead of counterattacking. You can also cut your friend or associate some slack by saying, "You may not have meant to hurt me, *but* what you said made me feel like...."

3. No hitting, spitting, hair pulling, punching, or destroying personal property.

This type of fighting is just plain wrong and has to be completely ruled out as an option. Parents and teachers should have helped everyone to know that this type of physical aggression will not be tolerated no matter how justified the fight might seem. It is necessary to resolve these fights with words and in an amicable way. (These physical reactions may sound extreme, but in my previous survey on business protocol, human resource managers noted that there had been incidents of firing employees within the last year due to physical altercations.)

4. Be direct. Avoid sarcasm.

Sometimes sarcasm is so subtle, it is hard to even know the point that someone is trying to make. Trying to resolve a dispute is not the time for sarcasm and convoluted verbiage or wording. Be clear and to the point.

5. Give your "opponent" time to react to what you say.

Fighting fair requires that you give your "opponent" time to react to what you say. It may take her a few seconds, minutes, or even hours or days to think over the issues you raise and see your side of things.

6. Listen, don't just talk.

Rarely is there just one side to a fight. Usually there are misunderstandings or hurt feelings on both sides, to a lesser or greater degree, that lead to the fight. If you take the time to listen to your opponent's reasons or feelings, you might find out that some of your anger or reasons for the fight were based on misperceptions.

7. Agree to disagree; you can both be correct.

Sometimes just realizing that you can both be right may defuse your fight. You don't have to agree on everything just because you're friends or classmates. You can disagree and yet both be "right."

8. Agree to a "time out" or a "cooling off" period and return to re-evaluating the issues, arguments, or disagreements at that time.

Fighting fair also means allowing each other time to reconsider your disagreements in light of the new information that you've gained about the situation or about each other. It's too easy to end a friendship or relationship in the heat of the moment when you're both worked up over disappointments. Perhaps you thought your friend didn't care when she cancelled your Friday night out at the movies, or you assumed she'd cancelled with you in favor of a last-minute date with a new guy, but it turned out that she had a bad cold and needed to stay home and rest.

9. Avoid gossiping about each other or about your fight with others.

Especially if you want to try to save this friendship, avoid gossiping about your friend—no badmouthing—or retelling the story of your fight with others who will spread it around, making it that much harder to put the fight behind you. (If you do need to share about it, try to share with someone outside your circle, such as a sibling or an old friend in another town or city who isn't connected with this friend or the group you're part of now.)

10. Keep confidences even if you're tempted to blurt out those entrusted secrets in the heat of the fight.

Fighting fair means that if you do decide you have to end the friendship, you still maintain a loyalty to each other by keeping the confidences that were shared when you still were friends. Even if you no longer feel a loyalty to your friend, others may question how you will treat them and their confidences if they see you failing to maintain your trustworthiness to your former friend.

If you decide at a later date to revisit this relationship or friendship and try to reconnect with your friend, it will be that much harder if you had compounded the fight with feelings of betrayal because you broke a promise of discretion. The same is true for your friend about your confidences as well.

Playing the "You Remind Me Of " Game

Sometimes a friendship at work or in business is moved along, or halted, because someone you meet unconsciously relates to you as if you are someone else from his or her past. If you find a workplace relationship that could become a friendship is either moving too quickly along the road to friendship or that the road has been blocked prematurely, try asking yourself the following questions:

- Does this person remind me of someone from my childhood?
- Who is that person?
- What was my relationship with that person?
- In what ways do they seem similar? Different?
- Why is that unconscious association or comparison motivating me to befriend this person (or, conversely, discouraging me from moving the relationship forward)?
- How can I separate this new or current person from the past associations that are clouding or distorting this fresh relationship regardless of my past?

As noted in Chapter 8, "Dealing With Conflicts," the associations could be as superficial as hair color: a co-worker has the same hair color of a friend from sixth grade who betrayed you. It could be race: you may have grown up in a neighborhood where you lacked opportunities to befriend anyone who was not the same race as you. It could be religion: friendships have always been with those who shared your religion. It could be the way someone smiles: you had a friend in first grade who smiled like that and you are naturally drawn to someone with the same smile. The association could be on a deeper level as well: a customer wants to be in charge of all the details of your business dealings and that reminds you of your domineering younger sister.

Vikki, mentioned earlier in the chapter, relates how she initially ended a friendship because her friend had a problem that reminded her of her father but, at a later date, she was able to reestablish the friendship, providing an admirable insight into the family roots of her friendship behavior:

> When I was in college, I had a friend who had many problems including an alcohol problem. Due to my own history—an alcoholic father—I could not deal with this and ended the friendship. We did not have contact for four years, but then we got together again and now I would say that she is a close friend. She is living in another town but we talk on the phone a lot.

Although Debbie's story relates to a personal friendship, her example merits sharing because it demonstrates the way that early childhood patterns can influence someone's connection to a friend and even how easily, or with difficulty, someone recovers when that friendship is severed. Debbie is a 35-year-old married secretary who lives in the West, with two teenagers. She is having tremendous angst over the ending of her one best friendship of fifteen years. She points to the possible childhood roots of her difficulty in trying to get over the end of the friendship and in cultivating a new friendship:

> Growing up my parents constantly moved so I never had an opportunity to develop lasting friendships. My husband on the other hand is Mr. Popular. Everywhere we go, someone knows him. He has so many friends that it astonishes me. Although I've realized now that I am a package deal, I have friends but only because of him.

Debbie's son left an item at her friend's house and the item got lost. Her friend then offered to pay for the item. But "when we accepted, they were angry and cut off the friendship."

For two years Debbie tried to win back her best friend, but the friend has refused to talk to her. Recovering from the end of this friendship has been difficult for Debbie who, even after two years, still feels "betrayed, angry, used, and bitter…I don't think I will ever get over the loss."

As so often happens when there is a conflict or a loss, it may bring up all the other unresolved relationships in someone's life, especially the primary ones. As Debbie, who is currently seeing a therapist, notes:

> I've failed in almost all the relationships that I valued the most: my father died, I have a bad relationship with my mother, sister, and younger brother, which is why I don't want or need a "best friend." I feel they are too much work and I don't want to get hurt again. My husband is great but he feels that I need to have a friend because I depend on him more than ever for everything from conversation to companionship.
>
> My doctor thinks I've been through a lot and should avoid any close friendships until I am ready to deal with and accept the loss of this friendship...I must not be a good friend, daughter, or sister. I would like to make sense out of all of this.

Hopefully through therapy and self-analysis, Debbie will stop exclusively blaming herself for all the failed relationships in her life: her best friendship as well as her relationships with her parents, sister, and brother. She also needs to dwell on those relationships that are positive in her life, namely her marriage and her relationship with her own children.

Therapy offers Debbie a chance to reprogram herself toward friendship and to work through the feelings she has for her late father. If she is able to handle it, she could also actively try to work on the relationships she has with her mother, sister, and brother, not just through therapy but in face-to-face get-togethers, e-mails, letters, or phone calls.

For me, spending a week with my mother did as much for improving my friendship relationships as it enhanced how I get along with her. For years I wanted to take the time to try to work through all the old unresolved issues directly with my mother but my late therapist discouraged me, suggesting that I wait. So I would talk with my late therapist about my mother, and try to work things out that way.

But then my therapist died suddenly, and I realized that I could either find a new therapist or go back to the original source of those issues that I wanted to work through. For once since leaving home as a teenager, I chose to try to work it through directly with my mother.

We went to London for one week, just the two of us. My mother agreed to help out at the booth I had taken at the London

Book Fair; it gave us something to do each day and a business focus to the trip. But we had dinner together each night and we also had those long plane rides to talk, and talk we did.

When my father was alive, I could always talk to him if there was a conflict with my mother. He would help us to resolve any disagreements. But my father died a few years before so the only parent now available to me was my mother; I so wanted to have a better relationship with her.

That week in London, I spent more quality and quantity time with my mother than I had at any time since leaving home for college at the age of sixteen. I felt a nurturing and a bonding that I had always hoped I might have, but there were always so many other people that my mother had to deal with: my father, my siblings, as well as her demanding career as a kindergarten teacher.

My wonderful husband was back home taking care of our two sons so I gave myself the gift of time with my mother and that week together. Yes, there were some tough spots here and there but overall we got along quite well. I listened to her, and she listened to me, so that after that week, I would have more to give back to others including my friends and family.

But not everyone can or should do what I did. Working out early childhood issues through a therapist, in individual or group treatment, through self-analysis, or through a combination of therapy, self-therapy, and going back to the significant person with whom there has been a conflict may be what's needed.

Each situation, each personality is unique in what will work. If your current friendships at work or in your personal life are not what you would like them to be, if you are not as trusting of work friends as you want to be, if you are too trusting, or if you have had a friendship betrayal and it has left you paralyzed with fear about finding and cultivating a new friendship, you may need professional help. That help could be the catalyst to gaining the insights you need to understand the current and early roots of the friendship challenges you're now facing.

14

School as a Training Ground for Work Relationships

> "My friends in college were like my family."
> —Kassin Laverty, graduate student

> "School is all about work. You need someone to talk to at times, like lunch period. You don't want to be doing work all day and not saying a word to a person. You have to be social in school, at least some [of the] time."
> —Suzette James, ninth grader and part-time model

W hy is it usually so natural to find, and form, friends at school but having friends at work often seems so complicated? Let's look at the similarities and differences that might explain this dichotomy.*

School Friendships are Usually with Peers

Although in college or graduate school sometimes teachers and students develop a friendship, especially after graduation when a student is no longer in the student role, and certainly during the formative elementary, middle school, and high school years, school

---

* Some of the examples in this chapter were previously published in my article, "Wise College Students Find Friends For Life," originally posted to the *Wall Street Journal*'s online publication www.collegejournal.com on February 14, 2001.

years, school friendships are between fellow students who are of the same status.

Befriending a teacher or someone working in the office or the cafeteria would be atypical even if a student said, "I like so-and-so," or, "I feel like my teacher is my friend." Most of the time, the term *friend,* when used in a school setting about anyone besides another student, usually expresses a positive friendly attitude toward the authority figure rather than a reciprocal friendship.

Friendship is Considered a Priority during School Years

It is widely accepted that the friendships that are formed and maintained at school are as essential to a child's, teen's, and young adult's emotional growth as the knowledge that he or she gains is for intellectual growth. Fellow students also educate each other so that there is an additional benefit as well. It is this combined emotional and intellectual value of friends at school that make the peer group one of the key factors that go into school choices at every level, including college and graduate school. Students learn from each other as much as they learn from teachers, books, or the Internet.

School Friends Help Youths to Define Themselves

During elementary, middle school, high school, college, and graduate school years, friends help children and young adults to find out who they are as individuals outside of their families. Friends also offer opportunities for others to care about them outside of their immediate family. As 17-year-old Maren Walsh put it when she was a senior at Stamford High School:

> When you're growing up, you need someone to be there for you. You don't always want your parents because you know they're going to be there for you. Your parents *have* to be there for you. Your Mom has to tell you that you're great, but you want someone else, who doesn't really have to, and they just want to tell you, so I think friends are *very* important.

Friendship choices define someone during his or her formative years as much as a choice of a major may limit a career path once someone attends college, graduate, or professional school.

Throughout the school years, friends are a pivotal way to cope with school and even life experiences that for some may be stressful, demanding, and confusing.

Sharing with other students of equal status helps children, teens, and young adults to deal with authority figures, especially their parents and teachers. The "you and me against the world" mindset helps school friends to be united. (That is also one of the reasons that friendships between co-workers are easier in the workplace than those between boss and subordinate.)

Friends at School Provide the Intimacy of a Family

As youths navigate the challenging task of separating from their family of origin as they start their own family or establish an adult single lifestyle, school friends offer a substitute family. As Kassin Laverty, a 22-year-old graduate student explains:

> When I got to the university, I was about a thousand miles from home, and knew not a soul. My friends and I would really keep each other in check. Study at the library together, study over coffee, quiz each other between TV commercials, and of course, we'd pull "all nighters." We'd eat together, celebrate holidays and each other's birthdays, run errands for each other, do favors. We grew together. Being independent, being away from our families and our comfort zone, it made us come together, support each other as we branched out into new territory.

School Friends Offer Bonds and Help Throughout Life

The bonds of friendship, for those who are fortunate to have made at least one close or best school, college or graduate school friend, may last years, decades, or throughout your life. (As noted later on, it is never too late to reconnect with school friends, or to see if a casual school friend might become a closer contemporary.)

David Hochberg, Vice President of public affairs for the Lillian Vernon Corporation in Rye, New York, says: "I had a party recently and two of my oldest friends were there. They are my oldest, most intimate friends to this day, twenty years later, [and they are] people I met freshman year of college."

Living in the dorm, David Hochberg was able to spend time getting to know his friends. Says Hochberg: "College offers an incredible opportunity to bond with your friends, to get to know them well." For Hochberg, the opportunities to bond that he had in the college dorm are not duplicated in the nine to five, Monday through Friday work environment since the school dorm experience was 24/7. "It's just totally impossible [for me] to duplicate in the work environment the quality or quantity of time together" that you have during the college or graduate school years.

Dr. Wendy Oliver-Pyatt, a 37-year-old Reno, Nevada-based married psychiatrist with two children, who is also author of *Fed Up*, met her best friend Vicky, who now lives in Florida with her husband and three children, through the housing office during their freshman year at the University of Denver. Dr. Oliver-Pyatt explains:

> She thought my card said I was from WV (West Virginia), which was where her mother was from, so out of all the random numbers of people looking for roommates, she chose my name. The card actually read NV, because I'm from Nevada. I got lost in my car on the way to our meeting point at a restaurant. She waited over an hour for me, desperate to make a new acquaintance. I eventually made it there. We met, managed to get tickets to a sold-out Elton John concert, got into the concert, and we've been best friends ever since. We even look and sound like sisters.

Dr. Oliver-Pyatt's friendship with Vicky helped her through a rigorous transition from one university to another as well as making the demanding shift from growing up in the small town of Carson City, Nevada to a huge university situation. Says Dr. Oliver-Pyatt: "Not knowing anybody [at the University of Denver] I think just having one good friend [Vicky] was all I needed to grow and feel comfortable there. There was this emotional bond. It felt safe."

Friends Make School More Fun

Think back on your childhood, teen, and young adult years. In the midst of the studying for exams, term papers, and required classes hopefully there are memories of friends at school that made each day more fun. Whether right at school, playing or studying after school, on the phone, or through e-mail or instant messaging, friends offer some of the defining moments to those school years. Says 13-year-old Suzette James:

> Friendship is important because you need people in your life who care and are there for you when you need them. In school, it would be really boring to play by yourself in gym. Today we had to pick a partner and make shoots with the basket and that was really fun. If you were left alone to throw balls at the hoop, that would be really boring. It was really fun with the partner activity.

Friends at School Provide a Chance to Learn How to Socialize

Friends at school can also be a distraction if a student spends too much time socializing and talking. He or she may also spend an inordinate amount of time on the Internet or on the phone in the evening hours and not enough time listening to the teacher or studying. Working out a balance at school so that interacting with friends is done at the appropriate time, and in the right amount so it supplements and aids rather than detracts from learning, is a life lesson that will prove beneficial in the workplace.

Here are the ways that school friendships develop and thrive to keep in mind when you analyze your workplace relationships:

Truisms about School Friendships

- School friendships are usually with peers.
- Friendship is considered a priority during the school years.
- Friends help children or teens to define themselves.
- Friends help students relieve stress.
- Friends aid in dealing with parents and teachers, the authority figures.

- Friends at school provide the acceptance and closeness of a family based on choice.
- School friends offer bonding and help throughout your life.
- School provides the time and opportunity to befriend someone.
- School offers a place to meet a friend who could become a lifetime bond.
- School friends make school more fun.
- Unless a teacher or professor wants to give only so many A's, by and large, in school you can go as high as you can and are in competition with yourself (although there can be only one valedictorian).

Truisms about Workplace and Business Friendships

- Workplace or business friendships are less complicated if between peers.
- Friendship (or workships) should be considered a necessity at work or in business.
- Friends at work help you to define yourself.
- Friends at work help you relieve stress.
- Friends aid in dealing with bosses, the authority figures, with employees, as well as customers or clients.
- Workplace or business friends provide the closeness of another family in addition to the family of origin, husband-wife, and parent-child relationships.
- Workplace or business friends offer bonding and help throughout your life.
- After the school years, work or business provides the time and opportunity to befriend someone.
- Work offers a place to meet a friend who could become a lifetime bond.
- Friendship makes work and business more fun.
- As you go up the ladder, there are usually fewer spots at the top. Whether you are the one who is envied, or the one feeling envy, try to look past a promotion, a raise, or a career accomplishment as taking away from anyone else's upward climb.

Keeping Up with School Friends as a Training Group for Maintaining Future Workplace Relationships

You're working hard to become successful. You've probably developed new friends at your current job or school. You might have romantic pulls or even hobbies and additional training you want to pursue in whatever free time you have. But since graduating from school—elementary, middle, high school, college, graduate school, or professional school—going your separate ways is one of the classic *friendshifts*®. How do you manage to keep connected to your school friends? How do you make time for your school friends, especially if they live far away?

Here are suggestions for keeping up with friendships that began at school:

- Join your alumni association and get involved by going to local meetings and annual activities such as Homecoming.
- Stay connected throughout the year, not just at school-related functions, through e-mail, letters, phone calls, or visits.
- If you have relocated to another town, city, state, or country, consider finding local fellow alumni with whom you connect informally or through formal monthly, semi-annual, or annual social events.
- Make sure you notify your old friends of any changes in your name or address so they can keep in contact with you.
- Notify your schools of any name or address changes so old friends who want to find you can do so. (If you have any misgivings about giving out your home address, use a mailing address, such as a post office box or a rented mailing address.)
- Join Classmates.com or the other reunion web sites that help school friends to find each other and communicate.
- Build new memories with your school friends so your friendships are contemporary, and not just nostalgic.
- Take the time to find out how you and your school friends have changed, or stayed the same. Exchange photos of family members and reminisce about the old days so you can dispel any outdated myths about each other that you and your school friends are still carrying around in your memory banks.

- If you read about a school friend in the newspaper, take the time to send a note and applaud your friend's accomplishment. It could be the beginning of reviving that friendship. (Of course, if you read something sad about your friend or his or her family, a condolence card or note would be appreciated.)

Reconnecting after You've Lost Touch

There are numerous reasons why you and your school friends may have lost contact with each other, from drifting apart to moving away to unresolved conflicts. You can, however, reconnect at any time, as long as you can find your friend and he or she agrees to revive your previous friendship.

Some services have developed that might be useful if you are trying to find a school or college friend, such as Gradfinder.com and Classmates.com. Although initially specializing in relocating high school buddies, it now also lists colleges and universities and has added searching for military and former work colleagues, that you might contact for alumni information.

If you know your friend's current name, as well as what city and state your old school friend might be living in, you can also try to find him or her through Switchboard.com. Don't overlook your high school, college, or graduate school alumni functions. Check if your college has a club in a major city, such as the Harvard Club or Cornell Club in Manhattan, where you might have dining or social opportunities. Join your alumni association so classmates can find you. Make sure your listing is up-to-date in the alumni directory.

Reevaluating Your School Friendships and How They Might Relate to Friends at Work

Take some time to reassess your old school ties. What information about you and about your friendship choices can you discover that might help you improve the work friendship choices you are currently making?

Other considerations are "the way you were" during your school years. Were you so shy that you found it hard to initiate friendships? Did you go through awkward stages physically that made it harder for you to reach out to friends? Were you dependent on your parents to drive you places because your friends from school lived far away but they were unavailable to take you places?

If you have changed since your school years, through self-analysis, therapy, or through a natural maturational process, your workplace or business friendships can reflect who you are now.

You need not repeat the patterns from your school years, especially if those experiences were downright negative. By the same token, if you find your current workplace friendships are negative, but your past school friendship patterns were positive, you could reassess your school experiences, as well as what you were during those years to discover what changed for the worse.

If your school friendships were strong, positive, and fun, and if you apply the same principles at work that were effective for you at school, you will have an advantage in your workplace relationships.

If your school friendships were negative or non-existent, you now have the opportunity to develop or enhance your work friendships. Those friendships could be every bit as nurturing, emotionally rewarding, intellectually stimulating, and long term as your school friendships could have been (and for those who did form at least one school friendship that still exists today, it still is true).

For those who look back on the high school years or the four years of college as the optimum time for forming lifetime friendships, work provides even more years together especially if you stay at a shared job for six or eight years, a decade, or more.

Some work experiences are almost universally associated with workplace friendships, such as firefighters, police officers, and professional team sports. In other work situations, there are conditions at a specific office that fosters workplace friendships at one investment banking firm versus another, or at one publishing company and not another. The type of work is not, in and of itself, friendship-related, such as for the firefighter or the professional football player, but it could be if attitudes and activities are present that create a pro-friendship and workship environment. You could start a business with a friend, do projects together, or work in the same office but for your own companies, rather than someone else's.

School is an excellent starting place for learning the skills that help you find, cultivate, and maintain friendships. But it is not the only place. Maren, a college freshman, learned invaluable lessons about work and friendship by working about thirteen hours a week during her senior year of high school. She explains:

> I work in a bagel store. I like the people I work with. I get along with them but there is this one co-worker. She almost quit because of me. We like each other outside of the job but we hate working with each other. We're comfortable enough with each other that I tell her, "I hate working with you but I love you." She tells me things too. "You with the job is horrible but you're awesome as a person."

If business workships and friendships are given the emphasis given to school friendships, you may find business people enjoying their jobs much more; positive workships and friendships at work makes work a better place to spend eight or more hours a day.

For entrepreneurs, college faculty members, especially those who only teach part-time, writers, and small business owners, it may be harder to develop friends at work or in business because there may be lots of travel or atypical workdays; working alone may be more common than having people around everyday.

Looking back on my school, college, and graduate school years, my closest college friendship began during the summer I took my required science course. Because it was over the summer, the course was daily for two months. Joyce and I sat next to each other; we had a chance to get to know each other through the shared class experience, a chance I notice is often lacking for many college students who attend some classes only once or twice a week.

Creating that consistency of contact so a workship and then a friendship might ensue, which is the way that relationships naturally grow during the typical school or college experience, will benefit your current relationships. Try to volunteer on a committee so you spend more time with your colleagues, make an effort to get repeat business, if you are an entrepreneur or a freelancer.

Go to a week-long or weekend seminar where you are more likely to meet like-minded individuals and where you may also have the time to get to know each other with family and workday pulls temporarily set aside. Long-term friendships will have more of a chance to start and flourish if you at least have some uninterrupted time together to get to know each other and to share as most did so spontaneously and naturally during the school years.

15

Personality Traits You May Find at Work

> "We all have to work together; you have to know the personalities and the likes and dislikes of the people you work with to be effective."
> —Male personnel manager from Arkansas

As you form various types of workships or friendships throughout your career, you will encounter a number of different personality traits that will affect each relationship.* Recognizing the personality of the colleague with whom you are working may be useful to how you interact. (These personality types are in addition to the four key positive workships discussed in Chapter 4 and the fourteen types of foes in the workplace discussed in Chapter 10.)

While these are just general traits, you might find it useful to see what traits fit those you work with as well as how you might be characterized by others. For example, if you believe that someone with whom you have a workplace relationship has the need to be parental, you may want to think twice about playing into this need by seeking out his or her advice. Or if you consider someone a "tell all," you would want to avoid making any comments that you fear might

---

*This chapter is an edited and expanded version of the 17 types in Chapter 9 of Business Protocol (Wiley, 1991; Hannacroix Creek Books, 2nd edition, 2001). The types were expanded to included 26 types; those types were presented as an information sheet for a keynote presentation, "Personality Types You May Encounter at Work, in Volunteer Situations, and in Life," delivered by the author at the U.S. Navy's 7th fleet CO/XO Spouse's Conference held October 8th, 2003.

be shared inappropriately. Some of the types described below are more negative than others, while others simply require your knowing how to deal with that type so his or her dominant trait does not negatively impact on your success at work.

The Optimist

The Optimist believes everything will work out okay. Optimists are much more pleasant to be around, compared to the other extreme, The Pessimist (see below), but only if the optimism is realistic and not Pollyannaish. If the optimism is based only on a generalized positive personality, the trait can be annoying when you are trying to get real concern for issues that need to be addressed. "Don't worry, it will all work out" only goes so far. If you know you are dealing with The Optimist you can put it to your advantage by saying, "I know you are an optimist and you think this is going to work out okay and that's fine, but here are some real issues that we need to address." Then state the facts, clearly with as much supporting evidence as possible, and The Optimist is more likely to hear you and respond in a timely and appropriate manner.

The Affable

This friendly and good-natured type is an idealist, usually smiling and cheerful. Why do you have to consider how you will deal with this type if you have him on your committee or if you are The Affable? Shouldn't someone who is The Affable only be an asset? The challenge for The Affable is that he or she could be taken advantage of by others because he or she is prone to only seeing the good in situations or other people.

If there is a Saboteur in his or her midst, or a Bully, The Affable type may be slow to recognize and deal with those personality types who could undermine a department or committee's best efforts. If you are dealing with someone who is The Affable type, and you suspect that that personality trait is getting in the way of seeing clearly what others are up to, you might say, "I know you lean toward seeing the positive and pleasant aspect of every situation or personality, but you might want to consider that there are negative motives or insidious personality traits at work here that, unchecked, might sabotage our efforts. For example...."

The Coach

Listens and guides, based on instinct, experience, and research, without getting too analytical. The Coach is an asset to most work and volunteer-related situations, but if The Coach also has to be the student, he or she needs to be comfortable with someone else being in The Coach role.

The Benevolent Leader

Combines the right blend of leadership with respect for the opinions, values, and talents of others. Leads others but is open to listening and giving credit where credit is due. This personality type is a team player, not the lone despot.

If you are dealing with The Benevolent Leader, be aware that he or she has to—needs to—lead. Taking instructions, or being a follower, is tough for this personality type. There are, however, ways to still deal effectively with this type without necessitating him or her leading every minute, all the time. Helping The Benevolent Leader to delegate is one way that he or she could be the primary leader but others would lead (and have other leaders who are also responsible) within the committees or smaller groups.

The Parent

The Parent has a need to be parental and to take an authoritarian role in giving directions and advice, whether asked for or not. In a positive workship, this personality trait may be found in the role of a mentor and can actually be helpful in advancing your career. However, others who display parental personalities may be driven by motives that are not in your best interest so you have to take their advice and direction with a grain of salt. Once you've spotted this personality trait in a potential workship, you can deal with it by showing appreciation for his or her help, while continuing to use your own judgment.

The Nonconformist

This type always has to object to the status quo; blending in or going along with the majority is stressful for The Nonconformist.

If you are The Nonconformist, or if you are dealing with one, reassure yourself that being part of a team just this one time does not mean you are doing a complete personality makeover. Also, it may be possible to use this trait in a positive way: The Nonconformist tends to think outside the box. Call on him or her to offer a different perspective; even if that view is contradictory or considered and rejected it could make a positive contribution to the committee or department's overall performance.

The Pessimist

Working with or for The Pessimist could wear you down before long since he or she voices the doom and gloom prognosis that nothing will work out, or work out well. Even if you know things are moving along in a positive way, The Pessimist finds something to worry about and fear. You can diffuse The Pessimist's orientation by responding in a similar way to The Optimist but wording it in the reverse: "I know you think this won't work out, but here are the reasons I think we're on the right track." Once again, the best defense with The Pessimist is concrete evidence that something or someone does have a chance at meeting or exceeding expectations.

The Workaholic

Workaholics are campaigners in their commitment to their job, so you may have to hear about how hard they work, and what sacrifices they make for the job. Be sympathetic and congratulate them on their dedication. Avoid analyzing the psychological components of such a lopsided existence, since work is the defense that those who are frightened of relationships and free time hide behind. Workaholics will probably remind you throughout your meeting that they really do not have time for a leisurely talk—they should already be at work—so accept whatever time they can give you as the best they can offer. Workaholics have more of a need to tell you about their work than to hear about your own, so be a patient listener.

The Braggart

You have to listen patiently to every personal and professional achievement that The Braggart has accomplished. Try to avoid drawing attention to your own triumphs; braggarts are insecure and want the platform all to themselves. It is best to let braggarts get their fill of bragging before going on to the business at hand. Without being too obvious, give praise throughout the meal to boost the much-too-low ego of The Braggart. For example, compliment his or her choice of restaurant (if he or she selected it), how he or she handled the waiter, or ask for any recommendations for dishes he or she may have already tried on the menu.

The Show Off

This type is similar to The Braggart. Whereas The Braggart uses words to try to gain attention and approval for his or her abilities, The Show Off relies on actions. If a report is due by Friday, The Show Off will try to get it in early. If there is a quota for sales in the department, The Show Off will work hard to beat it, and then try to get the results posted so there is no question about who is the high achiever. Working for or with The Show Off can wear you down since he or she needs to be in the limelight. You can use it to your advantage, however, by learning how The Show Off manages to achieve such exceptional results and then meeting or exceeding those achievements, but without resorting to the obnoxious bravado that pushes others away.

The Tell-All

The Tell-All needs to relate every minuscule detail of what went on right before your meeting. For example, at a morning meeting, a single man or woman who had a date that was particularly pleasant or traumatic the night before might want to share the experience with you. You might just as well sit back and enjoy the tale that The Tell-All shares. Be supportive, empathetic, and nonjudgmental, but also be cautious since The Tell-All just may repeat to others anything personal or professional that you relate to him or her.

The Controller

Watch out for this type since everything, from what is said to who picks up the check, can be manipulated by this type, who needs to control the situation. The Controller is really an insecure person who is unable to trust his or her instincts as situations unfold, so he or she tries to manipulate every sentence, every situation. Stay calm and pleasant since you understand the manipulator's game.

It may help if you are dealing with The Controller to give him or her input over some of the details, perhaps even the less significant ones, so you can still maintain actual control of your committee, department, or project. If you have to organize a dinner, ask The Controller to do the research and come up with suggestions for the restaurant or location for the dinner, or composing the wording for the invitation. Others can then take charge of the myriad of other details so it is truly a shared effort although The Controller may still see himself or herself as the key organizer of the event.

The Courtship Personality

A colleague with this trait needs to be courted before making any decisions. If you are dealing with this personality type, avoid pressuring him or her into a "yes" or "no" on a particular subject at your first meeting. With courtship personalities you are better off having several meetings, putting some time between each one, rather than trying to get an answer right away.

For The Courtship Personality, the wooing and getting a person to say "yes" is as pivotal as the final decision. They will prefer working with you if you indulge their indecisiveness by giving them even more items to choose from, several projects that might be worked on, or a variety of ways of completing a certain task.

The Need for Closure Type

In contrast to the Courtship Personality, the Need-for-Closure person must come to closure by the end of your meeting. To deal with this trait, make something concrete happen, such as "I'll call you on Monday," or "I'll send you a copy of that article I told you about," especially if you want to avoid a "yes" or a "no." Since there is this need for closure, you have to be careful that this personality type does not provoke a "yes" or "no" just to finalize the matter. Acknowledge this person's needs—"I know you want to finish up this project"—but introduce your different approach by saying, "but let's keep the door open another few weeks." Allay his or her fears by emphasizing that closure is not too far off: "Don't worry. I know we'll nail down this campaign by the middle of next month."

The Hidden Agendist

The Hidden Agendist gets you to a meeting on one pretext; it is only by being astute and a good listener that you learn, sometime during your meeting, that there was a completely different motive for the encounter. For example, a co-worker might ask you to lunch on the pretext of discussing a report you are working on together. It is only halfway through the meal that you realize The Hidden Agendist wants to find out if you would give this person a recommendation if he or she were to give your name as a reference to a headhunter he or she is seeing.

It is important when meeting with a Hidden Agendist to switch gears easily from the presumed to the actual reason for the meeting, and to be cautious for the remainder of the meeting since the motive for the meeting might even switch again.

The Lay Psychologist

The Lay Psychologist has a need to analyze everything you say or do. Do not take it personally. However, this person does need affirmation, so humor the Lay Psychologist by saying something like, "How astute of you," or "That's quite an insight; you could have been a psychologist."

The first thing you want to avoid doing with a Lay Psychologist is asking for his or her interpretations of anything. Try not to tell him or her about the dream you had the night before. Keep in mind that while he or she is usually well meaning in his or her impulse to analyze, this may be driven by his or her own projections of unconscious conflict and an unrealized need to be analyzed themselves.

The Official Host

The Official Host is the kind of person who is always calling meetings. When more than two of them are at a meeting, however, you can lose sight of this distinction as others may take over this role. Official hosts may be insulted if their official host capacity is questioned or overthrown. Who is seen in this light may also determine who picks up the tab or brings the meeting to an end.

The Unofficial Host

This is the person who takes on the role of host, even though it is really someone else who set up the meeting and is responsible for the check. The unofficial host is a strong personality type that rarely feels comfortable in the subordinate role. If you are dealing with this type, it is best to share the decisions at the meeting, such as where people will sit, who picks up the check (if meeting at a restaurant), and what time the meeting is over, rather than make the unofficial host uncomfortable and anxious.

The Nervous Wreck

Avoid laughing when a nervous wreck knocks over water glasses, mistakes the half-and-half for milk that someone can drink, or gets his or her sleeves in the coffee. Nervous Wrecks cannot help it, and the meal setting only exacerbates their nervousness. People with this personality trait are best seen in whatever calmer setting where they are most comfortable. But sometimes breakfast, lunch, or dinner meetings with them are necessary and then it is best to be tolerant and compassionate about their nervous habits and accidents.

The Success Story

The Success Story has achieved something that the other person (or persons) at a meeting have not yet done and feels the need to share that story with the others, whether they want to hear it or not.

The Success Story has a need to share and educate, and you just might as well sit back and listen and possibly even learn something, because they need to tell it to you anyway. It could be a happily married woman telling a recently divorced woman how to meet someone and get married again. It could be a vice president telling a new manager how he made it to the top. Since you understand that The Success Story has a need to share his or her tales with anyone, do not take it personally as a put-down of your own achievements.

The Complainer

No matter how well things go for The Complainer, he or she dwells on his or her problems or setbacks. Being overly positive with him or her can just be infuriating, so listen patiently and agree that life can be a struggle without being condescending or becoming as depressed as he or she seems to be. Avoid bringing up all the joys in life as a counterpoint since this only fuels The Complainer's angst.

The Flirt

Be cautious with The Flirt and avoid saying anything that could be misconstrued as giving credence to his or her fantasies. Dress appropriately, avoiding anything even somewhat risqué. Similarly, avoid using any sexual phrases or expressions, or alluding to anything personal that could be taken as approval, on your part, of this person's behavior or flirtatious orientation.

The Furious

The Furious appears to be furious almost all the time and it has nothing to do with you, even though it may be directed at you during the workday. Things may not be going well in The Furious' life right now, or this could be a life-long pattern. Confronting The Furious about his or her anger is probably useless since he or she may be unaware of how others see him or her. If you have to work with an angry colleague, or your boss is angry, remind yourself that it has nothing to do with you. If you simply have to say something, make sure you express it from the "I" point of view, rather an accusatory one: "I feel as if I'm making you angry. I don't mean to. If I'm causing you to get angry, please explain to me what I'm doing so I can do things differently."

The Perfectionist

The Perfectionist has a need—to the point of obsession—for everything to be "just right." Rechecking every detail, beyond just being careful, causes others associated with him or her to also second-guess themselves.

Aiming for excellence is a realistic standard; perfectionism may cause undue angst and stress as tasks take longer than necessary and The Perfectionist unfairly criticizes others for failing to perform at that level of flawlessness.

If you are dealing with The Perfectionist, point out that his or her standards, although exemplary, are unrealistic for a particular task at hand. Discuss a realistic compromise of excellence that is attainable. Suggest that it is perfectly all right to have two standards, for The Perfectionist and for everyone else, praising him or her for having self-scrutiny that others lack. Without criticizing or putting down The Perfectionist, explain why it's okay for the others to strive for excellence rather than perfectionism. In that way, there is an increased likelihood that the deadlines for an activity or project will be met and the group's morale will remain high.

The Aggressor

The Aggressor comes on strong; this type always has to approach or initiate rather than waiting to be contacted or asked.

Dealing with The Aggressor first requires that you don't let his or her need to push people away by coming on so strong push you away so you do not even want to communicate or connect.

Realize that The Aggressor probably has this façade of harshness as a self-protective mechanism. Engage The Aggressor slowly and carefully, rather than coming on so strong or being so timid that you are repelled or ignored.

Let The Aggressor set the tone and pace of your interactions, even to the point of asking for input: "When would you like to start?" or, "Would you like me to contact you by phone, e-mail, or would you like to get together in person to discuss this?"

The Blamer

Everyone and anyone is to blame for his or her mistakes or problems. This personality type is often most dangerous to himself or herself as the ability to learn and grow from recognizing and dealing with mistakes is minimized or eliminated since he or she refuses to take any responsibility for his or her behavior.

The Blamer can become a detriment to your career if he or she needs to place blame on others, even though unjustified, whether it is you, undermining your advancement, or someone else. That would cause you to bear witness to such undeserved blame, putting you in the quandary about possibly "telling" on your colleague.

Although The Blamer may be in need of therapy to deal with the deep-rooted causes of this tendency from his or her earliest years, it is possible that just pointing out the reality of each situation will cause The Blamer to keep this inclination in check. The Blamer probably had an extremely critical and authoritarian parent who punished physically when he or she did something wrong, so denying guilt became the path of least resistance.

For that reason, try to be the kind Parent, the understanding and positive co-worker or boss, so The Blamer is more likely to trust you. With his or her fear of being yelled at minimized, there is a greater likelihood he or she will take the blame (or at least not falsely accuse others for his or her mistakes or shortcomings).

*

Here are some overall questions to ask yourself about the above 26 personality types at work and in business:

- Review the above types. What type best describes how you behave in most workplace or business situations?
- How does behaving like that help or hinder you in your workplace or business relationships?
- Is there another type that you'd like to become that might help you to be more effective in your work or business relationships? Is yes, what type is it? (Especially review the first six personality traits: The Optimist, The Affable, The Coach, The Benevolent Leader, The Parent, and The Nonconformist.)
- What are three steps that you plan to take to become more like that type?

16

30 Insights on Workplace Relationships

> "We're spending so much time at work as a society, we do consider our work another family. It's important we feel good about the relationships at work."
> —Human resource manager at healthcare company

B ased on my research, consulting, and observations over the last two decades, I have put together a list of 30 ideas concerning workplace relationships that I want you to share with you:

1. Developing workships or friendships is an ongoing process, especially since the people with whom you form these relationships will change jobs and even careers. It's not something you can do once and for all; you have to continually cultivate your workplace or business (and personal) network.

2. It is easier and more comfortable to form workships or friendships with those at your own level rather than upward or downward. Workships or friendships with superiors or subordinates are possible but you have to be careful about being accused of favoritism (if you befriend upward) or of having your status compromised (if you befriend downward).

3. If the friendship precedes working together, you can work with a close or best friend more easily if you discuss the conflicts that might arise because of your friendship, and how you might handle them, before you even start working together.

4. Same sex workships or friendships may be easier to cultivate and maintain than opposite sex workships or friendships. Opposite sex workships or friendships may be easier to maintain if one or both friends are romantically involved with others outside the workplace. To keep opposite sex workships or friendships from generating gossip, be careful about when and where you get together. Avoid badmouthing one's romantic partner or sharing details that are too intimate or personal (that might unwittingly "turn on" the opposite sex workship or friend). If a workship becomes an office or work romance, there are different relationship and work considerations.

5. Although it is usually better to do advance networking so that you will already have some point of reference to those that you meet in a new situation, it is not always possible to do so.

6. It is also important to learn how to walk into a room full of strangers and to quickly make positive connections so you can turn trade shows and meetings into positive networking experiences. In the long run, this can be as critical as having longstanding workships who will vouch for you and possibly even send you referrals or recommend you for jobs.

7. Take your time developing a workship or a workplace or business friendship. Observe, listen, and be as certain as possible that this person will aid, not betray, you because the stakes are too high—your work, your professional reputation, and economic livelihood—to guess wrongly.

8. Moving a workship away from the place where you met, e.g., working together at a company or seeing each other at the monthly association meeting, may move your relationship one more step closer toward a tried-and-true friendship.

9.	If you decide that keeping your work and personal friendships separate is best for you, that's fine. But avoid sending mixed messages, such as having a work-related dinner party at your home. Instead, entertain at a restaurant or after work in the conference room.

10.	Avoid name-dropping or blatantly using your workships or friends for career advancement. If a workship or friend volunteers to help, decide on a case-by-case basis if you even want to accept his or her help.

11.	If you're having trouble making workships find someone who has excellent "people" skills at your job or in your business. What separates them from the rest? What do they do that you could do, too?

12.	If you're shy, you need to work at getting over it. In most careers, it will stop you from advancing as far and as fast as you could and even how much daily enjoyment you get out of your work because your shyness stops you from having workships. Fortunately, there is help for those who are shy, from individual or group counseling to support groups as well as self-help books on overcoming shyness.

13.	Men and women, in general, define friendship differently and they also share information and feelings in unique ways. Those variations will show up in the workplace and in business as well. Neither approach is right or wrong. What counts is an understanding of someone's approach, and whether or not it is working for his or her career or personal work and relationship goals.

14.	Being honest at work and in business is not the same thing as keeping to yourself and avoiding the sharing or feelings and thoughts that may not be in your best interest to share at work.

15.	Even if a friendship started and is maintained solely in the workplace or in business, when those relationships end because one friend changes jobs, or dies, it can be as devastating as when a personal friendship ends. Mourn that loss, make a commitment to keeping in communication (if there was a job change), but also to make a concerted effort to develop new workships or work friendships.

16. Workships often grow into close or best friendships and that's fine, but even if the relationship remains a workship, it's still valuable and key to career and personal fulfillment.

17. E-mail and the phone, although useful in moderation, should not substitute for in-person meetings and get-togethers with friends. Less than ten percent of communication is verbal; the rest is tone of voice and body language. It is preferable to meet someone, as early on in a work relationship as possible, as long as proper precautions are taken to ensure it is a safe, comfortable, and appropriate in-person meeting.

18. When economic times are challenging, and the number of equally qualified applicants soars, the "who you know" and "who you could know" becomes even more important than only "what you know."

19. Maintaining workships or friendships takes time and energy. Remembering workships or friendships at the holidays is a good first step, but you also need to try to do a lot more than that. Keep a dialogue going so your workships or friendships know what you're up to; celebrate their milestones, such as anniversaries at the company; keep up on what's going on in their personal lives. Workships and friendships are part of an ongoing process that starts in childhood, continues through the school years, then into the workplace and, after retirement, into doing volunteer work or participating in community or special interest activities.

20. At each stage in life, workships and friendships make life more enjoyable. To quote a man in one of my friendship workshops, it's all about "connecting." Connecting reaffirms us whether it occurs in the sand box, at school, at the corporation, at a professional association, at an annual meeting, or as a retiree.

21.	You don't have to like everyone you work for, or who works for you. You do need mutual trust, respect, and a shared belief that you're being honest with each other. However, having a boss who is also a Mentor or Advocate will get you farther faster in your career.

22.	When someone does something in a business capacity that makes you feel criticized and pushed away remember that it's business; separate your feelings from the work-related context.

23.	If possible, try to turn around unfriendliness, especially if it is someone who could help you and your career (and if the unfriendliness is not turned around, could hurt or hinder you). If it is not possible to turn the unfriendliness around, move on without self-blame.

24.	Even after you retire from work, there are workships available to you through volunteer opportunities, community associations, or even keeping up with former co-workers through informal or formal alumni get-togethers.

25.	Be aware of cultural differences that will impact on your workships and workplace friendships. With so much business today transacted internationally, you may find yourself more than ever before, because of the Internet, open to potential relationships with men and women from around the world and not just within your department or company. Keep in mind that there are cultural differences in how friendship is viewed in different countries and take the time to get to know what those similarities and differences are. Of course letters and phone calls have been ways to connect internationally, but the Internet makes it faster, easier, and less expensive to develop and maintain international relationships—including workships and friendships.

26.	Delegate tasks, not relationships.

27.	Workships and friendships have as much to do with emotion and feeling as with logic and intellect. You can try to "do the right thing" and behave in a way that makes you more likeable but you can't force someone to like you. Take the hint if someone rebukes your friendly overtures to become a workship or friendship.

28. With each relationship, and with each job situation, you may have to decide if the work or the friend comes first. Ideally, you won't have to make that choice or you will be able to put the job first without your friendship suffering. Workships and friendships are not chiseled in stone. Relationships at work have to be revisited often since people may go through a metamorphosis because of career or personal ups or downs. Observe those changes and respond accordingly.

29. Here's a way to remember how to focus on excellent listening skills, an aid to every workplace or business relationship:

    L—Look your workship or friend in the eye when she or he speaks to you.

    I—Indicate you are listening by nodding your head when you agree, smiling, or through other gestures.

    S—Show interest by reframing what your workship or friend says or by asking questions about what you've heard.

    T—Take the time to listen carefully, time that your workship or friend deserves.

    E—Empathizing with what your workship or friend is saying will get you farther than criticizing or judging.

    N—Never interrupt before your friend has finished a sentence or completed his or her thought or point.

30. Apply workship and friendship protocol: respond in a timely manner to all e-mails, phone calls, letters, or requests; attend events that you are invited to, such as seminars, product launches, or parties, or have a good reason to decline. Definitely RSVP yes or no; if invited to a personal function, such as a birthday party or a wedding, and if you feel uncomfortable accepting and attending, have a believable

reason why you have to say "no" and, if possible, send a token gift anyway or at least make a donation to a worthy cause in celebration of the occasion that you are avoiding. Be an asset to your workships and friendships so they want to know you, work with you or for you, and help you to succeed.

17

Summing Up

"Your relationships drive how successful you'll be."
—Connie Duckworth, one of the first women partners at
investment banking firm Goldman Sachs, quoted in *Fortune*

The need to connect at work and in business is stronger now than it has been at any time since I started studying the business world two decades ago. There are definite changes in attitudes about relationships at work, including friendship—a decided openness and acceptance with an increasing awareness of the benefits. It is rare to hear someone comment on socializing at work as a "waste of time," as it was often viewed in the 1980s. The contemporary, enlightened attitude is that those conversations and connections have as much to do with increasing productivity, teamwork, creativity, and innovative ideas as they do with improving worker satisfaction and worker retention. Rarely is it considered the negative gossip or idle chit-chat that such activities aimed at fostering workplace connections used to be mislabeled.

Companies now stipulate how you get along with co-workers a measurable part of your performance review. They may even ask colleagues to rate you on such areas as teamwork, sharing, and your ability to get along with others.

Change is afoot as typified by Company of Friends, a grassroots networking movement started by *Fast Company* magazine, which has grown to tens of thousands in numerous cities throughout the United States. In 2002 in Chicago, marketing director Leslie Banks organized their first Company of Friends breakfast get-together.

Banks says: "We had space for forty people and it was standing room only with people on the waiting list. The second event had thirty-five people showing up so I was pleased about that as well."

Banks explains that not coming on too strong is important at these business/social functions: "Most of the people I have met that I would like to get to know more, either through a business context or as friends, have been people who are not aggressively trying to 'network' and sell me on whatever services they represent. That can be annoying." Other Company of Friends activities around the country include networking lunches, dinners, or evening seminars.

The name of this grassroots movement, Company of Friends, highlights how much the workplace and work has, for so many today, become the new "village green" where the community used to get together in bygone days to "chew the fat."

Coffee shops throughout the United States, such as Starbucks,® are meeting places for entrepreneurs as well as for nine-to-fivers, before or after work, for finding new workships or friends as well as reconnecting with old ones, like the pubs of England, or the cafes of Paris.

Ten years ago, Media Bistro was started in New York City by Laurel Touby. Those in the media, including writers, editors, publicists, and photographers, meet and share business leads, contacts, information, and where business connections might ensue. Now their events are held in major cities in the United States including Boston, Chicago, and Seattle, as well as in London and Paris. Their website contains free listings for jobs in the media, updated daily, and upcoming events including seminars and classes.

Other Internet sites fostering friendship are flourishing, such as Friendster, which emphasizes personal, rather than work friendships, as well as dating, and Meetup, which connects those with shared interests who want to set up a meeting.

For some, friends at work have become the new extended family because family members have moved away or died, because they are single and unattached, or, if they do have a family, they lack time for cultivating friends outside of work. For those who are entrepreneurs or self-employed, friendships through their professional associations have become their new workplace family.

Patricia Schroeder, CEO of the Association of American Publishers, and a former congresswoman, shared the following anecdote that highlights this change that has occurred with the workplace becoming the new core of a town or village:

> When I was in Congress, I got a call one day from the White House saying they were doing a family thing and they wanted me to testify. My daughter, who was then eight years old, happened to be there that day because she was sick. She said, "Aren't you going to have kids testify?" and they said, "No," and she said, "Well, that's pretty stupid if you're having something without kids."
>
> Then she did something really interesting. She polled all the kids in her class. She asked them questions like "What do you think of when you hear the word *grandma?*" and most of them thought of the word *phone* or an airplane.
>
> "What do you wish you knew more about?"
>
> And just a huge number of them said, "We wish we met the people our parents work with because that's what they talk about at the table at night."
>
> And it suddenly occurred to me that we used to have extended families. People used to talk about Aunt Martha and Uncle Bill.
>
> Well these kids don't know them because they live somewhere else and it's just a name on a Christmas card. But what Mom and Dad talk about at the table are what Joe Smith said and what happened at work and these kids are saying, "Well you get to visit the school and meet my friends, why don't I get to visit [your workplace] and meet your friends?"

It can be wonderful to have friends at work or friends in business but it is still just one of the many pivotal relationships that are needed for a connected life, along with close nuclear and extended families and romantic partners.

If friendship is lacking at work or in your business, that does not automatically mean that you should get a new job, or search for new clients or customers who are friends. You can still have friendship in your personal life; you can still work at a job where you do not have friends. *It is blissful to like and befriend those you work with or those you do business with, but it's a desirable—not a necessary—condition of work.*

Friendship is indeed a magical and glorious relationship that cannot be forced, cajoled, bought, requested, or demanded. It has to be freely given and returned. (There are also examples in this book of workplace and business friendships that went awry.)

For a whole host of reasons shared in this book, from a wish to keep work and friendship separate to a reclusive personality, for you, or someone you know, friendship at work or in business may be missing.

One of the main goals of this book, however, was to dispel the myth that friendship at work is counterproductive. The opposite tends to be true: friendship at work contributes to greater productivity, worker satisfaction, and even employee retention.

Workships and friendships help you get jobs and land business contracts while close or best friends offer emotional support that transcends work or the workplace.

In this book, I have shared the essence of my research into the role that workplace relationships play in the success or failure of your career and in turn your personal life as well.

A 37-year-old married male engineer with one child, who found my survey on friendship by doing a search on the Internet by putting in the word *loneliness* into the search engine he used, shared with me that he does not have any friends at work and has only five personal casual friends. "I don't have any close or best friends now," he confided. He pinpointed—by the word he used to search for a survey on the Internet—one of the negative consequences of lacking a close or best friend: loneliness.

Is there a friend from work or in your business that's inspired you, and who you like, that you've been meaning to call for awhile or to get together with face-to-face? Make that call, send that e-mail, get together and reminisce as you forge forward with this friend, or go out for lunch with someone you just met at the job, or someone in your line of work, if you are self-employed, and see if a workship might evolve.

Ilene Harsip is a single Denver-based design manager in her 40s who recently had a reunion after twenty years with some of the women that she worked with at a publishing company in Boston. Ilene shares about the recent reunion as well as their original workplace relationships:

> We were a department of all women and it was like group therapy back when we were able to work together. We were all friends and fabulous co-workers. I would consider two close

friends of mine and the others more casual. But I could always go to any of them for professional assistance and probably personal support as well.

Although a few people have kept in touch over the years, it was nearly twenty years since most of us last connected. I came from Denver. Candy came from Maine. We met at Lorraine's house in the Boston area. I met with Pat, our boss, later in the week.

Many of us were friends while we worked together and others became closer afterwards, although the boss would have never allowed herself to become too close to any of us. [But] now that we don't have the restrictions of business relationships to contend with, many of us have grown closer.

What makes this departmental reunion and the long-lasting ties unique for Ilene is that it includes the entire department. As she explains:

I have always had a few friends from every job I have stayed close with, but never a whole department. I think the fact that we were all women and it was the early 80s, before e-mail, and world travel was so common, that we were really close to each other everyday. We shared births and deaths, divorces and weddings, promotions and demotions. We all have tremendous respect for each other in spite of our differences.

Keeping up with workships or friends from previous jobs helps to maintain those connections and adds to what I call the nostalgia relationships that we all need. Nostalgia relationships are those who knew us when; it adds to the continuity that we all seek in our lives.

Sites such as Classmates.com, which added a workplace division a few years back, help previous workers to find each other. As noted before, some companies have also added a reunion component to their websites, facilitating past employees continuing their corporate connection and relationship.

Reconnecting with school or college friends also helps to continue to open up your universe of relationships of colleagues and connections. I heard from a woman who made it her mission to find those who were in band together. She spent two-and-a-half years searching for the almost 1,000 students in the band from her high school, organizing a Band Reunion for students going back 15 years.

The event she organized even raised $3,000, which was donated to the school band program. She notes, "I've heard of several friends and groups of friends who renewed relationships."

Old friends, new friends. Friends from school or work become "just friends." As a 47-year-old married researcher from New England noted:

> While I know that work and friends don't always mix, I've never found that to be the case. Friends are friends wherever they're made.

Positive workships are as necessary for career advancement and are as pivotal to a productive workplace and to your worker satisfaction as close or best friendships are to a joyful personal life.

But what advice do I have for those who have never been so fortunate, or who once had supportive workplace relationships but now find themselves in negative situations? Use the suggestions in this book to try to turn the situation around but if you cannot, and it is possible to find a new job or cultivate other business, then do so.

However, if your job is worth keeping, you do not have to befriend everyone you work with even though that would be ideal. Just being respectful and receptive can go a long way in business.

By contrast, there are also some who spend so much time forming relationships at work, or maintaining the workships or friendships that they already have, that their work suffers; they need to put more time into just doing the work. A balance of maintaining relationships *and* doing the work is the winning combination.

Whether you are co-workers, boss/employee, employer/subordinate, service provider/client, business owner/customer, or employee/vendor, the choices you make in the platonic relationships you form at work are definitely a key factor in making or breaking your career or personal life. The goal of this book was to give you tools to make better choices about who to befriend, how to facilitate that connection, and how to deal with any conflicts that might arise.

It's been firmly established through social scientific research and anecdotally that friends lead to a longer and happier life. Through my workplace and friendship research, I have also learned that workships are necessary for a more productive and positive workplace as well as for more successful and happier workers. In the short run, it is not that important if those workships lead to friendships at work or, once the shared work situation is over, to personal friendships. But in the long run, those workships that become friendships will be the ones that have the greatest impact on someone's life, not just on his or her career.

I discovered a friendship group of eleven—six health care professionals and their five wives—that has been getting together for nineteen years. They meet a couple of times a year at a central location since its members live in different states in the midwest and east. It's an amazing friendship and skills-building network that defies the cliché of the isolated solo male healthcare practitioner. The group has a written philosophy and a mission statement; at the beginning of each meeting, those declarations are read.

It was founded with some basic ground rules: No missed meetings. Wives had to be included. Meetings would be a combination of educational and social activities.

From the beginning, the group's members made a commitment to each other, even meeting around the hospital bed of a member when a car accident left him temporarily comatose. One of the wives shared with me what a powerful feeling it is to know that if she needed something, with just one phone call, ten people would be there for her in an instant.

What an inspiration it has been to interview and then meet the members of that longstanding networking and educational group that has led to such powerful friendships with the men sharing the same profession.

Yes, I have been privileged to enjoy many wonderful friendships over the years, close and best friendships that have spanned decades. But a career is built on more than just a handful of close or best friends that those of us who are blessed typically have in our personal lives. Most careers today need scores, even thousands, who know about us and the excellence of our work, who want to help us to succeed.

It's taken me a very long time to heed the lessons that I learned in researching and writing this book. I know I would probably be further along in my career if I had understood the concept of workships much sooner.

Hopefully by reading this book, you have gained a better understanding of how what you say and do, and the relationships you make at school, work, and in business, impact on your well-being. If I succeeded in my goal for this book, you will be less likely to overreact if and when you are faced with the situation and question, "Who's that sitting at my desk?" because you know, whether a workship, friendship, or foe is sitting there, you need to effectively deal with, and ideally connect to, that individual.

I am reminded of a survey completed by a 34-year-old director of personnel. When asked how many friends he had at work, he wrote "340" and checked off "casual" as the category of friends. He also answered that there were 340 employees at his company.

After writing this book, I realized he probably would have used the term *workships* if he knew the term; it would most likely more accurately describe his relationship with those 340 employees.

While I was researching this book, I found out my membership application in a prestigious women's media association was approved. I know that getting into an association, although the first step, is just the beginning of a long process of taking the time to attend meetings, getting together with those I connect with, and investing the time and energy to go from a stranger to an acquaintance to a workship or a friend. I know that's important for me to do since, as a self-employed entrepreneur, writer, speaker, and consultant, I have to take the time to create teamwork opportunities and possible new workships or friendships.

When I learned I had been accepted into membership, I felt like Sally Field when she made that memorable speech in 1985 upon winning her second Oscar,[®] this time for her role in the movie *Places in the Heart*. Sally Field, as Sharon Waxman reports in her article, "The Oscar Acceptance Speech: By and Large, It's a Lost Art," effusively declared: "I haven't had an orthodox career, and I've wanted more than anything to have your respect. The first time I didn't feel it, but this time I feel it, and I can't deny the fact that you like me, right now, you like me!"

What is behind positive workships and friendships at work and in our businesses is the universal need to be accepted. Perhaps the reason Sally Field's acceptance comment for her second Oscar[®] resonated so loudly with so many is that her heartfelt outburst verbalized what most everyone thinks but few articulate: we all want, and need, to be admired for our work and also liked by our peers.

Selected Bibliography

Barkas, J.L. (Janet Lee). See Yager, Jan.

Baron, Gerald R. *Friendship Marketing*. Grants Pass, OR: The Oasis Press®/PSI Research, 1997.

Berkman, Lisa F. and Leonard Syme. "Social Networks, Host Resistance, and Mortality: A Nine-Year Follow-up Study of Alameda County Residents." *American Journal of Epidemiology* 109 (1979): pages 186-204.

Berman, Evan M., Jonathan P. West, and Maurice N. Richter, Jr. "Workplace Relationships: Friendship Patterns and Consequences (According to Managers)." *Public Administration Review*, March-April 2002, Volume 62, beginning page 217 (14 pages).

Birmingham Post, "Workforce: Friends at the Office May Last a Lifetime." October 12, 2000, page 26.

Bird, Laura. "Lazarus' IBM Coup Was All About Relationships." *The Wall Street Journal*, May 26, 1994, pages B1, B10.

Blieszner, Rosemary and Rebecca G. Adams. *Adult Friendship*. Thousand Oaks, CA: Sage, 1992.

Bloom, Allison. "Love is in the Air: Learn About the Bright Side of Workplace Romance." Posted at www.careerbuilder.com.

Bloom, Allan. *Love & Friendship*. NY: Simon & Schuster, 1993.

Bolles, Richard Nelson. *What Color is Your Parachute?* 2004 edition. Berkeley, CA: Ten Speed Press, 2003.

Bossler, Gregory. "Writers & Their Work: Eve Ensler." *The Dramatist,* March/April 2003, pages 4-13.

Bregman, Mark. "Networking: How to Build a Support System," *Choices*, October 1986, pages 11-13.

Bridge, Kennan and Leslie A. Baxter. "Blended Relationships: Friends as Work Associates." *Western Journal of Communication*, Summer 1992, Volume 56, Number 3, page 200.

Bryant, Mary. "Great Networking: From Courtship to Commitment." Presentation at the National Speakers Association, Tri-State Chapter, 2002.

California Department of Mental Health. *Friends Can Be Good Medicine*. San Francisco: Pacificon Productions, 1981.

Carnegie, Dale. *How to Win Friends and Influence People*. NY: Pocket Books, 1940 (1936), revised edition, 1981.

Carroll, Glenn R. and Albert C. Teo. "On the Social Networks of Managers," *Academy* of *Management Journal*, Volume 39, Issue 2 (April 1996), pages 421-440.

Coser, Lewis. *The Functions of Social Conflict*. NY: Free Press, 1956.

Covey, Stephen R. *The 7 Habits of Highly Effective People*. NY: Simon & Schuster, 1990.

Dickens, Wenda J. and Daniel Perlman. "Friendship Over the Life-Cycle" in *Developing Personal Relationships*, Chapter 4. Ed. by S. Duck and R. Gilmour. New York: Academic Press, 1981.

Duck, Steve. *Friends, for Life: The Psychology of Close Relationships.* Brighton, England: Harvester Press Limited, 1983.

Duncan, Lois. "How Not to Lose Friends over Money." *Woman's Day*, March 25, 1986, pages 20, 22, 25.

Early, Richard. "Seven Steps to Business Socializing." From *The Wall Street Journal online,* posted at www.careerjournal.com.

Faber. Adele and E. Mazlish. *Siblings Without Rivalry*. New York: Avon Books, 1998.

Fehr, Beverley. *Friendship Processes*. Thousand Oaks, CA: Sage Publications, 1996.

Fisher, Anne B. and Tricia Welsh. "Executive Life: Getting Comfortable With Couples in the Workplace." *Fortune,* October 3, 1994, page 138.

Freud, Anna. *The Ego and the Mechanisms of Defense*. Rev. ed. NY: International Universities Press, 1966.

Gabor, Don. *How to Start a Conversation and Make Friends*. Illustrated by Mary Power. NY: Fireside Books, rev. 2001.

Goleman, Daniel. "Stress and Isolation Tied to a Reduced Life Span." *New York Times*, Dec. 7, 1993, page C5.

_____ *Working with Emotional Intelligence*. NY: Bantam Books, 2000.

Gray, John. *Men Are from Mars, Women Are from Venus*. NY: HarperCollins, 1992.

Greenberg, Eric Rolfe. "The Libido and the Workplace." *Management Review*, May 1998, Volume 87, page 9.

Greer, Jane and Margery D. Rosen. *How Could You Do This to Me? Learning to Trust After Betrayal.* Garden City, NY: Doubleday, 1998.

Gurdin, J. Barry. *Amitie/Friendship: An Investigation into Cross-Cultural Styles in Canada and the United States.* San Francisco: Austin & Winfield, 1996.

Halpern, Howard. *How to Break Your Addiction to a Person.* NY: Bantam Books, 1982.

Hartup, Willard W. "Children and Their Friends," in *Issues in Childhood Social Development,* Chapter 5, pages 130-170, edited by H. McGurk. London: Methuen, 1978.

_____. "The Company They Keep: Friendships and Their Developmental Significance." *Child Development* 67 (1996): pages 1-13.

Hess, Beth. "Friendship and Gender Roles over the Life Course" in *Single Life*, pages 104-115. Ed. by Peter J. Stein. NY: St. Martin's Press, 1981.

Hillman, Carolynn. *Recovery of Your Self-Esteem.* NY: Simon & Schuster, Inc., Fireside Books, 1992.

Hoffer, William. "Friends in High Places." *Writer's Digest,* October 1986, pages 42-44.

Hymowitz, Carol and Ellen Joan Pollock. "The One Clear Line In Interoffice Romance Has Become Blurred." *Wall Street Journal*, February 4, 1998, pages 1, A8.

Isaacs, Florence. *Toxic Friends/True Friends.* NY: Morrow, 1997.

Izzo, John B. and Pam Withers. "Winning Employee-Retention Strategies for Today's Healthcare Organizations," *Healthcare Financial Management*, June 2002, pages 52-57.

Joseph, Sharon Simpson. *And How My Spirit Soars.* Atlanta, GA: Spirit Soars, Inc., 2002.

Kanter, Rosabeth Moss. *Men and Women of the Corporation.* NY: Basic Books, 1977.

Karr, Albert R. "It's Who You Know." *Wall Street Journal,* Oct. 16, 1990, page 1.

Kelly, Michael. "A President-Elect with a Way with People." *New York Times,* November 4, 1992, pages 1, B2.

King, Florence. "The Misanthrope's Corner: Linda Tripp, Friendship and Morality." *National Review*, September 1, 1998, page 56.

King, Mary E. "When to Keep Your Mouth Shut." *Self,* November 1988, pages 76, 78.

Kirkpatrick, David. "I Get By With a Little Help From My Friends of Friends of Friends." *Fortune*, September 30, 2003. (http://www.fortune.com/fortune/subs/columnnist/0,15704,49`3`3 ,00.html)

Lazarsfeld, Paul F. and Robert K. Merton. "Friendship as Social Process: A Substantive and Methodological Analysis." In *Freedom and Control in Modern Society*, pages 18-66. Edited by M. Berger, T. Abel, and C. Page. New York: Van Nostrand, 1954.

Leonard, John. "Private Lives: On Losing a Friend Your Private World Can Least Afford." *New York Times*, March 2, 1977, page C14.

Lewis, Robert A. "Emotional Intimacy Among Men." *Journal of Social Issues* 34 (1978): pages 108-121.

Lichtenberg, Ronna. *It's Not Business It's Personal*. NY: Hyperion, 2001.

Liebow, Elliot. *Tally's Corner*. Boston: Little, Brown, 1967.

Lindsey, Karen. *Friends as Family*. Boston: Beacon Press, 1981.

Lopate, Phillip. "What Friends Are For." *Utne Reader*, Sept./Oct. 1993, pages 78-85.

MacKay, Harvey. *Swim With the Sharks Without Being Eaten Alive*. NY: William Morrow, 1988.

Marelich, William D. "Can We Be Friends? (Managers and Employees)" *HR Focus*, August 1, 1996, pages 17-19.

Maxwell, Bill. "Sex Scandals Cast Shadow on Workplace Friendships." *Rocky Mountain News,* March 3, 1998, page 36A.

Mitchell, Jack. *Hug Your Customers*. NY: HarperCollins, 2003.

Montaigne. "Of Friendship" in *The Complete Essays of Montaigne,* pages 135-144. Ed. and trans. by Donald M. Frame. Stanford, CA: Stanford University Press, 1958.

Mosle, Sara. "The Importance of Being Busy." *The New York Times Magazine*, November 15, 1998, Section 6, page 132.

Naegele, Kaspar D. "Friendship and Acquaintances: An Exploration of Some Social Distinctions." *Harvard Educational Review* 28 (1958): pages 232-252.

Nardi, Peter M., ed. *Men's Friendships*. Newbury Park, CA: Sage, 1992.

Newcomb, Theodore M. *The Acquaintance Process*. NY: Holt, Rinehart & Winston, 1961.

Newman, Mildred and Bernard Berkowitz with Jean Owen. *How to Be Your Own Best Friend*. New York: Ballantine Books, 1971.

Norman, Michael. *These Good Men: Friendships Forged from War*. NY: Crown Publishers, 1989.

Overell, Stephen. "Work Moves to Home Ground: Life in the Office," *Financial Times*, August 2, 2001, page 16.

Paul, Robert J. and James B. Townsend. "Managing the Workplace Romance: Protecting Employee and Employer Rights." *Review of Business*, Winter 1998, Volume 19, pages 25-31.

Pogrebin, Letty. "Work Friendships Are Very Difficult," *Bottom Line Personal*, February 15, 1987, pages 11-12.

Pool, Ithiel de Sola and Manfred Kochen. "Contacts and Influence." *Social Network* 1 (1978): pages 5-51.

Powers, Dennis M. *The Office Romance: Playing with Fire Without Getting Burned*. NY: Amacom, 1998.

Putnam, Robert D. *Bowling Alone: The Collapse and Revival of American Community*. NY: Simon & Schuster, 2000.

Ross, Judith A. "Human Resources: Does Friendship Improve Job Importance?" *Harvard Business Review*, March-April 1997, Volume 75, Number 2, page 8.

Rowe, Dorothy, *Friends & Enemies*. London: HarperCollins, 2001.

Rubin, Lillian Breslow. *Just Friends*. NY: Harper & Row, 1985.

Sanders, Tim. *Love Is the Killer App: How to Win Business and Influence Friends*. NY: Crown Business, 2002.

Sapadin, Linda A. "Friendship and Gender: Perspectives of Professional Men and Women." *Journal of Social and Personal Relationships* 5 (1988): pages 387-403.

Shellenbarger, Sue. "Layoffs Wreak Havoc on Office Friendships." From the *Wall Street Journal* online posted at www.careerjournal.com.

Shanley, Mary Kay. *She Taught Me to Eat Artichokes*. Illustrations by Paul Micich. Marshalltown, Iowa: Sta-Kis, Inc., 1993.

Sharpe, Anita. "How to Find Guys to Hang Around and Do Stuff With." *Wall Street Journal*, May 9, 1994, pages 1, A6.

Sheehy, Sandy. *Connecting: The Enduring Power of Female Friendship*. NY: Morrow, 2000.

Simmel, George. *The Sociology of George Simmel*. Trans. by Kurt H. Wolff. NY: Fress Press, 1950.

Solomon, Robert C. *The Passions*. Garden City, NY: Anchor Books, 1977.

Stern, Barbara Lang. "Is Jealousy Healthy?" *Vogue*, October 1988, pages 350, 352.

Stewart, Nathaniel. *Winning Friends at Work*. New York: Ballantine Books, 1985.

Strauss, Alix. "Schmoozing Without Losing: The Art of Networking." *Dramatists Guild Quarterly,* Spring 1997, pp. 10-14.

Stuart, Julia. "So Who Needs Friends Anyway?" *Independent,* November 7, 2001, page 7.

Suarez, Ray. "Office Romance," transcript of "Talk of the Nation" radio show, National Public Radio (NPR), October 7, 1998. Guests: Jan Yager, Gary Neuman, and Gary Mathiason.

Tannen, Deborah. *Talking from 9 to 5: Women and Men at Work*. New York: Quill, 2001.

Taylor, Shelley E. *The Tending Instinct*. NY: Times Books, Henry Holt and Company, 2002.

Thompson, Michael and Catherine O'Neill Grace with Lawrence J. Cohen. *Best Friends, Worst Enemies.* NY: Ballantine Books, 2001.

Tice, Lou. "Learn to Win and Mentor Others." *Personal Excellence*, Premier Issue, n.d.

Vault, Inc. "Office Romance Survey." Press release received February 11, 2003.

Van Dusen, Christine. "Business Partners Are Also Close Friends." *The Atlantic Constitution*, September 11, 2001, pages D1.

Wall, Bob. *Working Relationships*. Palo Alto, CA: Davies-Black Publishing, 1999.

Walsh, Anna. "Working Relationship." *Accountancy*, November 2000, page 47.

Waxman, Sharon. "The Oscar Acceptance Speech: By and Large, It's a Lost Art." *Washington Post*, Sunday, March 21, 1999. Posted at http://www.washingtonpost.com/wp-srv/style/movies/oscars/speeches.htm.

Welty, Eudora and Ronald A. Sharp, eds. *The Norton Book of Friendship*. NY: Norton, 1991.

Wells, Rebecca. *Divine Secrets of the Ya-Ya Sisterhood.* NY: HarperCollins, 1997.

Wheelis, Allen. *How People Change.* NY: Harper, 1975.

Yager, Fred. *Rex.* Stamford, CT: Hannacroix Creek Books, Inc., 2001.

Yager, Fred and Jan Yager. *Just Your Everyday People.* Stamford, CT: Hannacroix Creek Books, Inc., 2001.

_____ *Untimely Death.* Stamford, CT: Hannacroix Creek Books, Inc., 1998.

Yager, Jan (a/k/a J.L. Barkas). *Business Protocol: How to Survive & Succeed in Business.* NY: Wiley, 1991; 2nd edition, Stamford, CT: Hannacroix Creek Books, 2001.

_____ *Creative Time Management.* Englewood Cliffs, N.J.: Prentice-Hall, 1984.

_____ *Creative Time Management for the New Millennium.* Stamford, CT: Hannacroix Creek Books, Inc., 1999.

_____ "The Dual-Career Couple: Making Time for Each Other." *Modern Bride,* Oct./Nov. 1989, page 150.

_____ *Effective Business and Nonfiction Writing,* 2nd edition Stamford, CT: Hannacroix Creek Books, Inc., 2001.

_____ . "Finding Friendship." *ParentGuide,* September 1997.

_____ . "Friends, Friends, Friends." Issue #1. Posted to http://www.janyager.com/friendship/e-zine/e-zine-one-6-2002.asp.

_____ . *Friendship: A Selected, Annotated Bibliography.* New York: Garland, 1985.

_____ "The Friendship Factor in Marriage." *American Baby,* March 1988, pages 65, 78+.

_____ *Friendshifts®: The Power of Friendship and How It Shapes Our Lives.* Stamford, CT: Hannacroix Creek Books, Inc., 1997; 2nd edition, 1999.

_____ . *The Help Book.* New York: Scribner's, 1979.

_____ . "How to Stay Connected With Your College Crowd." *Wall Street Journal*'s www.collegejournal.com, Released February 14, 2001. (Part 2)

_____ . "The Impact of 9/11 on Friendship," Issue #2. Posted to http://www.janyager.com/friendship/e-zine/e-zine-9-2002.asp.

_____. "Is She a Toxic Friend?" Posted to the *Ladies' Home Journal* website (http://www.lhj.com), December 6, 2002.

_____ *Making the Office Work for You.* New York: Doubleday, 1989.

_____. "Marriage and Friendship." *Modern Bride,* Feb/March 1987, pages 500, 502.

_____ "Perspectives on Friendship." *International Journal of Sociology and Social Policy.* Volume 18, Number 1, 1998, pages 27-40.

_____. "The Power of Friendship." *Executive Update,* October 2002, pages 41-43.

_____. *Single in America.* NY: Atheneum, 1980.

_____. "Ten Friends Every Woman and Man Needs," Issue #3. Posted to http://www.janyager.com/friendship/e-zine/e-zine-11-2003.asp.

_____. *Victims.* New York: Scribner's, 1978.

_____. "What to Do If You're Fired." *Parade,* May 31, 1992, page 16.

_____. "Why New Mothers Need New Friends." *McCall's,* Jan. 1988, page 41.

_____ *When Friendship Hurts: How to Deal with Friends Who Betray, Abandon or Wound You.* NY: Simon & Schuster, Inc., Fireside Books, 2002.

_____ "Wise College Students Find Friends for Life." *Wall Street Journal*'s www.collegejournal.com, Released February 14, 2001. (Part 1)

_____. "Working with Your Husband: Blessing or Curse?" *Modern Bride,* Dec./Jan. 1981, pages 20, 28, 30.

Yager, Scott. "He Says-She Says: Friends With Benefits: Are There Any?" *The Westword,* February 2003, page 36.

Zajac, Robert J. and Willard W. Hartup. "Friends as Coworkers: Research Review and Classroom Implications." *Elementary School Journal*, Sept. 1997, Volume 98, Number 1, pp. 3-11.

Zetlin, Minda, "Mixed Company: Balancing Business and Friendship." *Management Review,* January 1991, page 59.

Zey, Michael G. *The Mentor Connection.* Homewood, IL: Dow Jones-Irwin, 1984.

Resources including Websites

Here you will find a sample of membership associations and organizations that focus on work-related concerns; some have state affiliates or local chapters. These associations may provide a way for you to meet new workships or friends through a formal group that shares your interests. Check your local newspaper, or your community's web site, for similar listings to the ones that follow.

Inclusion in the following list does not imply an endorsement of any association, agency, or company by the author, nor does omission imply criticism. For space and other considerations, the listings that follow are selected. Furthermore, since agencies change names, and associations may merge, cease operating, or relocate, the accuracy of any listing cannot be assured.

Business-Related Networking

American Management Association (AMA)
1601 Broadway
New York, New York 10019
http://www.amanet.org
Membership association for management; seminars and newsletters.

CEO Club (Chief Executive Officer's Club, Inc.)
457 Washington Street 1st floor
New York, NY 10013
http://www.ceoclubs.org
Networking association for CEO; organizes international trips to find out about doing business with other countries.

Company of Friends (CoF)
c/o *Fast Company* magazine
375 Lexington Avenue
New York, NY 10017
http://www.fastcompany.com/cof
CoF is a business networking; local groups have get-togethers, with and without guest speakers.

Mediabistro.com
http://www.mediabistro.com
New York-based website for relationship building for media professionals including educational courses as well as local networking events throughout the United States and in selected international cities. Also posts job listings at the site, updated daily.

National Association for Female Executives (NAFE)
P.O. Box 156
Congers, NY 10920
http://www.nafe.org
Membership, networking, and educational association.

National Association of Women Business Owners (NAWBO)
1595 Spring Hill Road, Suite 300
Vienna, VA 22182
http://www.nawbo.org
Networking and educational association of women business owners with local chapters; annual national conference.

Women's Media Group
P.O. Box 2119
Grand Central Station
New York, NY 10163-2119
http://www.womensmediagroup.org
Invitation only membership association for women in the media; monthly luncheons; sponsors a college summer internship program.

Friendship Associations or Organizations

Friendship Force International
57 Forsyth Street, N.W. Suite 900
Atlanta, GA 30303
http://www.friendship-force.org
Founded in 1977, this is a program with "citizen ambassadors" traveling to live with host families in 45 countries.

Help Finding Friends including Old Classmates or Former Co-workers

http://www.gradfinder.com
http://www.asd.com (American Alumni Directory) (Annual fee)
http://www.reunion.com
http://www.curiouscat.com/alumni
http://www.switchboard.com (Internet directory)
http://www.alumni.net (school and work)
http://www.coolbuddy.com (school and work)
http://www.classmates.com (school and work)

New Friends

http://www.friendster.com
http://www.entertainmates.com

New Business Connections

http://www.fastcompany.com/friends
http://www.linkedin.com
http://www.mediabistro.com

Organizing Local Interest Groups

http://www.meetup.com

Major Internet Search Engines

http://www.google.com
http://www.altavista.com
http://www.hotbot.com
http://www.yahoo.com

Where to Find Professional Help

If shyness, low self-esteem, insecurity, or social phobia stops you or someone you care about from developing workships or friendships, help is available from a wide range of trained counselors, psychotherapists, psychiatric social workers, psychologists, clinical sociological practitioners, family therapists, or psychiatrists. In addition to asking a family physician or friend for a referral, recommendations to professionals may be available from these services or professional associations:

1-800-THERAPIST Network
2923 Sandy Point, Suite 6
Del Mar, CA 92014
http://www.1-800-therapist.com
Therapist referral service run by Kevin Grold, Ph.D.; Christine Hartline, M.A. is in charge of media relations.

ADAA: Anxiety Disorders Association of America
11900 Park Lawn Drive, Suite 100
Rockville, MD 20852
www.adaa.org

American Association of Marriage & Family Therapy
1133 15th Street, N.W. Suite 300
Washington, D.C. 20005-2710
http://www.aamft.org

American Psychiatric Association
1400 K Street, N.W.
Washington, D.C. 20005
http://www.psych.org

American Psychological Association
750 First Street, N.E.
Washington, D.C. 20002-4242
http://www.apa.org

National Association of Social Workers
750 First Street, N.E. Suite 700
Washington, D.C. 20002-4241
http://www.naswdc.org

National Mental Health Association
1021 Prince Street

Alexandria, VA 22314
www.nmha.org

For Conflict Resolution Assistance

American Arbitration Association
335 Madison Avenue, Floor 10
New York, NY 10017-4605
http://www.adr.org
Makes referrals to arbitrators.

Association for Conflict Resolution (ACR)
1527 New Hampshire Avenue, NW 3rd floor
Washington, D.C. 20036
http://www.acreresolution.org
Association of dispute resolution professionals providing networking
and educational opportunities. Sponsors conferences and maintains a
mediator referral list and a directory.

For Relationship and Friendship Researchers

The International Association for Relationship Research (IARR)
http://www.iarr.org
Professional association of social scientists and communication
experts focusing on friendship, family, or romantic love. Sponsors
bi-annual international conference and publishes a journal.

Web Sites Dedicated to Friendship

www.friendship.com.au
Global Friendship
P.O. Box 1259
Camberwell VIC 3124   Australia
Created in 1996 by Bronwyn Polson, it provides quotes and poetry
about friendship and information about Friendship Day in August.

www.janyager.com/friendship
Includes excerpts from Jan Yager's book, *Friendshifts*® and selected
article reprints. Sign up for the free friendship-ezine or read about

the annual May National New Friends, Old Friends Week, founded in 1997:
www.janyager.com/friendship/nationalnew-oldfriendsweek.htm

www.WhenFriendshipHurts.com
The official website for Jan Yager's book, *When Friendship Hurts* (Simon & Schuster, Inc., Fireside Books, 2002). Includes the book's complete Introduction, a list of foreign editions, a media kit including "5 Steps to Try to Save a Friendship," and related links.

Web Sites Dedicated to Business Information including Business Relationships

www.forbes.com
Informative site of business articles maintained by *Forbes* magazine.

www.fortune.com
Useful business articles and columns provided by *Fortune* magazine.

www.janyager.com
Business article reprints or book excerpts by Jan Yager on business protocol, time management, workplace relationships, and writing.

www.careerjournal.com
www.collegejournal.com
www.startupjournal.com
Wall Street Journal online sites with current and archived articles on such topics as business relationships, job searching, and etiquette.

www.workingwounded.com
Site about workplace relationships and issues maintained by Bob Rosner, author of *Working Wounded* (Warner Books, 1998).

Acknowledgments

Thank you to all who participated in the research that formed the basis of this book, whether named or anonymous, whether the interview took place in person, on the phone, or their contribution was a completed questionnaire.

Of course I want to thank my cherished friends who have been there for me: Joyce, David, and Davida Patton, Mary Tierney Kelley, Sharon Fisher, Judy Copeland, Annette Ott, Rhonda Ginsberg, Suzanne Vaughan, Marcia Hoffenberg, Sheila and Art Kriemelman, Joseph Novoa, Elia Schneider, Pramilla Poddar, Paula Fins, Gail Tuchman, Ginny and Jim Mugavero, Abra Wilkin, Mitzi Lyman, Jennifer Ash, Nona Aguilar, Sue Margolis, Ed, Candy, and Mollie Craven, Tahasha Impastato, Illa Howe and Bernie Adams, my writers group, the Writers Bloc, my sister, Eileen Barkas Hoffman, my brothers-in-laws and sisters-in-law Richard, Joel, Billy, Becky, Sissy, Christina, my cousins Phyllis, Carol, Daryl, Stuart, Fran, Keith, and Arlene, my nieces and nephews—Sky, Nancy, Coral, Ariel, Trish, Seth, Lilly, Vanessa, Courtney, Harlen, Colleen, John, Natalie, Julia, Billy, Billy Jr., Gracie, Barbara, Laura, David, Ryan— my aunts and uncles, my Mom, Gladys Barkas, my mother-in-law Mary, and the memory of my late father, William Barkas, D.D.S., my late brother, Seth Alan Barkas, and my late father-in-law, William Yager.

There are mentors, researchers, and advocates to thank in my school and work life, including Patricia Schroeder, Betsy Lampe, Joanne McCall, Caryl J. Frawley, Penn George, Nella Barkley, Irwin Zucker, criminologist Richard Quinney, who encouraged me to go back to school for my doctorate, Nancy Creshkoff, who took me under her wing by hiring me for my first job in publishing, Mary Claycomb, who was my second boss in publishing, John E. Glass, who shares information about sociology, and Beatrice Salzman, my high school English teacher who believed in me and my ability to write.

I also want to thank Lillian Vernon, David Hochberg, Jon Chakoff of iForum,com, Leslie Banks, Mark Sanborn, Don Gabor, Gerald R. Baron, Jan Nathan, Terry Nathan, Lisa Krebs, Gundhild Lenz-Mulligan, Ruth Winter, Jim Blasingame, Christine Hartline, Judy Kaufmann, the late C.H. Rolph, Ib and Bebbe Lauritzen, Lora Fountain, the late Helene Raude, Alexandre Civico, Maria Camila Perez, Elfiede Pexa, Sabine Schultz, Shoshi Grajower, Michael Meller, Franka Schmid, Lia deBoer, Dirk Demuynck, Maya Papayannapoulou, Lily Chen, Duran Kim, Karin Schindler, Anna Droumeva, Lucie Strakova, Alexander Korzhenevski, Tanja Tuma, Susanne Sinclair, Ajeet Khurana, Alexey Ilin, Predrag Milenkovic, Milena Lukic, Ana Milenkovic, Sanja Bastajic, Tamara Micic, June Badcock, James DeFalco, Monica Wang, Bobae Jung, Fr Joe Eruppakkatt, Hideai Matsuura, Koji Chikatani, Tony Herold, Evelyn Lee, Andrew Lee, Simona Kessler, Antonia Kerrigan, Asli Karasuil, Dr. Luc Kwanten, Vinelle Pan, Makiko Takeuchi, David Tayne, Norio Irie, Sunnie Lim, David Fewster, Maria White, Karin Taylor, R.H. Sharma, Folly Marland, Katie Blough, Anne Garinger, Dr. Luis Castaneda, Ashwin J. Shah, Penny Chen Peng, Sandra Stringer, S.R. Wadiker, Manuel Fernandez, the late Dr. David Leeds, Jim Cox, Caryl Frawley, Allison Hunter, Anette Moos, Peggy Stautberg, Larry Stybel, Joy Tipping, Al Walker, Mary Bryant, Dr. Terry Reilly, Sheila Moore, Gaye Tuchman, Arlynn Greenbaum, Mary Lou Brady, Diana Sokolow, Andrew M. Greeley, David Carradine, Susie Glennan, J. Barry Gurdin, Daniel Perlman, Diane DiResta, Rob and Rande Davis Gedaliah, George Tabbert, Nili Landon, Albert Ellis, Rosemary Blieszner, Steve Duck, Rebecca G. Adams, Carole Copeland Thomas, Scott Mikeloff, Terri Lonier, Whitney Fleming, Josh Piven, Carl Sanger, Jane Pollak, Brian Tracy, Tim McCormick, Andrea Reynolds, Helena Lehrman, Dorothy Malstad, and David and Michelle Riklan, Mike Toth, among others.

Index

About the Author

Relationships and workplace expert Dr. Jan Yager is the author of numerous highly-regarded books, translated into more than 25 foreign languages, including books on work relationships, friendship, and business issues such as: *When Friendship Hurts; Friendshifts®: The Power of Friendship and How It Shapes Our Lives; Business Protocol; Work Less, Do More,* 2nd ed; *Creative Time Management for the New Millennium; Grow Global; Productive Relationships; 365 Daily Affirmations for Happiness; Effective Business & Nonfiction Writing;* and *The Fast Track Guide to Speaking in Public.*

Dr. Yager, who holds a Ph.D. in sociology (City University of New York, 1983), has a masters in criminal justice (Goddard College, 1977), and did graduate work in art therapy (Hanemann Medical College). She has taught at the University of Connecticut, Penn State, St. John's University, Temple University, and The New School.

The former J. L. (Janet Lee) Barkas, Jan Yager is often interviewed by broadcast and print media including *The Oprah Winfrey Show, The Today Show, Good Morning, America, Sunday Morning, The View,* CNN, MSNBC, NPR, *The Wall Street Journal, USA Today, Investor's Business Daily,* and *The New York Times.*

A member of the National Speakers Association (NSA), she lives in Connecticut with her husband Fred; they have two grown sons and a grandson.

To book Dr. Yager as a speaker, contact your favorite speaker bureau or send an e-mail to: yagerinquiries2@aol.com. Speaker or media inquiries only: Fax (203) 968-0193.

Although personal replies cannot be guaranteed, Jan Yager welcomes hearing from readers with your comments about this book as well as any friendship or workplace stories—positive or negative—for her continuing friendship and work research.

Dr. Jan Yager
1127 High Ridge Road, #110
Stamford, CT 06905 USA
www.drjanyager.com
e-mail: jyager@aol.com